Everyday Phenomenology

Everyday Phenomenology

By

Derek Mitchell

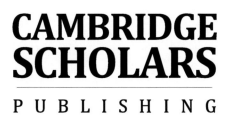

Everyday Phenomenology,
by Derek Mitchell

This book first published 2012

Cambridge Scholars Publishing

12 Back Chapman Street, Newcastle upon Tyne, NE6 2XX, UK

British Library Cataloguing in Publication Data
A catalogue record for this book is available from the British Library

ISBN (10): 1-4438-4114-5, ISBN (13): 978-1-4438-4114-6

To Gilda

TABLE OF CONTENTS

ACKNOWLEDGEMENTS

I would like to acknowledge the inspiration and support that I have received from the groups that I have been teaching for the Workers Educational Association in Tenterden, Ashford and Herne Bay, who allowed me to work through much of this material in my courses. I would also like to thank my friend Megan Stern who introduced me to the works of both Sebald and Bachelard, and my cousin Phil Davies who advised and assisted me in finding a publisher for this book.

CHAPTER ONE

INTRODUCTION

I have chosen to entitle this book *Everyday Phenomenology* because I am interested in how the world appears, not in its immediate and obvious manifestation but in the philosophical sense of how it comes to appear. I will be using the term phenomenology in the way suggested by Gaston Bachelard in his book *The Poetics of Space* when he describes phenomenology as "consideration of the onset of the image in an individual consciousness".[1] I will try to approach this bringing forth of the image into perception in a number of different ways, but my aim will remain an examination of how we can come to experience what is there, or that which can appear. In this way I will combine a study of how consciousness works in the world and how the world fits in with consciousness.

I have chosen the work of four very different thinkers to facilitate this enterprise, these are: Gaston Bachelard, Martin Heidegger, Hans-Georg Gadamer, and W.G. Sebald. I have settled mainly on these four because I think that they all represent oblique approaches to the acquisition of knowledge and provide a means by which the world can be approached and understood, and one which can help us to avoid the distortion and reduction that more direct approaches necessarily bring. I think that the fact that these four thinkers offer very different routes to the same end point gives strength to the argument in ways that would not be possible if I had chosen a group of writers more traditionally thought of as philosophers and who took similar approaches. By using the work of these four, I hope to be able to approach the subject from a number of different angles and, by doing so, preserve the fragility of the enterprise. It has been suggested to me that the work of other thinkers, for example, Fouccault, Rorty, Wittgenstein and Derrida,[2] may have been equally appropriate in helping me to achieve my aim. This may well be so and I am happy to defer to the familiarity that others may have with the works of such writers. To some extent it does not matter that we might come to the same conclusion by other means, in fact my conclusions in this work will only be strengthened if this is true. For my own part, the understanding that I have gained of the works of Bachelard, Heidegger, Gadamer and Sebald revealed resonances between their very different approaches which, to me, seemed to deserve further elucidation. This book is my attempt to elucidate a strand of thinking which they all share. I was also pleased to be able to use the somewhat more accessible works of W.G.Sebald and (to a lesser extent) Gaston Bachelard alongside the more inaccessible works of Heidegger and Gadamer, as it is at least a part of my intention to show that philosophy, and in particular epistemology and phenomenology, are perhaps not quite so difficult to explain and communicate as we might think. I hope that I have used some of the kinds of books that people might read for pleasure and that this will make my message more easily understood. This will also mean that the method of approach that I have chosen will make this book sometimes seem most unlike a work of academic philosophy. I trust that my more academically inclined readers will bear with me through these parts of the book and be able to allow the argument to appear where I have chosen not to state it explicitly. It is my intention that the kind of thinking that I will be advocating will emerge gradually as the work progresses. This will require a delicacy of touch in the writing and an equal patience in the reading if we are to be successful.

Before setting out the course of the argument in this book I want to say some things about the two terms which make up its title, both as a means of beginning to pose the questions that I will be addressing and in order to indicate the direction of travel that the argument will take as we proceed. I will also define what I mean by a couple of key words which will figure prominently in this book.

Everyday

The use of the term 'the everyday' is well known to anyone with even a passing familiarity with Heidegger's work; it is also a familiar term in everyday speech. It is largely because of this dual aspect that I have chosen 'everyday' in that it will enable me to use the philosophical insights provided by Heidegger and those like him, while at the same time providing a constant reminder of the sheer ordinariness of the kinds of things that I am going to talk about.

The everyday is everything, including that which goes unnoticed. It is the totality of that which can be revealed as phenomena, that is, all that can appear. It forms the background to the whole world which can be accessible to us through appearances; it is both ubiquitous and unexamined. In its everyday state the everyday is therefore not 'understood' to any extent nor is it appropriated or critically appraised by our consciousness, it is merely there. The everyday is inescapable, it is everything that there is, it is all around us all the time. The everyday is thus not only everything that is there but also everything that can be there. It is the whole world, it is just everyday.

Only when we notice it does the everyday stand out and become something meaningful for us, that is, it appears in our world. This development of an everyday phenomenology is an attempt to see how we come by this world; that is, to show how it can appear. To this extent it is an attempt to give an account of the world not as a collection of things that accumulate but as a whole world. Moreover it is an attempt to understand how consciousness comes by this world through appearances, and to understand something of the nature of the world before it comes to the notice of consciousness. This will be undertaken through an examination of the process of its becoming noticed, or appearing, in a wide variety of ways. From this examination we should be able to understand what is happening when the everyday is noticed and appears, and to thereby give some kind of an account of the process of appearing. We will, however, be attempting to understand something which usually lies just beyond the reach of consciousness and herein lies the paradox of the everyday. It is that which is all around us and to which we seem to have no unmediated access, that is; it is there but our encounter with it is always through our noticing. If the everyday is just beyond our reach, or out of appearance, it seems that we should never be able to know it for what it really is at all. This is because whenever we engage with an entity we bring it forth out of the everyday background and put it to use, we interfere with it and make it into something else, something relevant or useful to us. To circumvent this problem it will be necessary to make our attempt on the everyday indirectly and to allow answers to emerge. If we try to stick pins in the butterfly of the everyday will we miss it altogether.

Heidegger describes how entities from the everyday are used by conscious beings but only come fully to notice when they fail to meet their expected performance or when they obstruct rather than facilitate the work.[3] This calling forth (appearing) also occurs when we first come to learn a task and the tools that we need to use are unfamiliar to us. Typically, as the task becomes familiar, these entities, the tools, recede once more into the inconspicuous everyday. In the normal course of events in which the work proceeds smoothly, the entities which make up the everyday remain inconspicuous, we do not notice them and they do not stand out. The everyday is noticed as it intersects with the projects of conscious beings because in this way it gains significance. While we do not use all of the everyday in each of our projects, each instance in which an entity emerges from the everyday, as equipment, also gives us notice of the manifold from which it has emerged, this manifold is the everyday. We are seeking here the nature of that, which for the most part, remains inconspicuous, that which has yet to appear. Only if we solve this conundrum can we begin to understand what it is to appear.

The key difficulty is that our very act of recognition, description, discussion, and differentiation seems to remove us from the possible access to the everyday as it is in itself. This does not mean that the everyday is not there before we are conscious of it; we do not dispute the existence of the world in a skeptical fashion. We do not live in a kind of subject centered world in which the existence of objects comes to depend on their being perceived. Even though concealed, before they are noticed by consciousness, the elements of the everyday must have some kind of being however 'mere'. To discover what this might be we must find ways that take note without noticing. To put it another way we must find a way of remembering before we have forgotten, that is to gain an access to the everyday which does not depend on any kind of fore-knowledge or fore-having. On the other hand we must endeavour to preserve the utmost philosophical rigour and avoid any descent into vague mysticism. This is one reason why phenomenology is the method of approach that I have chosen.

Phenomenology

Heidegger says,

> We shall maintain that phenomenology is not just one philosophical science among others, nor is it the science preparatory to the rest of them; rather the expression *"phenomenology"* is the name for the *method* of *scientific philosophy in general.* (Heidegger, 1988, p.3)

This places phenomenology at the centre of this kind of enquiry with its dual emphasis on the entities that appear, and on scientific methodology. At least for Heidegger phenomenology is pre-eminent as a mode of investigation and, for the purposes of this work, I will follow his lead. Phenomenology is simply the study of appearances and this makes it the appropriate method to use in approaching the appearing of the everyday. Phenomenology also offers a quiet and gradual means of approach to the subject of our enquiry while at the same time providing a methodology which is robust and yet which accords with many of our common experiences of the way the world appears. By using the method of phenomenology we can concentrate exclusively on appearances and the answers to our questions can be allowed to appear. To this extent this book is itself an exercise in the kind of phenomenology that I will be describing. It is my intention that the way that this book is written will itself be an example of the ways of thinking that I am trying to elucidate. This deliberate ploy is based on the assumption that, that which appears cannot necessarily be made to appear, and in some cases the very attempt to make it appear forestalls appearance. This work is a discussion of appearances and of their appearing. The very fragility of these notions demands a method of approach which will not only illuminate these ideas but preserve them. A more strictly empirical or analytic philosophical method would obscure or change the nature of, rather than illuminate, what is there. When we begin to describe, analyze, dissect and categorize, as philosophers will, we tend to lose sight of what we are looking at.

Our problem here is one of naming; the activity of discussion is a species of description and therefore of differentiation. If our awareness of the everyday is to remain undifferentiated then we must find other ways of talking about our engagement with the everyday, other ways of allowing it to appear, for example through silent observation or a kind of reverie. We may hope to make some progress in this direction by these more indirect methods of approach which may then give us some understanding of the everyday without calling forth. As I have said, to achieve my aim I will use the writing of some thinkers who do not think like philosophers, this is because the assumption of the fragility of appearances underlies most of what I am going to say and they have been chosen because the style of their work protects this fragility. I hope that their less than philosophically orthodox approach will show that, sometimes at least, appearances need to be taken as it were by surprise

My aim then will be to pursue phenomenology, and therefore appearances obliquely, in a number of areas. Predominantly these will be the appearances of; houses, landscapes, places, people and history, but it is my intention that these individual studies will eventually coalesce into a more general theory about appearances, place and time and thereby provide a phenomenology of the everyday. In this pursuit I will not only use philosophical methods and devices but also examples and work from the fields of literature and art (mainly painting) in order to circumvent the apparent paradox of the ubiquity and inaccessibility of the everyday. This will make my work wide ranging and extensive but I hope that by the end a coherence and unity will have emerged from the bringing together of these different avenues of approach to appearances.

Spaces and Events

Finally, before setting out the course of the argument, I will make two important distinctions. I have deliberately used the term 'place' rather than 'space' because my intention is to address the questions with regard to the former rather than the latter. By 'place' I will take to mean a space which is in some way imbued with meaning for the individual consciousness. While it will be necessary at some points of the argument to use and explore theories of the more abstract notions of space and spatiality my main focus will remain spaces which have meaning, or 'places'. I see phenomenology as an essentially human activity and, while more abstract musing on the nature of endless space is interesting in its own right it is not what I am concerned with here. In some ways the same also goes for the notion of time. My use of this word will also include the human dimension, in the sense that I might have subtitled this work 'The Phenomenology of Places and Events'. I will take 'events' to mean times which have meaning in the same way that places are spaces which have meaning. Once again theories of time and temporality will have their place in the following arguments and discussions but they will be there to support less abstract discussions and arguments about the nature of places and events. In short I am interested in the relationship between the phenomenal world and consciousness, the nexus where the onset of the image, or appearing, takes place. The rest of this book will be divided in to eight further chapters as follows.

Summary of Contents

The next chapter will look at houses, their appearance and their meaning. For this I will primarily use the work of Dennis Severs and Gaston Bachelard who have both written beautifully and enigmatically about houses. I will pay particular attention to Sever's idea of 'the space between' and Bachelard's use of the terms 'psychogeography' and 'transcendental geometry' and his idea of dreaming.

Dennis Severs' book *18 Folgate Street – The Tale of House in Spitalfields* is an evocation of a time and place that fascinated the author. This remarkable work is a striking attempt to facilitate appearing and reveals some of the way in which this takes place.

In *The Poetics of Space* Gaston Bachelard is conducting an explicit examination of the working of poetic imagery but his work has much in common with Severs as is witnessed when he say, "One must be receptive, receptive to the image at the moment it appears"[4] and when he speaks of, "the very ecstasy of the newness of the image".[5] In particular in this chapter I will address what Bachelard calls, "the problem of description".[6] Severs would recognise this kind of language and it is clearly it is a language that speaks of appearances of all kinds, the manifestation of all the stuff of the world.

Chapter Three will present further examples of descriptions of the kind that Severs has given and which appear to fit the analysis given by Bachelard. The first three are in Rainer Maria Rilke's novel *The Notebooks of Malte Laurids Brigge* which pre-dates Bachelard's work. The others are in W.G. Sebald's *The Rings of Saturn* and are later than Bachelard. In the course of setting out these descriptions of encounters with houses and places it will become clear that Rilke and Sebald are in the same phenomenological territory as Severs and Bachelard and that the descriptions of places in all four has much of significance in common. In this section it will also begin to emerge that the work of all four of these very different writers rests on the philosophical and phenomenological ground set out by Heidegger.

I will then look at some of Heidegger's work in *Being and Time*, and *The Basic Problems of Phenomenology* which will underpin these earlier discussions and begin to provide a sound philosophical basis for understanding Severs, Bachelard, Rilke and Sebald's work on the nature of place. In particular I will look at his discussion of Rilke in *The Basic Problems of Phenomenology* along with some parts of *Being and Time* which stress our involvement or engagement with the world.

In Chapter Four I will look at the appearance of landscapes through the work of Dutch painters of the fifteenth and sixteenth century and some more of the writing of W.G. Sebald. I have chosen here to consider paintings because they involve the creation of an appearance or an image, and they themselves appear as what they are, that is as images of images. In a number of ways they can provide useful metaphors about appearances which will inform the discussion.

As well as illustrating what is going on when we perceive a landscape (or to put it another way when a landscape appears) this will centre on a discussion of the nexus between seeing and knowing, a distinction which is essential to the entire project. I this chapter I will show how the work of the painters of the Dutch Republic of the seventeenth century provides a demonstration of the Being-in-the-world of Dasein as set out by Heidegger in his work of 1926-1929. I will seek to describe a few of the paintings in Heidegger's terms and to show how the enterprise of painting itself illustrates Being-in-the-world. In this I will use specific landscape paintings and Sebald's descriptions of the landscapes he experiences. In particular I will begin to open up the idea of the uncanniness of what we perceive and the idea of reverberation which will continue in the next section

In Chapter Five my aim will be to demonstrate that truths about certain kinds of places (houses and landscapes) are also true of all of the places we can find ourselves in and therefore say something about the more abstract notion of a place as a space with meaning. This will extend the discussion of uncanniness and reverberation and begin to place consciousness somewhere in the world that appears.

This will extend and deepen the ways of thinking presented by both Bachelard and Sebald and try to see which way their thinking really points, not only in terms of specific houses and landscapes but in terms of spaces in general and, in particular, places. I will also look at some of Gadamer's work, specifically on the nature and role of play. This will take us closer to the mystery of "the onset of the image".

Chapter Six is concerned with the notion of memory and the ways that it contributes to the construction of our experience of the world. The complementary notions of remembering and unforgetting are closely associated with the idea of memory and some preliminary definitions and clarification of these terms will be given. Once again in this part of the work I will use Sebald's evocative works but now with reference to more explicit philosophical texts, in particular Gadamer's *Truth and Method* and his idea of Bildung or culture, as it is sometimes translated.

I will also discuss two specific items through which memory is apparently recovered, these are photographs and gravestones. Discussion of these examples will further illuminate the way that memory supports present experience.

In Chapter Seven I will move on from the idea of personal memory to history. This move is essentially a move from personal past experience to collective or group memory. For this I will make use of the work of Sebald (again) and the more recently rediscovered work of Irene Nemirovsky (*Suite Francaise*) in an attempt to explore the idea of historical witness. I will also consider some more of Gadamer's work, specifically on tradition and on the festival. This will bring out the key concepts of memory, reverberation and the recovery of past times; it will also complete the earlier discussion of uncanniness and throw some light on the ways in which we understand the intersection of places and times in our lives.

The notion of personal identity is prominent in Sebald's work and there are many instances in all of the works which seek to address this notion. In Chapter Eight I will select and describe a few which I think summarise his thoughts on identity and which point towards some interesting and difficult problems with this most personal of notions. I will discuss the appearance of our own selves to others and to our own selves in a discussion of faces which will embrace not only portraiture and self portraiture, but also some recent controversies about face transplants and the covering of faces. This will amount to a phenomenology of faces and lead into a discussion of the phenomenon of personal identity. I will be fundamentally concerned with the self that appears and I will attempt to understand how that appearance is possible. I will link this discussion with Hegel's discussion of self-consciousness in *The Phenomenology of Spirit*, Descartes *cogito*, Sartre's demonstration of the existence of Others in *Being and Nothingness* and Heidegger's notion of Mitsein or being-with.

In the concluding chapter I will be able to show that I have built up a picture of connected discussions, commentaries, and theories which add up to a phenomenology of place, time and consciousness and, in addition I will have shown by my method of approach that the fragility of appearances can both be illuminated and preserved. The value of this approach will be reinforced by a worked practical example, as far as is possible in a work if this kind, of a specific branch of knowledge. I will consider the ways that clinical knowledge and understanding, in its practical aspect of application to patients, can benefit from this kind of thinking. This example will show how the kind of thinking that I have been setting out has practical implications and applications beyond the rather esoteric thinking of academic philosophy, and how it can have meaning in our everyday lives.

Finally I will have shown that Heidegger's ideas of the emergence and reticence, Sebald's spectral materialism, Bachelard's oneirism, and Gadamer's notions of tact and inescapable Bildung represent oblique approaches to the everyday and provide a means by which the everyday can be approached and understood in its everydayness. Gadamer's tact, Heidegger's reticence, Bachelard's oneirism and Sebald's oblique approach to his subjects, all these tell us about ways of encountering the world which may appear to be unnecessarily laboured, superficial or even pretentious. By the end of this book it will be clear that if we want to see what is important about the world, and in particular to see the structures which enmesh us all in the world, then these avenues of approach will prove much more fruitful, rather than deficient, in allowing us to see and to understand the richness and complexity of the world.

As I have said, philosophically speaking my main guides through all of this will be W.G. Sebald, Gaston Bachelard, Martin Heidegger and his sometime pupil Hans-Georg Gadamer. I will also gain lesser assistance from a few others, notably Descartes, Hume, Hegel, Rilke, Nemirovsky,

Sartre, and Severs, although I will endeavour to add some insights of my own as we go along. To begin with, houses.

Notes

[1] Bachelard, 1958, 1994, p.xix.
[2] Upshur, R, 2011, p.905.
[3] Heidegger, 1962, H.73-75.
[4] Bachelard, 1958, 1994, p.xv.
[5] Bachelard, 1958, 1994, p.xv.
[6] Bachelard, 1958, 1994, p.6.

CHAPTER TWO

PHENOMENAL HOUSES:
YOU EITHER GET IT OR YOU DON'T

Dennis Severs' book *18 Folgate Street – The Tale of a House in Spitalfields* is an attempt to set down in words the tours of his house which Severs conducted for his visitors; in effect it is an evocation of an evocation. Severs' whole exercise is an attempt to make the house appear, or more accurately to allow the house to appear, in ways it might have been in the past. Even the way that the book is presented is extraordinary and goes beyond the conventional devices used by writers to illuminate meaning. Severs uses illustrations, some in colour some in black and white, some are no more than diagrams others are collages, many of them are framed in unusual shapes like circles and as though seen through a keyhole. He uses different font sizes within the text to create emphasis and a sense of space, and both text and illustrations blend together to form a seamless stream of evocation. The book is less an account of what Severs has done with his house and more like an example of the kind of thing that he has done; it is as much something to look at as it is something to read and it is certainly something to think about. All in all this remarkable work is a striking attempt to facilitate appearing and reveals some of the ways in which this takes place.

Peter Ackroyd[1] in his introduction to this book describes Severs as conducting "his own experiment in recovering past time".[2] He describes Severs' intentions as to have the house "recover its origins"[3] and says that; "The house became a living story with each of its rooms as a separate chapter".[4] Ackroyd's careful use of language begins to show us what he thinks Severs is trying to do (or at least what he is not trying to do or trying not to do). The essence of Severs' enterprise is a *living* recovery and not the presentation of an ossified assemblage of historical artefacts. The house is not intended as a museum or mere collection of objects from the past; it is intended as an evocation, complete in itself and immediately available to us as such. Severs' visitors were presented immediately with the house as a living entity and were, so to speak, injected into the life of the house and the family that Severs has contrived to inhabit it. In this way the house is allowed to appear. To paraphrase Bachelard when he describes phenomenology as consideration of the onset of the image, Severs is facilitating the onset of the image of the house through his enterprise at 18 Folgate Street. Severs himself says;

> Pigeonhole intelligence is not going to win by ruining the picture I paint in the space between us. You will not return what I create in your mind by reducing it to a palette of paint with a name and number for each ingredient. (Severs, 2001, p.64)

Severs insists that we resist the temptation to disassemble his creation as a means of understanding it; we are urged to take it as it appears and as a whole. It is interesting and revealing that Severs is already using the artistic metaphor of painting a picture rather than simply presenting an entity; pictures are completed with the last brush stroke, their power is not in the accumulation of paint on paper or canvas but in the way that all the elements combine to give us meaning. We will see more of this later in the specific consideration of painting as a phenomenological event, but Severs' use begins to point to the necessity for this kind of approach when looking at appearances.

Severs had much more in mind than the creation of an eighteenth century replica; in fact this is exactly what he says he is not doing. He was trying to provide the visitor (or reader) with an immediate impression (appearance) of what it was like to live in this house during the mid-eighteenth century; simply by being there, you will either get it or you won't. You must not try to understand the house through the usual intellectual processes of description, definition and interpretation; in this context the notions of description, definition and interpretation are the archenemies. The appearance is fragile and must be allowed to appear rather than be forced. Severs understands this danger only too well and asked his visitors not to talk during their visit; he knew that even this level of articulation would have destroyed the immediacy which was central to his enterprise. He says,

> To be smart, no fancy must get in the way of what our mind's eye can plainly see. Our success at physical and mental co-ordination depends on a lack of any slack between our self and what we see. To admit to seeing the invisible – the space between – is to the gang, at least weird, infantile or retarded. (Severs, 2001, pp.53-54)

So, simply, "You must close your eyes to help you to see".[5] Appearance is not just about simple seeing and Severs was trying to allow the visitors to experience the house in its immediacy without the conventional interactions we might have in a museum or a visit to a stately home. In this way the visitors notice the space between as that which separates them from the house and in which it can be apprehended without comprehension, thus drawing to attention, in an indirect manner, the everydayness of the house. It is as if we begin to notice the everyday almost by not noticing. We will see, as the argument in this book develops, that this notion of immediacy and its counter notion of mediation will form a crucial nexus in the understanding not only of Severs' project at 18 Folgate Street, but throughout the discussion of place and time; it is part of the story of our access to the everyday.

Severs is clearly interested in much more than the appearance of individual objects which make up the house, and he wants to use the idea of the 'space between us' as the space in which this appearing happens. Consequently he has some interesting and thought provoking ideas about the scenes which he had created. Ackroyd captures this when he says,

> This book is also about 'the space between', the air between objects which becomes charged with their presence, that intangible and ineffable 'aura' which holds being together in it capacious embrace. (Severs, 2001, p.ix)

And Severs himself explains further about this "space between" when he says,

> The Space Between is the invisible, shared third element that lies between any two sides. It contains all we have in common with anyone else. Good or bad it is the place where sharing being alive happens… Like the varnish over the painting a healthy space between brings together, bonds and then protects the whole picture. (Severs, 2001, p.100)

Appearing takes place in the space between. It is as if that which apparently separates us from the entities and from each other is that which unites us to these same entities and to others. It ties us into the reality in which we exist, a reality in which all we have of the entities is their appearance. The entities are, it seems, less important in themselves, while the space (relationship) between them creates the aura or context which Severs finds so rich in meaning. Without wishing to pre-empt later parts of this discussion we might already begin to infer Heideggerian insights from this kind of talk, but for the moment we may let it lie simply as a means of rejecting an empirical or essentialist approach to the house as an approach which will fail to reveal the origins of the house, and which fails to recover past time. Severs was providing his visitors with a phenomenology of his house by allowing it to appear. By using phenomenology, he was able evoke responses to the house, and the situations he created, which go beyond the kind of responses which might have been provoked by a simple description or tour of the house. In enabling the house to appear he is positioning the visitor within the world of the house rather than providing them with a spectatorial position from which to view the house. He was trying to avoid a representational model of the world and of perception and instead conducting an experiment in existential phenomenology, that is, he was seeing what happened when the house appeared, and when people experienced it.

Severs' interest and indeed fascination with appearance and context begins to reveal a deeper understanding of the nature of his enterprise and an appreciation of the more fundamental notions of place and time of which I think he was only instinctually aware. He begins to describe his relationship to these entities and to really clarify his central enterprise when he says,

> As time went on I began to see the shape of a bottle or a milk jug of a particular period as having the same general outline as that age's fashion and design. And by its similarities to other objects – including architecture and music – I could eventually work out what the *mood* was that once related them all: the spell which once constituted an 'age'. From there I would assimilate what I had heard of real history: politics, legislation, battles, dates and so on. Again for me everything had to be related, and what little I do know about English history, I know this way. I can only dig into the air for the core of a subject and then work outwards from there. Human nature first, history later, as proof. I call it working *inside out.* (Severs, 2001, p.6)

Severs' use of the words "mood" and "spell" indicates once again how we need to approach these phenomena obliquely and through a more imaginative and less empirical route, a route which will lead us not to a crude factual understanding of the history of the house but to a rich experience of the past of the house. This experience, he hopes, will take us beyond where a simple description of the historical past of the house would take us and will allow something else to appear, that is, the house itself. It is important to note here and onwards that Severs is not propelling us towards some kind of mystical appreciation of the house. Although the language he is forced to use might suggest mysticism we will gain more purchase on the method that Severs, and the other thinkers like him that I will discuss use, if we take their aim positively as one which moves us away from crude empiricism and towards a more imaginative conception of our experience of the world.

What we have here from Severs is much more than a simple statement that each historical era has a style that we can read through the artefacts that remain. Although this is undoubtedly true, the more interesting and deeper point is surely that there has to be a more fundamental relationship between the entities and their time. In effect these entities help to constitute 'their time', so that their appearance to us makes this 'time' reverberate in our time. This further implies that the entities themselves are temporal, that is, they exist not simply in time but with time as part of their existing. There is a specific historical context in which these entities feature, they come to us like flies in amber and they can evoke this time and place, by their appearing together. In this case it is a house in East London in the middle of the eighteenth century, but we will see many other examples of the same kind of thing in the chapters that follow. This constituting of an age, or temporalizing, is a product of the temporality of these entities and denotes something which is central to their being. At this early stage we should also note that there is a further context in which these artefacts are set, a context of more generic notions of place and time which Severs notices and which he acknowledges gives them their power. Severs calls this context 'the space between' while others, like Sartre, have referred to the nothingness which separates us all from each other.[6]

We shall see as the discussion moves forward that this is the level at which the meaning of these entities is revealed, the space between is the ground of their appearing. The key to Severs' work, and his attempt to evoke a place and a time, is his understanding of the nature and importance of context, the space between in which things can appear. This includes all of the entities and structures, indeed the whole house, including the space it occupies and encompasses. We, and his visitors, are set into this context in such a way that we cannot stand back and watch what is going on but are straight away and forever mixed up in it. Our experience and the appearing of the entities, including the house, are simultaneous and unmediated to the extent that we can only come to understand the house, and the situation that Severs is creating, through this unmediated immersal. Once we have been immersed our later rationalization, description, understanding, and application of historical and other frames of reference, comes to seem less, not more, real than our unmediated first impression. We become enmeshed in the appearance of the house and it seems that this is the only way in which the house can appear to us. In his book Severs gives us one example of this kind of engagement with the world; that is with a single house; however I think that it is already becoming apparent that the kind of thinking that Severs is illustrating can be extended.

From my own experience I have found visits to battle sites particularly illuminating. It is immediately striking, for example, to stand on Senlac Hill from which the Saxons fought the Battle of Hastings in 1066, and to see the space they saw and out of which came the Norman army. Our present day immediate (unmediated) perception transcends the knowledge we have of events before, during, and after the battle and gives us another insight into what happened there. This new insight is not available to us from factual history alone. It is as if, by occupying the same space, we partake of some of the experiences of those who stood there before. We stand where the Saxons stood and we look out across the ground over which the Normans advanced. A similar feeling is evoked at the now disused paper mill in Verla, Finland.[7] This mill is preserved as it was on the day it closed in 1964 with its everyday artefacts complete. We can see the marks left by those who occupied the space while working in the mill, including a deep groove in the wooden floor created by one single woman who worked in the same place in the mill for fifty-two years. Verla gives us a powerful evocation of the lives of all of the people who worked there. This original, unmediated evocation and appearance retains its power by providing us with the ground upon which later mediation fits the experience into our consciousness, our memory, and our everyday patterns of understanding. We synthesize what we learn from the guide about the facts of the history of the mill with our unmediated first impressions and through this synthesis we fashion a rich understanding of our experience of Verla. We leave Verla with the words of the guide almost forgotten in the intensity of the sheer experience of the place and its times. These three, Severs' house, Senlac Hill, and the paper mill at Verla, are all examples of the same kind of imaginative evocation, and our encounters with them reveal more than merely factual reality and knowledge, they provoke a kind of imaginative understanding.

Severs' work is limited in that it is specifically confined to his house in Spitalfields and to the middle of the eighteenth century, and Senlac Hill and the mill at Verla are similarly isolated examples. However, I think that all three provoke a discussion about time and place which can be taken further. I will now look at the work of Gaston Bachelard in *The Poetics of Space* to see particularly how the points raised by Severs can be taken deeper and applied not simply to the evocative appearance of an individual historical house but to houses in general.

However, before embarking on this it is necessary to admit that the enterprise is fraught with difficulty. How far the approach taken by Severs and Bachelard can be preserved is in some doubt when we begin to describe, analyze, dissect and categorize. One way, perhaps the only way, in which to express what is being said and unsaid would be to respond to poetry and art with another piece of poetry or art. I have chosen not to take this route partly because I am no poet or artist and partly because I think that the attempt to interpret, in philosophical terms, the ways in which places and times appear is worthwhile. So, to this…

The Phenomenology of the Image

I shall begin with a warning. By using the words "the phenomenology of the image"[8] Bachelard seems to mean that the image comes before the thought so that, "the image has touched the depths before it has stirred the surface".[9] This is of course a poetic image in itself, but one which conveys the difference between a descriptive or analytical (mediated) process and the sheer immediacy of what we like to call real life. We will see as we go further and deeper into Bachelard's work that his words have a multiplicity of meanings; this multiplicity reflects the complexity of the world of experience and it is his intention to reveal, or to allow this richness to appear. At the outset we should be clear that Bachelard is no mystic and any attempt to interpret his work in such a way will miss the point entirely. We must remain aware of the complexity of experience through all our consideration of Bachelard's work over the next few chapters. Bachelard uses poetic imagery and appeals to our own imaginative impulses to suggest a different way of seeing and understanding the world and in this he has much in common with both Severs and W.G. Sebald. This makes his approach fragile and we should be careful to preserve this fragility. It is, therefore, important to acknowledge that any attempt, including this one, to discuss the kind of work that Bachelard gives us runs the risk of destroying the poetry of the image and with it the almost ethereal substance of Bachelard's method. I hope that by acknowledging the danger I might be spared the criticism.

Right at the beginning of his beautifully written book *The Poetics of Space* Gaston Bachelard echoes Severs when he says,

> it is not a question of describing houses or enumerating their picturesque features and analysing for which reason they are comfortable. On the contrary, we must go beyond the problems of description … in order to attain to the primary virtues, those that reveal an attachment that is native in some way to the primary function of inhabiting. (Bachelard, 1958, 1994, p.4)

For Bachelard the house is going to be more than just bricks and mortar; it will not be the geometry or the materiality of the house which will interest Bachelard, and it will not be this physical manifestation which will give us the reality of the house. Bachelard is explicitly moving beyond simple description and simple appearance in a way that Severs only hinted at. It is clear by now, from both Severs and Bachelard, that there is more to it than just empirical appearance, or perhaps more accurately, appearance is no longer simple. In accord with Severs, Bachelard recognizes that the appearance must be preserved, and, in common with Severs, this is going to be more than a simple visual appearance and much more like an unmediated impression so that,

> by approaching the house images with care not to break up the solidarity of memory and imagination we may hope to make others feel all the elasticity of an image that moves us at unimaginable depth. (Bachelard, 1958, 1994, p.6)

Memory and imagination are central to this impression and if they are preserved we may have some hope of communicating our experience of the house to someone else, a kind of communication that would be impossible were we to confine ourselves to facts about the dimensions of the rooms and the colour of the brickwork. Bachelard is conducting an explicit examination of the working of poetic imagery and he speaks of, "the very ecstasy of the newness of the image".[10] Severs would recognise this kind of language and it is clearly a language that speaks of appearances of all kinds, the manifestation to consciousness of all of the stuff of the world.

Coming from the perspective of the philosophy of science Bachelard admits that it is difficult to shed the kind of reasoning he has always used, but in turning to poetic images he recognises that the methodology he has previously espoused, a methodology of description and categorization, masks what he now calls, "the primitivity of the imagination".[11] Along with Severs, Bachelard is now interested in immediacy and we may consider Severs, in providing his tours of his own house, to be indulging in the kind of 'poetry' that Bachelard is trying to get to the bottom of, but while Severs' evocation is confined to one house in one place, and can merely hint at the power of evocation, Bachelard's more generic approach means that he can explore the nature of evocation itself.

Bachelard hopes that by developing a poetic phenomenology he can help us to recapture what we have lost and to regain specific realities so that;

the reader of poems is asked to consider an image not as an object and even less as the substitute for an object, but to seize its specific reality (Bachelard, 1958, 1994, p.xix)

It is in poetry that we are asked both to seize the immediacy of our impression and to allow the often multiple meanings of the words to appear. We are specifically asked not to simply attend to the words as they might appear in a works manual or instruction booklet, or for that matter in a work of academic philosophy. In essence Bachelard is showing us what Severs was doing, or more accurately what he was trying to do. In attempting to show the house in Spitalfields in an evocative manner Severs was creating a phenomenology of his house by presenting it in such a way and with such restrictions (no talking), that the immediacy of the phenomena (their appearing) was preserved. Bachelard is showing how this method is not simply the trick or gimmick of a good tour guide but is a way of capturing something fundamental about how we relate to the spaces around us and how both places and times are evoked. It is as if our perception, which describes, discusses and analyzes, drowns out something of what we are seeing and obscures the process though which it comes to appear.   He resorts to phenomenology because;

Only phenomenology—that is to say, consideration of the *onset of the image* in an individual consciousness—can help us to restore the subjectivity of images and to measure their strength and their transsubjectivity. (Bachelard, 1958, 1994, p.xix)

So that,

For a phenomenologist the attempt to attribute antecedents to an image when we are in the very existence of the image is a sign of inveterate psychologism. (Bachelard, 1958, 1994, p.xxix)

Bachelard wants us to get back to the beginning in our experience of phenomena, back to this event (the onset of the image) which is ours and ours alone, and which immediately reveals our connection to the world by its appearing. In this respect he once again reaffirms Severs' project when he says, "Imaginary reality is evoked before being described".[12] The equation of phenomenology and immediacy is vital. The appearance of the things makes them what they are and what they can become for us. By dealing in the immediacy of their appearance we capture, or re-capture, a specific and unmediated reality which is prior to all understanding and which in fact provides the ground on which this understanding rests.

For Bachelard psychologism and psychoanalysis represent an approach which both masks and supersedes the primitive or primordial nature of phenomena, that of appearing. It is this appearing which gives us our initial access to reality, rather than the dissecting, de-contextualising and descriptive processes of science; in fact these processes are only possible on the basis of this access. We are driven back towards the images that are created by the poet in a way that leaves us open to the phenomena, but open in a way that it is difficult if not impossible to speak of.

Images of Intimacy – The Poetics of the House

Bachelard uses the house for his specific examination of our experience and understanding of space because he thinks that it "is a privileged entity for a phenomenological study of the intimate values of inside space"[13] and because, "A house constitutes a body of images that gives mankind proofs of illusions of stability."[14] Bachelard takes the house to be the first place of significance for us, that most intimate and primary of spaces imbued with all of the meaning we have given it and which it has accrued, meanings that go far beyond notions of geometric space and which can make such notions seem irrelevant. For Bachelard the house seems to provide a primordial nexus for the relationship between the individual consciousness and the notions of place and time. The house thus constitutes a psychological diagram for Bachelard, which can then be read and understood to the extent that,

> In this dynamic rivalry between house and universe we are far removed from any reference to simple geometric form. A house that has been experienced is not an inert box. Inhabited space transcends geometrical space. (Bachelard, 1958, 1994, p.47)

In *The Poetics of Space* Bachelard takes us on a tour of the house in a pre-echo of the way that Severs has done, but Bachelard's tour requires no specific house except the one that we can each imagine as our own. Bachelard has no geometric plan of this house but a phenomenological map with which he guides us around the space and time of the house. This method of transcendental geography, or psychogeography, takes us beyond the simple appearance of the house and into a world of imagination and memory in which are revealed the real meanings of the house. This transcendence envelopes not only place, but also time, because;

> beyond all the positive values of protection, the house we were born in becomes imbued with dream values, which remain after the house is gone.

Centers of boredom, centers of solitude, centers of daydream group together to constitute the oneiric house which is more lasting than the scattered memories of our birthplace. (Bachelard, 1958, 1994, p.17)

While Bachelard is perhaps over restrictive in focusing on houses in which we were born, particularly in a culture and an age in which most of us were not born at home but in hospitals, I think that his reasoning applies equally well to the house in which we were brought up, or the house in which we spent our childhood. The image of protection and origin works equally well for both of these. This dream like quality precedes any understanding and, although fragile, can remain with us. Memory is important but not necessarily essential and can itself, if we are not careful, become the kind of analytical dissection table on which the poetic image founders. The appearance of the house stays with us in much more than the visual sense; as Bachelard would have it, it is not an inert box that we simply see, but a space that we imbue with meaning and make into a place. We transcend the simple physical dimensions of the building and make it into a house, the space becomes a place. The unmediated nature of this experience of an appearance, or onset of image, is exemplified by Bachelard's account of a kind of half-conscious dreaming or imagining, as if we do not quite become fully aware of what is there; it is a kind of looking at the house through half closed eyes. In fact Bachelard thinks that we become more aware in this dreamlike experiencing, which tells us much more about what we are seeing than would be the case from a straightforward perception. In this way the house comes to have a transcendental geometry, specifically a geometry which transcends the simply apparent geometric features of the building, and which gives us imaginary dimensions. When we attend to it in the way that Bachelard suggests, the appearing of the house begins to reveal a kind of psychogeography which itself contains a region in which the appearing is taking place, a region which we can inhabit but not quite grasp and one which threatens to disappear at any moment. This sounds very much like Severs' notion of the space between.

Bachelard is keenly aware of the philosophical tradition of phenomenology in a way that Severs is not, and Bachelard is therefore much more explicit in his work not only in using the terminology of this approach but also in gaining critical purchase on phenomenological method itself. This allows Bachelard to go beyond what we might term a first order, or specific, phenomenological exercise and to extend the discussion to houses in general. In this way Bachelard is explaining to us what Severs is doing and the connection between them is made no more clear than when Bachelard says; "I must show that the house is one of the greatest powers of integration for the thoughts, memories and dreams of mankind".[15] It is as if this single most significant place opens up the access to a new understanding of all of our ways of seeing. Bachelard again reminds us of Severs' attempts to show his house when he says,

> For the real houses of memory, the houses to which we return in dreams, the houses that are rich in unalterable oneirism do not readily lend themselves to description. To describe them would be like showing them to visitors. (Bachelard, 1958, 1994, p.13)

Bachelard would thus both acknowledge Severs' difficulty in presenting his house as an evocation of this dream-like past, and applaud his attempts to make his tours as little like usual tours of historical sites as is possible. Severs was trying hard to make his visitors as little like conventional museum visitors as possible and in so doing to make his house as little like a museum as possible. Severs was striving to allow the house to appear rather than to show it, yet in spite of his efforts it is as if the very act of showing risks destroying the dream of appearance. Everything that Severs did was an attempt to create and to preserve the oneiric quality that Bachelard sees in the poetics of the house. It is precisely these poetic images of intimacy that Bachelard believes show us not only what the house means to us, but which reveal to us our underlying relationship to all places and times as appearances and events. Our experience of these phenomena must be immediate, we are within the house as we are within space and time; and this primordial relationship provides the ground for our later construction of more structured relationships with space and time and with houses and the spaces within them. In *The Poetics of Space* Bachelard specifically discusses corners, drawers, chests, wardrobes, nests and shells; all are the kinds of spaces with which we have a relationship. Standing aside and viewing houses as a spectator, or even in our memories, is a secondary relationship with which we first provide ourselves and then mistake for primary ground once we have forgotten (or destroyed) the poetic image. Both Bachelard and Severs are calling us back to this more primordial perception.

Bachelard's phenomenology applies equally well to the objects within the house. These objects are made to come alive, in a very specific way, a way which evokes both the reality of the objects and their context. He says,

> The minute we apply a glimmer of consciousness to a mechanical gesture, or practice phenomenology while polishing a piece of old furniture, we sense new impressions come into being beneath this familiar domestic

duty. For consciousness rejuvenates everything giving a quality of beginning to the most everyday actions. (Bachelard, 1958, 1994, p.67)

Our everyday experience of one object reveals a whole world of interconnections and appearances once we begin to practice phenomenology. Any one who has handled with fascination a piece of antique furniture, or any object of antiquity, will understand what is going on here. There is more to a seventeenth century chest than its dimensions or even the fact that it provides storage. It is an artefact with which we are involved in a successor relationship of function. It provides storage space for us in a way similar to the way it provided storage space for those who went before us. It appears to us as something more than just a box. Its ongoing use gives us its meaning through the context in which it exists, and by using it we understand and appreciate it. This recapturing of the immediate phenomenological experience, revealed through the everyday task of polishing, is at the very heart of what Severs is unwittingly striving to achieve; but even more, it is central to the way in which we come to know the world through our involvement in it and our engagement with entities in the world. Without this primordial experience no further understanding is possible. We cannot theorise about a world that we have not encountered phenomenologically, and there cannot be a world which cannot appear.

Bachelard sees the truth of this encounter as having a dream like quality, which is counterposed to what we might term the scientific or rational quality that we expect our judgements about the world to have. He wants to keep the dream going long enough for us to understand what is really going on. Our aim must be to guard the fragility of the appearance and to preserve its immediacy as a means of remembering what it really looks like and what it really means. He says,

> When we describe a daydream *objectively* this diminishes and interrupts it. How many dreams told objectively have become nothing but oneirism reduced to dust! In the presence of an image that dreams, it must be taken as an invitation to continue the daydream that created it. (Bachelard, 1958, 1994, p.152)

Severs' presentation of the house in Spitalfields was an invitation to daydream.

While it is often difficult to grasp exactly what Bachelard is trying to say about places and times (and this is as much a product of the nature of his enquiry as anything else) it is clear that he has uncovered something quite fundamental about the ways in which we inhabit space and time, and

one which deserves to be explored further. It is also evident that
Bachelard's work throws some light on Severs' project in 18 Folgate
Street, by explaining the kind of thing that Severs is doing. However it
will take more to understand the real contributions made by the work of
these two, and to uncover the foundations on which they rest, and to this
end I will return in particular to Bachelard in Chapters Three and Five
with specific reference to some more houses.

We need to find out what makes Severs' enterprise, and ones like it,
possible at all. In this way we will find out what is really going on between
place, time and consciousness. To do this I will next look at some further
examples of the dreamlike accounts of houses and other similar places all
of which use a literary approach. The first set of these will be from Rilke's
novel *The Notebooks of Malte Laurids Brigge* and the second from W.G.
Sebald's accounts of various places he visits in his Suffolk odyssey *The
Rings of Saturn*. These examples, combined with the work of both Severs
and Bachelard, will then provide a launch pad into Heidegger's work in
Being and Time and his "Thesis of Modern Ontology" given in the third
chapter of his work *The Basic Problems of Phenomenology*. This in turn
will illuminate the work of all four of these writers and set out both the
ontological milieu in which they are operating, and the fundamental
problems with appearances that they are highlighting.

Following that I will move onto an entirely different footing by using
some studies of paintings of still life and landscape made by Dutch artists
of the sixteenth and seventeenth century. I hope that this will bring to the
fore the important nexus between knowing and seeing which will further
illuminate our relationship with that which appears. I will also use some of
the accounts of landscapes provided by W.G. Sebald in his strange books
which I think will connect his thinking even more with that of both Severs
and Bachelard, and allow us to go even further in addressing some of the
uncanniness we sometimes feel in our encounters with the world.

Notes

[1] Ackroyd's own work, *London – The Biography*, though wider in scope and
grander in scale, is also trying to evoke in the same way as Severs.
[2] Severs, 2001, p.viii.
[3] Severs, 2001, p.viii.
[4] Severs, 2001, p.viii.
[5] Severs, 2001, p.54.
[6] Sartre, 1956, throughout, and defined p.633.
[7] www.verla.fi
[8] Bachelard, 1958, 1994, p.xx.

[9] Bachelard, 1958, 1994, p.xxiii.
[10] Bachelard, 1958, 1994, p.xv.
[11] Bachelard, 1958, 1994, p.xxvi.
[12] Bachelard, 1942, 1982, p.121.
[13] Bachelard, 1958, 1994, p.3.
[14] Bachelard, 1958, 1994, p.17.
[15] Bachelard, 1958, 1994, p.6.

CHAPTER THREE

HOUSES AND WALLS:
RILKE, SEBALD, BACHELARD, HEIDEGGER

I will now go on and present two further sets of accounts of the kinds that Severs has given and which appear to fit the analysis given by Bachelard. The first are from a novel by Rainer Maria Rilke and pre-date Bachelard's work while the second set, from W.G. Sebald's *The Rings of Saturn* are much later. I hope that it will become apparent in the course of setting out these accounts of encounters with houses and places that Rilke and Sebald are in the same phenomenological territory as Severs and Bachelard, and that the work of all four has much of significance in common. I will then look at some of Heidegger's work in *The Basic Problems of Phenomenology* and *Being and Time* which will underpin these earlier discussions and begin to provide a sound philosophical basis for understanding Severs, Bachelard, Rilke and Sebald.

Rilke - Houses that have gone

In his strange, and only, novel *The Notebooks of Malte Laurids Brigge*, Rainer Maria Rilke provides us with three epic accounts of his own experiences of houses. The first is his celebrated [1] account of an encounter with the end wall of a house the rest of which has been demolished but which bears the scars of use and, for Malte, the memories of the house as it once appeared and existed. The second is a ghostly encounter described between the young Malte and the burned out ruin of the house of one of their neighbours which he visits with his mother. The third is a kind of remembrance of the house of his grandfather. All of these accounts are striking in that they tell of encounters with houses which are in fact and substantially no longer there, but in all the cases something remains. These remains provide Malte with an appearance of the houses which is both shocking and unnerving, and which begin to say something about how we relate to the world around us and how this world appears to us. All three encounters engender a sense of the uncanny, [2] the first and third in the adult

Malte and the second in him as a child. I will discuss these accounts and see what we can learn about the way that houses appear and then to determine what factors there are in common not only between these three examples from Rilke, but also with the accounts of houses given by Severs and Bachelard.

First, to the wall. Malte is alone and impoverished in the Paris of the early twentieth century and, driven outside by the smoking stove in his room. While wandering the streets he comes across a row of terraced houses the end one of which has been demolished thus exposing the inside wall it once shared with the next house. It is to this exposure that Malte's attention is drawn,

> I don't know if I have already said that this is the wall I mean. But it was, so to speak, not the first wall of the existing houses (as one would have supposed) but the last of those that had been there. One saw its inner side. One saw at the different stories, the walls of rooms to which the paper still clung, and here and there the join of floor or ceiling. Beside these room-walls there still remained, along the whole length of the wall, a dirty white area, and through this crept in unspeakably disgusting motions, worm soft, and as if digesting the open, rust spotted channel of the water closet pipe. Grey, dusty traces of the paths the lighting-gas had taken remained at the ceiling edges, and here and there, quite unexpectedly, they bent sharp around and came running into the colored wall and into a hole that had been torn out black and ruthless. (Rilke, 1992, pp.46-47)

This wall and the marks on it make a vivid impression on Malte by pointing to the former existence of the house as somewhere where people lived. The lingering remnants of the interior, private, parts of the house show that it has been more than just another building, it also contained the lives of those who lived there and who made it what it once was. The bare remains of the wall bring forth the appearance of the house that was once there. But there is more to it than this, as he continues,

> But most unforgettable of all were the walls themselves. The stubborn life of these rooms had not let itself be trampled out. It was still there; it clung to the nails that had been left, stood on the remaining handsbreadth of flooring, it crouched under the corner joints where there was still a little bit of interior … it was also in the spots that had kept fresher behind mirrors, pictures and wardrobes; for it had drawn and redrawn their contours, and had been with spiders and dust even in these hidden places, that now lay bared. (Rilke, 1992, p. 47)

The walls themselves seem to contain something, something that was there before the house was demolished, its 'life', which now clings onto existence through the tattered remnants, and this too, whatever it is, appears to the increasingly appalled Malte, even though it is barely there at all. And yet it seems there is even more, he continues,

> And from these walls, once blue and green and yellow, which were framed by the fracture-tracks of the demolished partitions, the breath of these lives stood out—the clammy, sluggish, musty breath, which no wind had yet scattered. There stood the middays and the sickness and the exhaled breath and the smoke of years, and the sweat that breaks out under armpits and makes clothes heavy, and the stale breath of mouths and the fusel odor of sweltering feet. There stood the tang of urine and the burn of soot and the grey reek of potatoes, and the heavy smooth stench of ageing grease. The sweet lingering smell of neglected infants was there, the fear-smell of children who go to school, and the sultriness out of the beds of nubile youths. To these was added much that had come from below, from the abyss of the street, which reeked, and more that had oozed down from above with the rain. (Rilke, 1992, pp.47-48)

Not only the house but also the lives of the people who lived in it appear vividly to Malte as he comes upon this scene. The house still lives and is still filled with the lives of the people who once called it home. It is as if all of the work that Severs does in his house is unnecessary. The remains of the house that Malte finds gives us at least as much of the former existence and life of the building as all of Sever's efforts in his house can ever give us. Malte has a dream, or a nightmare, of a house, and all of those who were in it, and this dream is given in Rilke's account of what physically little remains of the house that has gone. Malte sees the wall of the house and yet understands so much more than is physically apparent. The being of the house is still there somehow in spite of its almost complete material demolition, it has no three dimensional existence. The house is apparent although it can no longer geometrically appear as a house.

Already we can hear resonances of Bachelard's oneiric house; Rilke's poetic imagery is seizing the specific reality of the house and opening up the possibilities of understanding the house in its "primary function of inhabiting".[3] The house, which is not really a house at all anymore, is yet more than an inert box and has become inhabited space and as Bachelard says,

> If we go from these images, which are all light and shimmer, to images that insist and force us to remember farther back into our past, we shall have to

take lessons from poets. For how forcefully they prove to us that the
houses that were lost forever continue to live on in us; that they insist in us
in order to live again. (Bachelard, 1958, 1994, p.56)

Rilke's account of the wall is transcendental in exactly the way that
Bachelard discusses, and it creates a transcendental geography or
psychogeography of the house through no more than the contemplation of
the remaining wall.

In the second example we have another house which is no more, when
Rilke gives an account of the visit of the child Malte to the house of the
Schulins. The Schulins house has been mostly burned down and "they
were now living in two narrow side wings".[4] Rilke describes a visit to the
Schulins in heavy snow and gives examples of the poor visibility as the
journey by sleigh proceeds; already the disorientation of the snowstorm
begins to give a dreamlike quality to the young Malte's experience. Then,
the sleigh driver apparently 'forgets' that the house is gone and pulls up at
the front door. The family, seemingly complicit in this mistake, walk up
the steps leading to the old terrace and "wondered that all was quite
dark".[5] The dream of the house grows with each passing forgetting. It is
only when the owners call out from another door, behind and to the left,
that they realise their mistake and enter the inhabited part of the house.
The devices of poor visibility in heavy snow, the 'mistake' of the sleigh
driver and the sheep like complicity of Malte's family combine to allow
the ghostly impression of the former house to appear. In addition Rilke is
using Malte's impressionable and imaginative child persona to enhance
the unreal and uncanny atmosphere of the setting. All of these give the
account of the visit, and the old house itself, the dream like quality
necessary to allow the long gone house to appear to Malte. Rilke goes on
to describe how the young Malte becomes so convinced that the old house
is still there that he is driven to go and look for it through a connecting
door and, even when pulled back by Viera Schulin, remains convinced that
the old house is still there. Eventually the house disappears but only after
an intensely fearful Malte seeks refuge in his mother's arms. Once again
we have an example of a dream of a house, or a house that, while it is not
really there to be seen anymore, still clings to existence, first in the mind
of the sleigh driver, then the in the adults in Malte's family, and finally,
and most enduringly, in the mind of the child Malte. The house has its way
of appearing after its physical destruction. The memories of the adults in
Malte's family, the sleigh driver, the Schulins, and the young Malte
himself bring back the house that was once there. All contribute to this
psychogeography. Rilke's highly imaginary accounts show that it is
possible to think of houses in this way and indicate further that the same

can be extended to other phenomena that are imbued in the same way with, not necessarily exceptional but merely everyday significance. We will see more examples like these in the work of Sebald. It is through the noticing of these seemingly insignificant everyday phenomena that we can understand our relation to the world through the appearing of things.

In this example from Rilke, the dream like quality of these kinds of experiences is to the forefront; the Schulin's house is clearly one of the "houses of memory".[6] The whole episode as described by Rilke is dreamlike and the dream only fades when Malte seeks refuge in the embrace of his mother. It is as Bachelard has said,

> When we describe a daydream *objectively* this diminishes and interrupts it. How many dreams told objectively have become nothing but oneirism reduced to dust! (Bachelard, 1958, 1994, p.152)

While the dream of the young Malte persists we are given something of the old house which indeed turns to dust once the dream is ended, but within the dream there is a persistent reality which is retained in the memory of the child. The source of this reality is our imagination.

In a third example (which Bachelard refers to in *The Poetics of Space*)[7] Rilke gives us an account of Malte's experience of the old manor house in which his grandfather lived when he says,

> I never saw again that remarkable house, which at my grandfather's death passed into strange hands. As I recover it in recovering my child-wrought memories, it is no complete building; it is all broken up inside me; here a room there a room, and her a piece of hallway that does not connect these two rooms but is preserved, as a fragment, by itself. (Rilke, 1992, p.30)

In this case the house is still there and it is his memory of the house that has decayed, but it is the decayed memory that gives Malte, and us, the house of his grandfather in a way that it could not have been given if the memory had been complete or the description perfect. Indeed the fragmentary nature of the memory opens up the space that we then use for imagining. Rilke goes on to say of the house,

> In this way it is all dispersed within me—the rooms, the stairways that descended with such ceremonious deliberation, and other narrow, spiral stairs in the obscurity of which one moved as blood does in veins; the tower rooms, the high-hung balconies, the unexpected galleries onto which one was thrust out through a little door—all that is still in me and will never cease to be in me. It is as though the picture of this house had fallen

into me from an infinite height and had shattered against my very ground. (Rilke, 1992, pp.30-31)

The very language that Rilke uses is extraordinary when we consider that he is giving an account of something as ordinary as a house, but by using the perspective of a child and the fragmentary nature of memory, Rilke's strange account of the house of Malte's grandfather penetrates to the heart of what this house was really like. We can read his account and know exactly what kind of a house this was, even though the account that is provided is, to say the least, less than orthodox. In all of these examples Rilke gives us the dream of a house. As Bachelard says,

> If we have retained an element of dreams in our memories, if we have gone beyond merely assembling exact recollections, bit by bit the house that was lost in the mists of time will appear from out of the shadows. (Bachelard, 1958, 1994, p.57)

Bachelard echoes Rilke's fragmentary account of his grandfather's house when he says,

> The old house, for those who know how to listen, is a sort of geometry of echoes. The voices of the past do not sound the same in the big room as in the little bedchamber, and the calls on the stairs have got another sound. (Bachelard, 1958, 1994, p.57)

This could apply equally to Severs house and to Rilke's account of the house wall; both are recalling the voices of the past and recognizing their distinctive characteristics.

Both Severs and Rilke are looking to awaken the dreams of houses that have gone in their presentations and accounts of houses and, just as we can see Severs as engaged in a kind of unwitting phenomenology, so Rilke is working in the same field, but in an explicitly poetic literary form. Rilke, by means of the novel, is showing that the houses and spaces that we inhabit have a character beyond the geometrically evident, and that once we have noticed this we can never really look away or forget. Severs is explicitly trying to get the house of memory to appear. Both Severs and Rilke are engaged in an enterprise described by Bachelard, an enterprise which involves remembering images and impressions rather than geometry because,

> Our memories are encumbered with facts. Beyond the recollections we continually hark back to we should like to relive our supposed impressions

and the dreams that made us believe in happiness. (Bachelard, 1958, 1994, p.56)

Bachelard's enterprise is one of disencumbering our memories and allowing the house to appear as it was to us when we first came upon it. It is through our feelings that this memory is reactivated and not through the precise delineation of the geometry of the house. We are thus allowed to imagine the house and to understand it in terms of our own subjectivity. We will see later, in Chapter Five, how Bachelard's thinking extends beyond houses and other defined spaces and comes to apply more widely to the view we can have of the entire world. For now we can conclude that houses seem speak to us and, as Alain de Botton has said,

> When buildings talk, it is never with one voice. Buildings are choirs rather than soloists; they possess a multiple nature from which rise opportunities for beautiful consonance as well as dissension and discord. (de Botton 2007, p.217)

To summarise, it seems that houses are more than just safe, warm, dry places to live. Houses are more than just appearances of houses. Houses are places not spaces, that is, they have meaning for us. There is more to the house than mere empirical appearance, houses are significant places, places in which things happen and have happened. In this way houses not only appear to us but seem to speak to us. When we ask, where they get this speech the only answer we can find is that they get it from us. We give houses their meaning and their meaning is given back to us in their appearance and by the way we attend to what we know about them rather than simply what we see of them. Severs, Bachelard, Rilke and as we shall see next, Sebald, are all helping us to see more than just the appearance, they are bringing to our attention the concealed meaning which transcends mere appearance. In this way it is not the appearing that gives us the meaning but the fact of meaning which allows the house to appear as a house. Houses could not first appear as houses unless they were already spaces with meaning.

Before going on to make any further connections between Rilke's examples and those worked through by Bachelard, and in advance of any specific philosophical examination of what may be going on here, I will look at some examples from the work of W.G. Sebald which will further widen the enquiry of places and how they appear. It will quickly become evident that Sebald goes well beyond the simple accounts of houses and spaces given by Severs, Rilke and Bachelard but I think that the resonances between his work and that of these thinkers will be clear.

W.G. Sebald – What I did on my holidays

Sebald was perhaps influenced by the writing of Rilke but his work is far more subtle and less overtly romantic. He moves from place to place in his works which are part travelogue, part novel, and part biographical and autobiographical exploration of his characters, and to some degree of himself. Sebald's style is quietly discursive and unspectacular, sometimes it is as if he moves through the scene without disturbing the environment in ways which reveal and preserve what is there. In his four novels and long prose poem *After Nature* he shows how our understanding of place, and the ways in which places appear, is very different from simply taking what we see to be there. In addition to reminding us of Rilke's accounts the form and style of his writing brings to mind both Bachelard's emphasis of the dreamlike quality of some of our experience and Severs notion of 'the space between'. The fact that Sebald's work is in literary form also takes us away from the simple fixity of visual appearance and enables us to penetrate further into the uncanniness of our experience of the world around us. I will begin with a look at some episodes in his book *The Rings of Saturn*.

In *The Rings of Saturn* Sebald ostensibly gives an account of a walking tour of Suffolk. On the first page he says,

> At all events, in retrospect I became preoccupied not only with the unaccustomed sense of freedom but also with the paralyzing horror that had come over me at various times when confronted with the traces of destruction, reaching far back into the past. (Sebald, 2002, p.3)

Already this echoes Bachelard's oneirism and the move beyond physical manifestation and geometrical form. Sebald is about to encounter specific realities.

While apparently giving an account of his holiday Sebald uses the occasions and locations of this period to dwell on the places he visits and to gain access to their deeper meanings and significances. In effect he gives us a circumstantial account of the places and buildings he sees and generates a phenomenologically rich account of them. In this way he penetrates into the being of places in ways that are both diverting and yet which illuminate their existence beyond the purely physical. This book is more than a travelogue, more than a kind of 'What I did on my holidays' it is a phenomenological tour of Suffolk and as such can tell us much about how we are related to, or are situated in, the everyday world. Sebald looks at the world in a different way, a way in which he calls us to see the things themselves as phenomenal entities. He does this in much the way that

Bachelard has done but using his own specific experiences and musings. Sebald's work, here and elsewhere, is certainly evocative; however I will argue that it is more than just this, Sebald is not simply drawing our attention to the quaint and coincidental. The basis of what Sebald is able to do, that is to evoke, is grounded not only in the kind of psychological processes that Bachelard describes, but even deeper in the fundamental relation of being-in-the-world and its phenomenological character. I will look later at how Heidegger sets out this character of the world.

It is a feature of *The Rings of Saturn* that almost all of the locations visited by Sebald on his tour become departure points for musings on all manner of things. It is even clear that those locations at which he does not stop, and merely lists as he goes by, have the same potential. Items and places that would pass unnoticed by the casual observer lead to extended discussions of art, history, philosophy, science and nature. Above all Sebald's work is imaginative and shows how everything is connected to almost everything else if we would only just think about it. It is not just the case that single entities, like walls and houses, can cling to their own past existence or just evoke that of their inhabitants. In Sebalds's world entities of all kinds bring to mind their connections with a wide range of other entities and events, past and present. Sebald ranges far and wide through a complex phenomenal context in which one thing may lead to another in often surprising and disturbing ways but always with a sense of their ultimate connectedness. In this way Sebald creates, or illuminates, a psychogeography which underpins our everyday being-in-the-world while going unnoticed for most of the time. In memorial to an earlier writer Sebald conducts an exercise in the recovery of past time but he does this at the same time as he reveals the phenomenal present in all its wondrous complexity.

A few examples from *The Rings of Saturn* will suffice to illustrate the point. Sebald's visit to the museum of the Norfolk and Norwich Hospital before he begins his tour leads to an extensive discussion of the life and work of Thomas Browne a seventeenth century doctor and author of the "part-archaeological and part metaphysical treatise *Urn Burial*".[8] This in turn leads to a speculation that the same Thomas Browne might have been present at the dissection of Aris Kindt, later painted by Rembrandt as *The Anatomy Lesson*. Naturally the painting turns out to be not quite as it would first appear; the corpse, when dissected apparently has two right hands, and this in turn leads to further speculation about the painter's motives. All of this follows from Sebald's own simple enquiry about the whereabouts of Browne's skull following his stay at the hospital.[9] His later stay at Southwold on the Suffolk coast brings to mind the Battle of Sole

Bay fought off the shore there in 1672. This includes considerable imaginings about the lives and experiences of the combatants and of those watching on the shore. When he visits Lowestoft we are treated to a discourse on the history of herring fishing along the east coast of Britain, its rise and its demise. Even more surprising is his account of the light railway which crossed the bridge on the River Blyth west of Southwold. Sebald speculates, on what can only be described as the thinnest of premise, that the railway and its engines were originally intended for the Chinese imperial family to connect the palace with the capital. This opens up the opportunity to tell the story of the Chinese empire, including the history of silk making, and its eventual collapse. In each instance Sebald appears to be doing more than simply telling a story that the particular place reminds him of, on each occasion he is able to recreate temporally past or physically distant events, and sometimes those which are both, and to such an extent that he himself appears to be there. Times and places overlap in Sebald's work so that, for example, we can feel the presence of the onlookers at the Battle of Sole Bay when we are taken by Sebald to Gun Hill in Southwold, this is what makes much of his work seem uncanny, like a waking dream.

Incidentally it seems in one way at least that Sebald's discussion of *The Anatomy Lesson* is curiously reminiscent of Rilke's earlier account of the wall and the way he talks about the anatomy of the house now exposed. While Rilke talks about "the open, rust spotted channel of the water-closet pipe" and "its unspeakably disgusting motions",[10] using explicit bodily metaphors, Sebald describes the cadaver and the ways in which its internal workings are exposed for all to see in the same way, as an *object* for science. Just as Rilke's house is more than just the walls, Sebald sees that the cadaver in *The Anatomy Lesson* is a man rather than just a body. It is interesting to speculate, as does Sebald, that Rene Descartes the originator of modern scientific subjectivity could have been present at the dissection depicted in Rembrandt's picture. Descartes work is responsible for many of the ways we look at and understand the world today and yet this exercise in rendering the individual down to a scientific subject, a Cartesian enterprise if there ever was one, is precisely the kind of enterprise that both Severs and Bachelard warn us against when they point us towards the imaginary. Through scientific dissection the doctors attempt to remove the imaginary dimension and to render the criminal a mere object, but, just as Rilke's wall gives us the house in all the richness of its meaning so Rembrandt's depiction of the dissected cadaver gives us the man; Aris Kindt. Both show us that individual bodies, be they houses or bodies have meaning which goes well beyond their mere physical manifestation. These kinds of meanderings are exactly the kind of thinking that Sebald's work provokes.

However the power and significance of Sebald's work in this book is more than a series of imaginatively set out coincidences leading to the revelation of times past. Through his moody melancholic style and his deliberate taking of oblique points of view on the things and places he finds, Sebald is revealing the embedded meaning in the scenes and entities which he encounters. By making the familiar uncanny and by getting us to see things from another angle, and in a different light, and by allowing free play of the imagination, Sebald shows us that there is more to it than meets the eye. He enables us to see things as they really are, not just as they simply appear. We will understand later that it is not a coincidence that Heidegger stresses the importance of mood in his search for the meaning of being in *Being and Time*. Sebald is conducting a Severs-like project but on the grandest of scales. His imaginative viewing applies not only to the history of the places and things he comes across, but to the lives and destinies of the people involved in them. Sebald exposes what might be termed the metaphysical interlining of reality; like Bachelard, Sebald takes "care not to break up the solidity of memory"[11] and, in so doing, helps to return us to a more primordial and imaginary basis for understanding the world in which we find ourselves. This is a ground of interconnectedness which must underpin all of our more sophisticated relationships with the world. It is a basis which we have in a significant way forgotten, and which through forgetting have lost the ways in which it can be said. Sebald's power is in his ability to bear witness to this primordial relation not by direct articulation but by quiet not-quite-saying. As Heidegger says, "Anyone who keeps silent when he wants to give you to understand something must 'have something to say'."[12]

Sebald reminds us that we have forgotten and helps us to un-forget. Forgetting has occurred inevitably as a result of the increasing sophistication of our thinking and the systematic differentiation given to us by scientific method. Forgetting has become a necessity of our everyday lives, a way of being ordinarily. Sebald's work is therefore a kind of remembering, a remembering of the way we really exist in the world and a way which is the real basis for all of our thinking about the world. We are returned to this primordial basis in Sebald's enigmatic prose. This is why the connections he makes go far beyond mere things and includes the ways in which these things have had meaning in the lives of those who used them. This is also something of what Rilke is seeing in the wall. The connections that Sebald makes with the long past and dead, and the seemingly incongruous melding of one experience into another both reinvests everyday life with its deep meaning and tell us that there is much there that is left unexplained. Paradoxically Sebald broadens our horizons by narrowing our focus back onto the inconsequential paraphernalia of everyday life. He makes these uncanny so that the latent becomes apparent through the familiar. In this way he is giving us glimpses of the everyday in its ordinariness by challenging our initial perception of entities and locations and asking us to see what is there. Sebald thus goes beyond the image while at the same time penetrating into the onset of the image, that is; the appearance. His accounts of places and houses are full of weighty, insistent meaning. In Sebald we find Bachelard in practice, operating in the world and applying the principles of phenomenology not just in respect of familiar domestic entities (houses, corners, cupboards, etc.) but to the entire corpus of perception.

Sebald is writing in the 'space between', that is, his writing is only possible because of the 'space between', the same space in which Severs carefully constructs the reality of his house, and the space in which we can see things, if not necessarily as they are, then as they might be. This has been called Sebald's spectral materialism[13] but I would rather think of it as his way of restoring the uncanny to all aspects of our everyday lives, and opening up the space in which we can imagine and in which phenomena can appear. Sebald clearly acknowledges that this can never be a simple process and admits openly and often that the truth given through this process can be unreliable. There are no simple answers. It is not simply a case of unraveling the multitude of perceptions past and present to reveal the reality within, it is more like unlearning one way of seeing and understanding and allowing another the room in which to develop. We will return to Sebald's work in Chapter Five but before that I will now begin to look at some of the philosophy which underlies his method

Heidegger Thinking of the Wall

It is already clear that Sebald and Rilke are engaged in something of the same kind of project. Both are using literary and poetic means to look at things in ways which reveal more than might otherwise be apparent, and both use their experience of everyday entities to make connections, with other lives, other places and other times. Both are also using the poetic literary form to create a dreamlike nature to the experiences of their characters which is reminiscent of Bachelard's oneirism. Although he was of course unable to say what he thought of Sebald's work, Heidegger famously seized on Rilke's account of the end wall of the house as an example of the kind of emergence of the everyday which supported his "Thesis of Modern Ontology".[14] I suggest that Sebald is similarly engaged.

To begin with, quoting Fichte, Heidegger says, "Gentlemen, think the wall, and then think the one who thinks the wall."[15] He then goes on to say in criticism of Fichte,

> There is already a constructive violation of the facts, an unphenomenological onset in the request, "think the wall". For in our natural comportment towards things we never think a single thing, and whenever we seize upon it expressly for itself we are taking it out of a contexture to which it belongs in its real content: wall, room, surroundings. (Heidegger, 1988, p.162)

The wall that Fichte is thinking is clearly nothing like the wall that Rilke is thinking, and the kind of thinking that Heidegger will suggest will have more in common with Rilke than with Fichte. In a similar but more memorable, and in a more poetic vein, in *Being and Time* Heidegger says,

> What we 'first' hear is never noises or complexes of sounds, but the creaking wagon, the motor cycle. We hear the column on the march, the north wind, the woodpecker tapping, the fire crackling. (Heidegger, 1962, H.164)

We can hear here echoes of Rilke's language as Heidegger describes the world and the things we find in it, but unlike Rilke Heidegger is explicitly pointing out the simple misconception we have about the nature of our relation towards the world, and is pointing us towards a new relation of contexture which includes us in the world. Philosophically speaking Heidegger is conducting a dazzling attack on the Cartesian and post-Cartesian model of a world made up of subjects like ourselves and objects which we can apprehend, and replacing it with a model in which we ourselves are inextricably included, thus,

> It is not the case that man 'is' and then has, by way of an extra, a relationship-of-Being towards the 'world'—a world with which he provides himself occasionally. (Heidegger, 1962, H.57)

We have no choice about our involvement and therefore no perspective to which we can retreat to get a view of the world separate from ourselves. We are not set aside from the world only to join in later, moreover,

> We say that the Dasein does not first need to turn backwards to itself as though, keeping itself behind its own back, it were at first standing in front

of things and staring rigidly at them. Instead it never finds itself otherwise than in the things themselves, and in fact in those things that daily surround it. (Heidegger, 1988, p.159)

This is because, "Intentionality belongs to the existence of Dasein."[16] In this way we can only understand the world and ourselves as essentially involved or engaged in the world. This is the engagement that both Sebald and Rilke are describing. The world that they give us in their accounts is one in which we are wrapped up, not one which we have to go out and apprehend, a world which appears when we allow it to appear. Furthermore this is not an accidental or an incidental engagement but one which is fundamentally constitutive of the kind of being that we are, and, as Heidegger says,

> As the Dasein gives itself over immediately and passionately to the world itself, its own self is reflected to it from the things. This is not mysticism and does not presuppose the assigning of souls to things. It is only a reference to an elementary phenomenological fact of existence, which must be seen prior to all talk no matter how acute about the subject-object relation. (Heidegger, 1988, p.159)

It is already apparent that mysticism is a charge that some may wish to level at the writing of Sebald and Bachelard but I hope that by showing how their work can be underpinned with Heidegger's explanations of being that this charge can be easily refuted. The connection with Heidegger is reinforced when he says,

> Poetry, creative literature, is nothing but the elementary emergence into words, the becoming-uncovered, of existence as being-in-the-world. For the others who before it were blind, the world first becomes visible by what is thus spoken. (Heidegger, 1988, p.172)

Rilke and Sebald are the kinds of poets to which Heidegger is referring and the significance of what they are doing begins to become apparent. This kind of pre-conceptual understanding is most reminiscent of Bachelard's daydreams but Heidegger is not prone to the same kind of potentially mystical language preferring instead his own philosophical expressions which lay bare the underlying structures of our being-in-the-world.

All of this places an appreciation of Rilke and Sebald at the heart of Heidegger's work as exemplars of the kind of poetic writing that is the key to becoming-uncovered.   Both Rilke and Sebald are writers of the phenomenal; that is they are trying to say something about the world in which we find ourselves by looking closely at the things they find. They are saying things in ways that recognizes the way in which they, and all the rest of us, are mixed up in these things and in the world. Heidegger supports this in direct reference to Rilke's account of the wall when he says,

> What Rilke reads here in his sentences from the exposed wall is not imagined into the wall, but quite to the contrary, the description is possible only as an interpretation and elucidation of what is "actually" in this wall, which leaps forth from it in our natural comportmental relationship to it. Not only is the writer able to see this original world, even though it has been unconsidered and not at all theoretically discovered, but Rilke understands the philosophical content of the concept of life. (Heidegger, 1988, p.173)

Heidegger is here applauding the immediacy of Rilke's account of the wall of the mostly demolished house and gives this immediacy philosophical significance in terms of the ways that we understand our own selves when he says,

> Self-understanding of the everyday Dasein depends not so much on the extent and penetration of our knowledge of things as such as on the immediacy and originality of being-in-the-world. (Heidegger, 1988, p.171)

Heidegger's emphasis on immediacy as against the extent and penetration of our knowledge of things is in direct contrast to the Cartesian and post-Cartesian basis of the scientific understanding of the world which has devalued imagination in the search for knowledge. This has not only led to an impoverishment of what we understand as knowledge but to an equal deficiency in the understanding of our own selves. It is not merely that Rilke has given us the wall and the house in his account, he has also given us his own self reflected in these things. The inextricable engagement we have with the world means that we cannot give an account of it without at the same time giving an account of ourselves. As a commentary on individual identity this will suffice for now as I will return to this subject at length in a later chapter.

If the things that Heidegger says of Rilke and his account of the wall are true then the same in even greater degree is true of Sebald. Sebald sees the original world and brings out that which is already contained within it. Even more, these things are not contrived or forced but leap forth from Sebald's accounts as elements integral to the places and things he sees. Through the literary form Sebald and Rilke are able to uncover this original world through the things they see and in a way that is inaccessible to traditional theory. They are able to show us the everyday in its everydayness and bring it to notice without undue violence to its character as inconspicuously sunken into our lives. Sebald's quiet approach allows us to see what is already there and reveals the ground upon which all later conceptualization can take place.

Once again Heidegger's insights support Rilke and Sebald's work when he says.

> The view in which the equipmental contexture stands out at first, completely unobtrusive and unthought is the view and sight of practical *circumspection*, of our practical everyday orientation. "Unthought" means that it is not thematically apprehended for deliberate thinking about things; instead, in circumspection, we find our bearings in regard to them. Circumspection uncovers and understands beings primarily as equipment. (Heidegger, 1988, p.163)

Both Rilke and Sebald may be said to be circumspect in their discussion of the world. Particularly in the case of Sebald it remains essentially "unthought" and the understanding that is thus uncovered through this method reveals the being of the things they find.

This is now a clear alternative to the mainly Cartesian or scientific model that had prevailed[17] when it came to consciousness and the world, and is a way of thinking that is much more in tune with both the intuitive approach of Dennis Severs and the approach taken by Bachelard. Like Rilke, Sebald, Severs and Bachelard, Heidegger's work is not so much philosophy by strict scientific method. He does not seek to systematically 'prove' everything about our existence, consciousness and world, but to illuminate and to reveal, and to disclose. In this way we are left to be convinced by ourselves. Heidegger's work provides the philosophical underpinning for the approaches taken by Severs and Bachelard and it is exemplified by Rilke and Sebald, they are the kind of poets who can call forth and make the world emerge as appearance.

Heidegger focuses our attention on the breadth of our experience and this parallels Severs and Sebald's approach by explicitly noticing what Severs has called the space between. Heidegger goes further and wants us to understand this way of experiencing the world as a totality, as fundamental, and prior to any further understanding or analysis so that,

> Our concernful dealings can let what is ready-to-hand be encountered circumspectively only if in these dealings we already understand something like the involvement which something has in something. (Heidegger, 1962, H.353)

It is perhaps still difficult, even at this stage, to recognise the full relevance of what Heidegger is saying about the enterprises of Rilke, Sebald, Severs and Bachelard, but it is at least clear that his overall methodology of disclosure and revelation has something in common with all of these. All of them are attempting to avoid an approach that seeks to determine, to analyze and to categorize entities and phenomena. Severs does this out of a wish to 'feel' reality rather than to 'understand', and Bachelard does it out of a recognition that spaces and things have oneiric quality which is obscured by analysis and description. Sebald and Rilke are both writing about the world in ways which make us recognize that there is more to it than might first appear. All of them have realised something particular about the world from their simple experiences. Heidegger has realised the philosophical inadequacy of Cartesian and post-Cartesian epistemology and can thus provide a new basis for understanding this new kind of experience that will ring true with such diverse characters as Rilke, Sebald, Severs and Bachelard. Heidegger's words resonate with all of them when he says that,

> When in one's concern, one lets something be involved, one's doing so is founded on temporality, and amounts to an altogether pre-ontological and non-thematic way of understanding involvement and readiness-to-hand. (Heidegger, 1962, H.356)

Heidegger reminds us that every day we come into contact with things in the world, and that for most of the time this contact is unmemorable and may even be unwitting. We navigate our way through the world and only occasionally stop and, as it were, make something of the world. Heidegger's central thesis is that the fact of this kind of pre-ontological non-thematic way of understanding is prior to any explicit conceptualization that we may undertake; it is the almost unheard background music of our existing, and those like Sebald, with their quiet approach, allow the music to be heard. Similarly a project like the one that Severs is pursuing is ontologically significant in Heidegger's terms both because it recognises the primordiality of the kind of unthought unmediated experience that it offers, and because, through this pre-ontological experience of the world, it supports the further analysis, determination and description of entities. Heidegger wants us to turn the usual process upside down, rather than taking a 'scientific' approach and analyzing objects in their isolation he insists, in the same way that Severs insists, that we take first the context, the space between, and arrive at the objects through their relationships within the context, a context which includes all of us. Bachelard is working towards much the same position by describing not space but our relation to specific spaces within the notion of the house. In simple terms we cannot hope to understand what the individual items in Severs house were (used) for in the eighteenth century not only without some prior understanding of what the period was like and how people lived, but unless we have an understanding of their being-in-the-world. Without the context the items are literally meaningless. Both Rilke and Sebald use the literary and poetic forms to demonstrate this kind of thinking in action in the real world. Heidegger's analysis supports the methods of Rilke, Sebald, Severs and Bachelard by affirming the primordiality of their approach which is direct, relational and without mediation. All of them are 'getting it' and Heidegger has begun to show how this is possible. I will return to Heidegger's work in later chapters and expand the view of the world and of being which he sets out as it becomes relevant to the theme of each chapter. In the next chapter I will go outside the house to look at the way that we perceive and understand landscape and the rest of the world through a discussion of its portrayal.

Notes

[1] Celebrated by Heidegger who quotes the entire passage in *The Basic Problems of Phenomenology*, pp.172-3.
[2] Throughout this work I want to us this term in the sense that Heidegger uses it; that is as the feeling of not-at-home (unheimlich).
[3] Bachelard, 1958, 1994, p.4.
[4] Rilke, 1992, pp.122-3.
[5] Rilke, 1992, p.124.
[6] Bachelard, 1958, 1994, p.3.
[7] Bachelard, 1958, 1994, p.57.
[8] Sebald, 2002, *The Rings of Saturn*, p.11.
[9] Sebald, 2002, *The Rings of Saturn*, pp.9-17.
[10] Rilke, 1992, pp.46-47.
[11] Bachelard, 1958, 1994, p.6.
[12] Heidegger, 1962, H.296.
[13] Santer, 2006, p.52.
[14] Heidegger, 1988, p.122-176.
[15] Heidegger, 1988, p.162.
[16] Heidegger, 1988, p.157.
[17] The best exposition of this position and the Heideggerian critique is given in Richardson, J. *Existential Epistemology*. Also see my own *Heidegger's Philosophy and Theories of the Self*.

CHAPTER FOUR

SEEING, KNOWING AND PICTURING: BEING-IN-THE-WORLD AND THE ART OF THE DUTCH REPUBLIC 1585-1718

In contrast to the discussion so far, I have chosen (in the main) in this chapter to consider some paintings and drawings, both because they involve the creation of an appearance or an image, and because they themselves appear as what they are, that is as images of images. I think that as this chapter develops the connections with what has gone before will become apparent. Furthermore the kind of figurative painting that I am going to consider seems to purport to provide images of the world in which we live, and everyday images at that. They seem to show us what we see. Importantly these particular paintings and drawings were created at a time when images were scarce and difficult to produce and therefore had a significance that is not easy to reproduce today, but which more easily reveals their meaning. A discussion of some of these paintings will provide useful metaphors about appearances which will inform the discussion in different ways to those we have already considered.

The fascination that the work of the artists of the Dutch Republic produced, and continues to produce, through their almost uncanny rendering of the everyday world has certainly stood the test of time, and exhibitions of their work still command great attention and attract huge crowds. They were no doubt great artists and they have left their mark on the world. However I am here not primarily concerned with what might be termed art theory. I leave speculation about the history and effect of art to those more closely versed in this kind of work. Although what I have to say may at least gesture towards some of this work my main interest is phenomenological. It centres on the nexus between seeing or sensing, that is, perceiving, in the widest sense of coming to notice, and knowing, which for the moment we can take to mean, being certain that it is the case. In the art of the Dutch Republic I am seeking illustrative examples of this nexus. I will try to show how the painters of the Dutch Republic, through their endeavours to render the world as image, and through the craft or work necessary to this endeavour, begin to reveal things about the world in which they lived which were not only not acknowledged at the time but, to some extent, ran against the new and rising wisdom of their time. I will try to show that the work of these artists illuminates features of our existence in the world which were not articulated philosophically for many years to come, but which were nevertheless crucial to their work. The works that I will use to illustrate my argument will primarily be landscapes, though I will also refer to some examples of still life and portrait. In this way I hope to move beyond images of houses that seem to speak to us, into a more general field of images of places in general that seem to speak to us, and in so doing say more about themselves, and about us, than is immediately apparent.

The Philosophical and Technological Context

I think that the philosophical and technological context of the art of the Dutch Republic is crucial to an understanding of the work, and I will spend some time setting this out before considering any particular works of art. The republic flourished at an extraordinary time for philosophy and for science. Beliefs about the world and how it works changed and developed more at this period than had ever before been imaginable. The effects of these changes were perhaps felt even more keenly in the Dutch Republic than elsewhere because of the relative intellectual liberalism allowed by Protestantism and the way in which new thinkers were driven from more conservative, and therefore more dangerous, Catholic Europe and concentrated in Protestant enclaves in the Netherlands and Britain. Philosophically speaking the work of Descartes and the early British empiricists provides the main intellectual context, along with the new scientific discoveries of Newton and others. At the ground level the new science was fed by technological development particularly in microscopy and magnification, and in the manufacture of more precise equipment through which to view the world. In short, at this time more new images were becoming available than at any time before and these images told much more about the world than had been known before.

Although the thrust of Descartes work was not empirical, by asking the pertinent questions about the world and how we come to experience it, he certainly provoked the development of empiricism which resulted in the rise of the British tradition of empirical philosophy and the great debates between the works of John Locke, George Berkeley and David Hume. Empirical philosophy and Newtonian mechanics, along with permission to question, established the intellectual climate for the Dutch painters. The availability of new materials and technologies for observing the world, like lenses, mirrors and the camera obscura, provided the means to take forward the enterprise of rendering the world as ever more perfect image. This enabled the artists to raise their craft to new heights and the results were works which appear almost real, or, as we might now say, photographic.

The artists of the Dutch Republic engaged with a will on a vast image making project of showing what was there to be seen, to reveal the wonders of nature and the world, and to make a profit out of selling these startling, never before available, images. Svetlana Alpers sums it up when she says,

> Attentive looking, transcribed by the hand... led to the recording of the multitude of things that make up the visible world. In the seventeenth century this was celebrated as giving basic access to knowledge and understanding of the world. (Alpers, 1983, p.72)

And even further commenting on Hooke's Micrographia,

> The eye, helped by the lens, was a means by which men were able to turn from the misleading world of Brain and Fancy to the concrete world of things. And the recording of such visual observations ... was to be the basis for new and true knowledge. (Alpers, 1983, p.73)

The creation of accurate appearances drives the enterprise like never before and brings into use more and more means of doing so. Empiricism provides the intellectual, philosophical and artistic background to the age, and the painters of the Dutch Republic can therefore be seen in this instance, by their creation of images, as purveyors of knowledge about the world as well as makers of decorative objects.

If we are even to begin to understand the circumstance in which the painters worked and in which the paintings were made, a further and important point that must be grasped is the sheer rarity of images. We find it almost impossible to imagine what a world without images could be like. Our present world is so dominated by the image, on television, in film, photographs and on computers that we cannot, without difficulty, transpose ourselves to a time when images of the world were rare. This present ubiquity of images makes any investigation into their onset very complicated and difficult. When the painters of the Dutch Republic produced their work they were almost the sole custodians of image making technology. Ordinary people had little or no access to any kind of image and probably only saw their own reflections and the reflections of their surroundings in pools of water. While lens and mirror technology was developing this would hardly be available to the population at large. Churches were often the only place where ordinary people saw fixed representations (images) of this world and the next. This gave the images that were available a magical and sacred quality and to their creators the same aura of wonder. The impact of the production of images of everyday life by the Dutch painters cannot be underestimated. For the first time ever people were able to see fixed images of scenes that they would recognise from their daily lives. In the land of the blind the one-eyed man is truly the king and the artists must have seemed like magicians to those who were not privy to their craft. We can hardly imagine the value that would be placed on an apparently perfect rendering of an image of objects and circumstances that were encountered every day, but never fixed. This perhaps came to a peak in the art of portraiture in which the look of my own self could be frozen in time for posterity, as well as being modified according to the taste of the day and personal vanity. In all of the following discussions the standing of the images produced by the Dutch artists must be borne in mind, they worked in a time when the onset of an image was a wonder. Fortunately for us the rarity of these images, by stripping away their present day ubiquity, makes a study of their onset more accessible.

Finally in considering the context for the succeeding discussion it is necessary to make explicit mention of the new technologies that were being made available to artists. While there has been argument in the past about the extent to which artists used mirrors, lenses and the camera obscura, and even in some cases whether or not these were used at all, I would argue that, following the work of David Hockney and his book *Secret Knowledge,* it is now beyond dispute that all of the great artists of the Dutch Republic used optical equipment to produce their striking paintings of the everyday. Hockney shows by practical demonstration that the method of projection and outlining had been in use for many years prior to the republic and remains dominant until the invention of photography in the mid-nineteenth century.[1] This means that these artists were engaged in producing an image of an appearance which they had cast using technological devices. They were not simply applying to the canvas an image which appeared, as it were, in their minds, they were apparently remaining external to these images. This is important when we come to consider the phenomenological import of these appearances and is the reason why these kinds of paintings can provide only metaphors in a discussion of the 'onset of the image' or phenomenology.

I do not agree with those who consider that the use of optical equipment devalues the work of those who used it, and certainly not the painters of the Dutch Republic. However I do think that the use of this technology combined with the prevailing climate of empiricism gave rise to the acceptance of a dominant metaphor of perception and representation of the world. In short these factors determined how these people saw the world and how they understood the world. The representational model of the perception of the world, the world as pictures or ideas, did not originate in the seventeenth century but its forward march into our modern consciousness was given a huge impetus and reinforcement at this time. Even now we find it hard to divest ourselves of this way of thinking and talking. It is however a metaphor for the world and one with which we must take great care. It will be central to the argument of this chapter that the representational model of perception is a misleading metaphor.

Painting Pictures – Seeing and Knowing

Having set out the philosophical and technological context I would now like to examine what it is I think these artists might have been up to, explicitly and then implicitly. I will couch this in philosophical terms since this is both my primary aim and my familiar vocabulary. I hope that what I have to say will ring true with regard to these kinds of pictures and begin to show what is really going on beneath the decorative surface. I will then consider four specific pictures in more detail. Although I am going to talk about specific pictures in this chapter there are no pictures in this book. The paintings that I have chosen to discuss work for me, but there are probably many other examples that will work in the same way for others, and finding and thinking about them is part of what any reader of this book will need to do as a way of understanding what I am trying to say. Meaning is given in the acts of searching and finding.

The examples of the representation of the everyday world by the painters of the Dutch Republic are legion.[2] Vermeer is acknowledged to be the greatest of these, although had Carel Fabritius[3] lived longer he might have achieved even greater things. I think that the empirical intent of Vermeer paintings like, *Girl Reading a Letters at an Open Window*, *The Milkmaid*, *The Lacemaker*, *Woman with a Water Jug*, and many others is indisputable. The striving for a sheer photographic quality of the images, a quality which, apart from their use of the camera obscura, Vermeer and his contemporaries would have had no real experience, is self-evident. They were trying to show it how it is, whatever 'it' is. This quality is found in many other paintings of this period and school. The flower paintings of

Van Huysum, Rembrandt's *Portrait of Jan Six*, and the interiors of De Hooch and others, all seem to show an uncanny reality and this is not confined to still life and portrait. There, in addition, are many landscapes; Vermeer's *View of Delft*, Cuyp's *View of Dordrecht*, Van Ruisdael's, *A Landscape with a Ruined Castle and a Church*, which seem to 'show it like it is'.

The motives for this striving are multiple. There is possibly a sense in which they did it because they could, as pure expression of their craft. They certainly painted for a market and to their patron's taste. Artists, like any artisans, were out to make a living and the better their pictures, the more perfectly they appeared to represent reality, the higher prices they could command. There may also have been a sense in which they saw themselves as part of the new science of revelation, showing the world as it appeared, as the new knowledge. A definitive collection of these kinds of paintings was drawn together in 1999/2000 in an exhibition at the Ashmolean Museum in Oxford called *Scenes of Everyday Life - Dutch Genre Paintings from the Maurithuis*. The sheer concentration of paintings of this kind certainly makes an impression in confirming the rampant empiricism of this tradition. Indeed it was this exhibition that in part inspired me, or challenged me, to write about this kind of painting in the first place.

The process of capturing a representation of the world is essentially a reductionist project, an attempt to reduce the entities we encounter in the world to their essential nature, to show them as they are. Particularly in the case of still life painting we can see the increasingly successful attempts to render the look of things as they 'really are'. We see the fruit and vegetables, the meat, the glass of wine, the flowers and the insects and we exclaim at how real they seem, and how we could almost touch or even taste them. We imagine that we could reach out and take them up from the picture itself. However in spite of their almost perfect representation of the world, the artists in a way tell us nothing new about the things and people that they painted. While their enterprise is empirical it is also second hand. Empirically speaking our encounter with these entities of everyday life is already complete when we encounter them. The pictures of them are nothing more than an imitating novelty, in this sense they are second hand images. The pictures painted by these artists taken as descriptions of the world lack almost everything that we have already found, for example in Rilke's accounts of houses. While it is true that the artists, through the sheer skills of their craft have given us lasting images of objects, and to some extent brought these objects forward to our attention at least empirically, there is, it seems, philosophically nothing more to see on this front. The paintings may be seen as no more than tricks, a two-dimensional representation, using coloured materials on a flat surface to deceive the eye into thinking that it is seeing a real object. In this they are much less even than the poetic musings of Rilke and Bachelard and less by far than the whole of Sever's enterprise in Folgate Street. In fact, and of course, we can get a lot more, empirically, from the looking at the object itself than we can from seeing a painting, however perfect a representation. We can touch, smell, and taste the lemon and the glass of wine, we can hear the milk as it is poured out of the jug, we can feel the wind on our faces and hear the rustling of trees in the wood, and these sensations give us our empirical ideas of the objects themselves, or so the empiricist would say. But if we are to go deeper and attempt to examine the onset of the image then the act of artistic creation itself may be able to tell us something else. Even as second hand and empirical, these pictures are still images and a discussion of their onset can throw light on the way that phenomenology, or the onset of images in general, is possible.

Perhaps Simon Schama had something of this in mind when he said,

> Before it can ever be repose for the sense, landscape is the work. Its scenery is built up as much from the strata of memory as from layers of rock. (Schama, 1996, p.6)

There is already an echo of Bachelard here and one which I hope will become louder. It seems that a simple urge to empiricism may not be all there is to these paintings, if it were it would be a barely worthwhile activity doomed eternally to fall short of what is available to everyday experience. The paintings would be no more than mere decorative curios and while it is true that the paintings give a permanent representation of passing phenomena this would hardly be sufficient to found their lasting impression. It is therefore to their modes of creation and the deeper purposes of the artists that we must turn. I hope that some consideration of the way the Dutch painters set about their work, and the kinds of images that they produced, will show us not only an example of the onset of an image but will begin to illuminate a relationship we all share with the everyday, a relationship which is more than mere appearance and which conveys to us something of that which makes these things possible in the first place. Through their paintings we are enabled to notice that which is unspoken, but evident, in the things they portray.

In order to attempt to describe this transition from seeing to knowing I will now discuss four specific works of art of the period which I believe begin to go beyond mere seeing, and which therefore begin to go further than even the artists who painted them had intended or could have understood. This analysis will involve careful and subtle distinction between seeing and knowing. The results of the investigation will reveal a new philosophical enterprise in which these artists were engaged, in spite of themselves, and which is in effect a kind of phenomenology. It will also begin to elucidate the true philosophical basis for this entire school of painting. In addition it will enable me to say something more about the work of the painters in producing the paintings, which will illuminate the act of creating an image and therefore have profound philosophical implications with regard to the onset of the image, and for the way in which we understand the world as a whole, and our own place in it. Following this I will look at some more of the work of W.G. Sebald and begin to examine the mechanisms which can enable us to go beyond simple representation in all of our understanding of the world. This will extend the range of this kind of thinking from the second hand images of the Dutch painters into all of the images and appearances which make up our world and thereby begin to point to the root of the onset of the image.

More than meets the eye

I am concerned in this section to deliver the master painters of the Dutch Republic from the relative triviality of assuming that they painted what they saw. I want to show that, at least in some cases, they were trying to paint what they knew, and that they were an important part of the new tradition of the display of knowledge of the world in the terms of their time. I will show that, in at least some of the pictures, the artist has gone beyond simple empirical representation, without explicit or philosophical intent to do so, and rendered not simply what they see but what they know, or think they know, to be there.

I will consider each of four pictures separately. These are: *Interior of the Burr Church, Utrecht*, by Pieter Saenredam;[4] *Panorama View of Dunes and a River*, by Philips Koninck;[5] *View of Delft with Salesman of Musical Instruments*, by Carel Fabritius;[6] and finally Samuel Van Hoogstraten's *Perspective Box with Dutch Interior*,[7] which is not so much a picture as a cross between a novelty and a technical tour de force.[8] While each of these exhibits, in a different way, the relationship between seeing and knowing I think that the conclusions that can be drawn from each individually can be brought together to show that something more fundamental is being glimpsed. Taken together, the underlying structures on which these and all of the other paintings of this kind rest can be revealed.

The first painting is a study of the interior of the church at Burr by Pieter Saenredam.[9] This artist specialised in painting interiors and in particular churches. The exceptional feature of this study is simply that, from where the drawing is made, not all of the individual features included in the picture can be seen. In fact Saenredam has used artistic license to enhance the picture. By so doing he has conveyed more information about the interior of the church than would a simply empirical rendering. As Alpers points out, the picture "clearly assembles two views on one surface",[10] that is, the artist has made two drawings from different viewpoints and combined the two into one picture. This may seem a simple and valid enough technique, however I believe that in this study Saenredam has crossed the fine philosophical line between drawing what he sees and drawing what he knows to be there, and has thereby embarked on an enterprise beyond simple empiricism. By taking the information accrued from two drawings and combining this into one finished piece the artist is carrying out a second order composition while still apparently 'showing it like it is'. It is true that both images are empirically derived, in that respect at least he has drawn what he has seen, but the final appearance of the picture is a combination of these images, a combination which conveys more about the interior of the church than could be achieved by a single representational image. Saenredam has begun to show that there is more to the way things can appear than that which we simply see. In fact he has appealed to the knowledge of the interior of this church that the people viewing the image already have, and in this way has represented to them not simply a view but a place which has meaning. The appearance of the church interior given in this picture represents not just a space but a place. Saenredam has created an image both from what is there and from what he knows the people who know the church already know. The image has its meaning from this fact of already knowing. This is a relatively minor example, artistically speaking, and in no way invalidates or denigrates the work of this or any other artist, some might even say that this move made by Saenredam could be seen as a prefigurement of cubism in which one of the aims is to show all aspects of the subject in one two dimensional plane. Putting artistic innovation aside I hope that the philosophical importance of this work and this move will become more evidently significant as we proceed to look at what is going on in the other three examples that I have chosen.

The second painting, *Panorama View of Dunes and a River*,[11] by Philips Koninck, shows a similar move. This apparently straightforward landscape is interesting in that there is no possible fixed point from which it could have been drawn, the artist would have to have been somewhere

up in the air in order to gain the apparent viewpoint. This does not mean
that the landscape is imaginary, the land certainly has (or had at that time)
the physical appearance portrayed, it is simply that there was literally
nowhere for the artist to stand to view the panorama. We may safely
assume that the artist did not have access to a helicopter or any other
means by which to view the scene. In this case Koninck has produced an
appearance which is made up of empirically derived elements with a little
added imaginative license, and in doing so has appealed to the knowledge
that those who view his work already have. In some ways this picture has
more in common with a map in that it is an interpretation of the landscape
rather than simply a view, and as such this connects it with the great Dutch
tradition of mapmaking that flourished under the republic, but then
mapmaking is already itself an explicit displaying of knowledge. As with
Saenredam, we see a move from pure empiricism to the incorporation of
accrued knowledge in an apparently simply representative picture.
Koninck is painting what he knows to be there rather than simply what he
can see; moreover it is what his viewers know to be there. They will have
been familiar with aspects of the view that he painted and it is this
knowing that gives the image its meaning. Again these are places which
have meaning and not just pictures of mere spaces. In a similar way to
Saenredam, who is combining two real viewpoints into one, Koninck is
giving us a real view from a position that does not exist. Again the
exercise is still mostly empirical but once again separate views are
combined into one appearance. The appearance of the landscape is
revealed to be not as simple as we might at first have thought; we
understand something more about the landscape because of the artifice
employed by the artist, he has shown us a place rather than a space and the
meaning which makes it so is the meaning that we are able to give it.

The third picture, *View of Delft with Salesman of Musical Instruments*,[12]
by Carel Fabritius, is a little more involved but the same kind of thing is
happening. In this picture the artist has not only used an optical instrument
(camera obscura), but furthermore he does not mind us knowing it and has
used the distortion produced to give us a much wider view of the scene
than would otherwise be possible. The result is a view in the round with a
sort of fish-eye perspective and with the figure of the salesman almost
incidental in the foreground. We have now gone beyond simple artifice
and almost into the realm of the surreal. There is no attempt to even trick
us into thinking that this is a view that we could simply see if we went out
and stood in the right place. We have to know what we are looking at.
There is clearly much more here than would have met the eye and
Fabritius is exploiting the technology to give us a picture of what he

knows, and what we know is really there, and what is meaningful for the viewer. In essence he is using new technology to show us new knowledge, telling us something else about the place. This is clearly a view of Delft but an appearance that has been carefully contrived to combine the two subjects of the title. This is the least purely empirical and most imaginative picture of the three I have so far considered but it is still part of the same representational tradition, even though it self-consciously mocks pure representation by showing that what we can see is not necessarily unique or as straightforward as we might sometimes think. We know that this is a view of Delft if we have seen Delft, but it is an appearance with which no-one is visually familiar, it therefore accrues some of the uncanniness which haunts work like that of Sebald. Once again the artist has created an image which has meaning beyond its mere appearance.

The fourth item is not really a picture at all in the tradition sense. Samuel Van Hoogstraten's *Perspective Box with Dutch Interior*[13] is a very successful attempt to take the art of depicting the interiors, so beloved of the Dutch painters, into a new dimension. The work exists as a closed box with painting on each inside surface. There are holes in the sides of the box through which the observer can peep. The paintings on the inside surfaces of the box are arranged so that, when viewed through one of the peepholes, the interior of a Dutch household in various aspects, is revealed in perfect proportion and with an illusion of three dimensions. The appearance is of a complete everyday interior. In order to achieve this, the individual paintings inside the box have necessarily been done in such a way that, if viewed independently, they appear grossly distorted; that is they do not appear true to life. The overall impression of the work when viewed through the holes is impressively vivid and much is gained over the simple picture format in the appreciation of the dimensionality and completeness of the 'picture' presented. However there is clearly more to this than simple empirical representation. Van Hoogstraten has constructed a trick, an illusion, and created an appearance in the same way that all of the painters have done, but this time the trick is explicit and open for all to see with no pretence, in a similar but even more imaginative vein to the Fabritius picture. Both Fabritius and Van Hoogstraten are beginning to challenge the simple empiricism of their genre and, ironically, both are doing so out of a motive to perfect the genre since both have achieved means to show even more than they, or their contemporaries, could have done by means of traditionally produced and presented flat pictures. Both are dependent on the understanding of their viewers, it is for them that the things represented in the pictures have meaning. This means that the viewers can 'make sense' of what they see by using what they already know.

All four of these artists are showing that appearance is more than meets the eye and the strength of the image, its impact on us as conscious thinking beings, is not straightforward. We combine what we see with what we know and this combining gives the image meaning. Particularly in the cases of Fabritius and Van Hoogstraten, the painters have produced pictures of places, spaces that are imbued with meaning, meaning which is provided by those viewing the images, that is, people who know Delft or people who live in this kind of house. Fabritius's picture of Delft is reminiscent of the kind of dream painting produced by the surrealists. In the case of Van Hoogstraten he has produced a picture of a house interior, and through the illusion of the peep box has imitated the dream like quality of Bachelard's vision of the house. In all four cases, by the way the appearance has been constructed, spaces have become places. Again perhaps Schama is beginning to think about the same thing when he says,

> the very act of identifying (not to mention photographing) the place presupposes our presence, and along with us all the heavy cultural backpacks that we lug with us on the trail. (Schama, 1996, p.6)

He gives us another hint when he says of his book,

> So *Landscape and Memory* is constructed as an excavation below our conventional sight-level to recover the veins of myth and meaning that lies beneath the surface. (Schama, 1996, p.6)

The only difference is that Schama is conducting a kind of historical archaeology while the territory that writers like Sebald and Bachelard inhabit is more like that of phenomenological archaeology, a ground which makes Schama's enterprise possible in the first place. The process of recognition is central to these diverse enterprises and Gadamer takes the analysis to a deeper level when he points out that,

> The essence of imitation consists precisely in the recognition of the represented in the representation. A representation intended to be so true and convincing that we do not advert to fact that what is so represented is not "real". Recognition as the cognition of the true occurs through an act of identification in which we do not differentiate between the representation and the represented. (Gadamer, 1986, p.99)

This means that,

> Recognizing something means rather that I cognize something as something that I have already seen. The enigma here lies entirely in the "as"... For what imitation reveals is precisely the real essence of the thing. (Gadamer, 1986, p.99)

These painters have represented not what they see but what they know and in ways that those who view their paintings will know too. In crossing the nexus between seeing and knowing they tell more than they know themselves, not necessarily about the subjects of their paintings but about phenomenology and our relation to the world as it appears to us. This is definitely not a conscious attempt by the artists to supersede empiricism and to embark on ontological investigation, but I suggest that this is an inevitable consequence of their enterprise given the underlying structures of the world, the nature of the relationship between the artist, the painting, and the work of producing the painting. In Gadamer's words we can begin by saying, "our perception is never a simple reflection of what is given in the senses".[14] While these artists may have begun to supersede simple empiricism it is still the case that the things that end up in their paintings are empirically derived, they are still painting things that they have seen, rather than things they have imagined. However I have argued that by combining a number of empirically derived images in a way that gives more meaning to their paintings, and to the subjects they portray, they have advanced from simply seeing towards knowing. They have not simply reproduced empirically the landscapes and buildings that were there for all to see. They have in Gadamer's words revealed "the real essence of the thing". This is because representation itself is no simple matter, as Gadamer also says,

> Imitation and representation are not merely a repetition, a copy, but knowledge of the essence. Because they are not merely repetition but a "bringing forth", they imply a spectator as well. They contain in themselves an essential relation to everyone for whom the representation exists. (Gadamer, 1975, 2004, p.114)

Gadamer's point is phenomenological and reflects some of what Heidegger had to say in the last chapter about the way we experience the world and ourselves in it. The fact that the Dutch painters are able to reveal this 'real essence' itself reveals the inextricability of our relationship with the world. The painters are working within a culture and in a tradition in which these imitations and recognitions can succeed. Their success is based on shared meanings which are already inescapable for both the painters and their public, and 'the real essence' is revealed when both partake of these meanings.

In summary then what we have here are two artists constructing artificial viewpoints and another two showing that what we can see might not be what is really there, and vice versa. Philosophically speaking we have an acknowledgement that what we see and what we know may be very different, with a complex and flexible relationship between the two. In their own way each of these four artists has produced in each of these works a statement of how they, and we, know the world to be, rather than simply how they see the world. In so doing they have gone beyond the simple empirical project and however unwittingly, hinted at something more about the world we live in and which they endeavour to depict. They have also begun to tell us more about the subjects of their paintings than we could obtain from our everyday encounters with these items. By calling them to our attention, through picturing them, they begin to reveal the underlying ontological structures that support everydayness. The fact that we can combine and invent viewpoints to show what we know about the world, and even simply distort what we see to take showing and knowing further, begins to reveal that the simple notion of reality which seems to have inspired most of the painters of the Dutch republic is not enough. There is more to it than simply that which appears to be there, we need to instil and then to understand the meaning these places have for us if we are to appreciate their true nature, and the true nature of these re-presentations. We should now look further to see what is really going on, to try to understand what we really know and what knowing itself is like. To do this we will need to consider more than these works of art. We will need to look at how individual meaning creeps into appearances not only of paintings but of all sorts of things and places.

Beyle and Ivrea

Before going on to consider the philosophical underpinnings of what is going on in these works of art I think that it will be useful to briefly consider a couple of minor but effective examples of the same process at work, which show how individual meaning comes to accrue to our experience of places, even when we are in error. These small examples both help to confirm the analysis with regard to the Dutch painters and show how the process goes beyond the work of painting landscapes and interiors. In the first part of *Vertigo*, in a kind of reverse example of the phenomenon which I have suggested is going on in the Dutch paintings, Sebald describes how another artist mis-remembers a landscape in much the same way that the Dutch painters remember what they know and add it to what they see. The first section of *Vertigo* is a brief essay on the early adventures of Henri Beyle, later the author Stendhal. Beyle was a soldier in Napoleon's army and described some of his travels through Italy with the army. Beyle's recollections show the way that memory plays him false when it comes to remembering the places he visited and the sights he (thought) he saw. Sebald says, "Beyle writes that for years he lived in the conviction that he would remember every detail of that ride, and particularly of the town of Ivrea."[15] But as Sebald continues,

> It was a severe disappointment, Beyle writes, when some years ago, looking through old papers he came across an engraving entitled *Prospetto d'Ivrea* and was obliged to concede that his recollected picture of the town in the evening sun was nothing but a copy of that very engraving. (Sebald, 2002, *Vertigo*, p.8)

This of course goes to show, as Sebald says, "even when memories are true to life one can place little confidence in them".[16] A further example is given when Sebald considers Beyle's memory of having seen General Marmont at Martigny resplendent in his robes as Counsellor of State. Sebald points out Beyle would have been well aware that the General must have been wearing his soldier's uniform and not the robes of state.

In both of these examples the image which Beyle has of these past events has been (mis)remembered as something more or something less than what was there, and yet for years for Beyle they become what he actually saw. Certainly if asked to describe these events Beyle would have given what he thought was a true and accurate account of Ivrea and of General Marmont, but these would not be accounts of what he saw but descriptions of what he thought he knew, a mistake only to be 'corrected' years later when he found the engraving. Other factors than simply the seeing have influenced and then determined his memory of those particular appearances. Factors like imagination, mood, and his existing stock of knowledge which were somehow combined to give to him his memory of these things and places. Both memories have turned out to be more than meets the eye in ways reminiscent of Saenredam's church interior and Konincks's landscape. But this is not to say that the method of exploring memory and the resonances of entities is itself unhelpful, indeed its very unreliability reveals the unevenness of the ground. Reality is not simple, and the process Sebald describes in the case of Beyle is not simply one of re-creation. Like the Dutch artists Beyle's experience emphasises the dynamic and imaginative relationship between knowing and seeing which can result in us both seeing what we know rather than simply what

appears to be there, and of knowing what we thought we saw even though
we could not have. Beyle's creation of the image of Ivrea, although false,
is based on the same kind of relationship to what he saw as was
Saenredam's and Konincks's work. If for example, Saenredam and
Koninck are giving us a view from a point which does not exists then
Beyle is giving us a view that does not exist from a point which does. Both
say something significant about how appearances are created on some kind
of pre-existing ground.

As McCulloch says about Sebald's description of his own homecoming
in the final part of *Vertigo*, "One of the lessons of 'Il ritorno in patria' is
predictably, that one simply cannot go home again. It is not the same
home; everything has changed."[17] The changing nature of things is the
changing nature of ourselves, not only do we return after time has ravaged
the places we know, but we ourselves are equally ravaged, we are not the
ones we were and we cannot see the same things and places.

Being-in-the-world and making pictures of it

I will try in this section to explain what it is I think the artists are
doing, as it were beneath the surface, although we need to be aware that all
spatial metaphors in this field tend to mislead. To do this it will be
necessary to look at some of Heidegger's work on Being-in-the-world and
the worldhood of the world. I hope that it will become clear as the
discussion progresses how this work is relevant to the enterprise of the
Dutch painters and how it can inform our understanding of what they were
about in creating images.

The representation, by making pictures, of everyday items cannot
portray their involvement with the specific projects of conscious individuals
no matter how vivid the representation or clever the composition. We have
to go further than merely seeing objects if we are to understand what they
are really for. We have to re-win the engagement with the entities in the
world if we are to even begin to understand them and to re-connect the
objects that are painted with their places and uses in the world. In
Heidegger's terms we have to re-visit the everyday and seek its meaning.
We have to move from seeing entities to knowing them, and we cannot
make this move under what are essentially conditions of perception and
understanding as representation. Access to entities in advance of our
explicit noticing is impossible if we think of them as mere representations
and we will forever miss the world if we use this model of perception. We
should not underestimate the way in which the representational model of
perception dominates not only our way of thinking about these questions

including the very language we use to discuss them. Our language not only propels us down lines of thought which may not lead anywhere but makes it difficult for us to accept any alternative view. This is a particular problem when using Heidegger's work because of his wholesale undermining, and rejection, of the fundamentality of a representational methodology, a way of thinking which goes all the way back to Descartes at least.

In the sections of *Being and Time* headed 'Being-in-the-world in General as the Basic State of Dasein'[18] and 'The Worldhood of the World'[19] and at the end of the preceding section entitled 'The Existential Analytic and the Interpretation of Primitive Dasein. The Difficulties of Achieving a 'Natural Conception of the World'',[20] Heidegger sets out the results of the preliminary investigation of the relationship of the Being of Dasein and the world. With the starting point of average everydayness he proceeds to show how the relationship to the everyday is fundamental to the Being of Dasein. Dasein is perhaps Heidegger's most important and difficult term and I shall not attempt to define it here. Suffice to say that it is not the Cartesian, or any other kind of subject, the most that it can be taken for in this context is a focus for experience, but the kind of focus which does not reify one particular focus and which necessitates understanding of the world through a variety of engagements or involvements. Dasein, like Being, in Heidegger's work is more like a verb than a noun.

He begins characteristically by saying clearly what he does not mean, "Everydayness does not coincide with primitiveness"[21] and then more explicitly,

> The Interpretation of Dasein in its everydayness however, is not identical with the describing of some primitive state of Dasein with which we can become acquainted empirically through the medium of anthropology. (Heidegger, 1962, H.50)

Heidegger is no kind of realist, naïve or otherwise, neither is he any kind of idealist. His work is constituted as a completed rejection of any kind of dualism whether it seeks to rejects one side or the other or to bring them together. With direct relevance to the work of at least some of the Dutch painters, and with some relevance to Severs comments, he says

> We shall not get a genuine knowledge of essences simply by the syncretic activity of universal comparison and classification. Subjecting the manifold to tabulation does not ensure any actual understanding of what lies before us as thus set in order. (Heidegger, 1962, H.52)

This chimes with what Bachelard has to say about the problem of description and the constant pressure we feel to differentiate and classify our experience. Heidegger's aim is to go much deeper into the onset of the image, because, as he continues,

> if one is to put various pictures of the world in order, one must have an explicit idea of the world as such. And if the 'world' itself is something constitutive for Dasein one must have an insight into Dasein's basic structures in order to treat the world-phenomenon conceptually. (Heidegger, 1962, H.52)

It seems that before we can have a picture of the world we must already have some notion of the world, and our conceptualization of what we find in the world rests on this notion. This begins to open up how the 'onset of the image' can be grounded and gives some indication of how the process proceeds.

For Heidegger Being-in-the-world is both an active and a unitary phenomenon if it is to be anything at all, and his view is very different from that of the empiricists and for that matter the painters. It is clear from this position, if Heidegger is right, that the painters' enterprise in providing knowledge of the objects they depict is doomed to failure, not due to any technical problem or shortcoming but because of the very nature of the enterprise itself. In Heidegger's terms, in their attempt to render images perfectly faithful to what they see, they have misunderstood the world. Heidegger is trying to get right away from the notion that Dasein, or the subject, or the self, or anything like this exists in a spectatorial position over and above the world. He rejects the notion of a position like the one apparently taken by the painters. He articulates this rejection through the development of a notion of being-alongside. Once again this is not simply a spatial metaphor; indeed it is not to be understood spatially at all, particularly in the way that the representational tradition would have us think. Specifically, the post-Cartesian notion that spatiality or extension is fundamental to the being of entities has no place here. In contrast Heidegger says very explicitly, "There is no such thing as the 'side-by-side-ness' of an entity called 'Dasein' within another entity called the world".[22] The relationship is much more one of active engagement than simple position, much much more active so that,

> The concept of "facticity" implies that an entity 'within-the-world' has Being-in-the-world in such a way that it can understand itself as bound up

in its 'destiny' with the Being of those entities which it encounters within its own world. (Heidegger, 1962, H.56)

This destiny is inescapable and Heidegger insists that we cannot take up our fundamental relationship towards the world as an option, occasionally choosing to join in and sometimes not. We are 'joined-in' permanently and inexorably. While we can take up particular relationships to this world in which we find ourselves these relationships are therefore by no means primordial, fundamental or definitive of either ourselves or of the world because,

> Taking up a relationship towards the world is possible only because Dasein, as Being-in-the-world, is as it is. This state of being does not arise just because some other entity is present at hand outside of Dasein and meets up with it. Such an entity can 'meet up with' Dasein only in so far as it can, of its own accord, show itself within a world. (Heidegger, 1962, H.7)

Particular relationships are grounded on our essential relatedness as Dasein. Heidegger describes how our specific relationships towards the world and the entities we find in it turns on the two kinds of relationship we have towards these entities. In the first place entities may be present-at-hand; that is they are merely there residing in the environment but with no specific or meaningful connection to us, in this sense they have no immediate meaning for us. We see them but we take little or no notice. Entities become equipment for us and are ready-to-hand when we are engaged or involved with them. They have meaning in terms of our intentions and we say that they exist in a way that is "for-the-sake-of-which".[23] This term, "for-the-sake-of-which", is used simply to denote the fact that engagements with entities in the world are given direction and purpose by the focus provided by the intentions of Dasein. These entities we then come to understand in the context of our projects, they now have meaning, and this is how we come to know them. It is through this kind of engagement that we usually come to know entities in the world.

We can now see that, in their painting, the artists first give us the objects they portray as present-at-hand. The objects in the paintings are isolated from us and are depicted in their unspecific generality, or as present-at-hand. They therefore have no meaning and we have no understanding of them. They seem to pass us by, however perfectly they may have been represented. This is the sense in which we recognize them as curious or quaint, or as simply provoking some aesthetic response. The artists paint what they see, and what they see are objects present-at-hand.

Once they begin to paint what they know they begin to move into the territory of ready-to-hand and a deeper understanding of the entities they depict. They do this, and begin to move to the world of engagements, by the way that they manipulate and combine the images which they produce. This is true even of Saenredam and Koninck who simply combine or invent empirical viewpoints and therefore still appear to be remaining within the empiricist enclosure. By beginning to paint what they know to be there the artists begin to produce work the meaning of which is dependent on the knowledge that the viewer already has, and thus the onset of the image is revealed as equally dependent on this coalescence. In Heidegger's terms they are in some way taking note of our pre-existing being-in-the-world and using this to communicate their meaning.

Even in the most perfect most empirical still life we can now begin to vaguely understand something about the entities pictured. Our impulses to take up the objects from the painting, to touch the wine glass, to eat the fruit, to smell the flowers, all of which we know to be impossible, give us an inkling of a more primordial and meaningful relationship with the objects portrayed. These are things that we can only imagine doing on the basis of an already present relationship with, and understanding of, objects like this. Only on this basis are we are thus able to imagine our own involvement with these objects. As Dasein, as Being-in-the-world, we are able to project a situation in which these objects become equipment and emerge from the present-at-hand into the ready-to-hand; in short we can imagine using them in our everyday lives. Ironically by drawing forth ever more vivid and veracious images the artists provoke a reaction which takes us beyond the simple empirical seeing of the present-at-hand and into the knowing ready-to-hand. This is the way that we can know that Saenredam's drawing of the church is the church we already know, and that Konincks's view of the dunes is a real view of real dunes. It is not merely the case that we have to know a church or a lemon before we can recognize a painting of a church or a lemon. We can know at all these things because we already have a kind of knowing in which these things can be true, and this kind of knowing is grounded in our inescapable being-in-the-world. Without this ground to rest upon our knowledge has no foundation. Essentially this means that all of our activity is grounded in a fundamental and constitutive phenomenological relationship with the world, and the relationships which we subsequently create, like subject/object, painter/picture, viewer/object, are rooted in this ground however much we might suppose that they subsist independently.

With respect to the pictures we can now see a bit more of what is happening, and how this is possible. It is clear that in some of the pictures the artist has gone beyond simple empirical representation. Neither Fabritius nor Van Hoogstraten intended to produce simple empirical representations but, without explicit philosophical intent to do so, these painters rendered not simply what they saw but what they knew, or thought they knew, to be there. In explicitly crossing the nexus between seeing and knowing they tell more than they realise. They appeal to the ability to know that we, the viewers, already have and which itself enables us to recognize the kinds of things that they have painted. As I have said this is definitely not a conscious attempt by the artist to supersede empiricism and to embark on ontological investigation, but it is an inevitable consequence of their enterprise given the underlying structures of the world and our way of being in it. Their straying from the simplicity of empirical representation starts to reveal ground that we did not before need to suppose existed but which we can now see must extend, not only to support the extension of empirical representation that I have described in the four specific pictures, but also to support all similar works whether in pictures, prose or poetry. All of the work of the Dutch painters of this period is grounded on Being-in-the-world, without this their enterprise would not be possible at all. They cannot create the fundamental relationship between themselves and the objects, or the relationship between any viewer and their pictures of the objects, they can merely choose its particular form, but in so doing they show that all of us are already bound up with the entities.

As Heidegger puts it, "The world is that in terms of which the ready-to-hand is ready-to-hand."[24], and moreover,

> An entity is discovered when it has been assigned or referred to something, and referred as that entity which it is. With any such entity there is an involvement which it has in something. (Heidegger, 1962, H.84)

Our whole view of the world and how it works is moved from the simple idea of presenting the world, as it were empirically, to an understanding of the world based not on our spectatorial view of it but from our active engagement in it, or from a continuing series of engagements. This may have its frustrations in terms of our being unable to step back and see the world for what it is, but it turns out to be the only way in which we can know the world and understand our relationship with the entities we encounter. This also applies necessarily to the artists themselves. The engagement of the artists with the craft of art, through the tools that they use, including their new scientific tools, is fundamental to their enterprise and connects them inextricably with what we term 'the work'. By taking their intentions to make images, and their use of equipment, they are taking forward a primary involvement with the world and doing so on the foundation of primordial Being-in-the-world, as it already is. So, while it may appear that this engagement with the objects and the artists' equipment creates a relationship between the artist and the world, it is in fact only a manifestation of an existing and inescapable relationship between all of us and the world, a relationship which grounds all of our experience and enterprise, including that of the artist. To understand this fully we should think more of the artist in the act of making the picture rather than just looking at the pictures themselves, for in creating an image of the world the artists reveal, each time, their own and our own pre-existing and primordial Being-in-the-world. In effect the onset of the image that they are creating, and of all images, rests on this relationship. This relationship is essentially active and we can no more divorce the results (pictures) from the activity of the artist, and view them in isolation, than we can understand any other entities we encounter outside their context of involvement and engagement. The work of the artists in making the pictures reveals to us the 'work' of engaging with the world by taking forward their intention to make a picture. In this way the artists can give meaning to the entities they portray, but only obliquely by using them in advancing the project of image making.

In short, unless there was already a ground and a primordial relationship between Being and world the artists endeavour would be groundless and impossible. Unless we are already engaged and involved in a world of entities the artist would be unable to paint the world at all, never mind allow us to understand what they paint. In all cases of human endeavour,

> As the Being of something ready-to-hand, an involvement is itself discovered only on the basis of the prior discovery of a totality of involvements. So in any involvement that has been discovered (that is in anything ready-to-hand which we encounter), what we have called the "worldly character" of the ready-to-hand has been discovered beforehand. (Heidegger, 1962, H. 85)

Summary

The Dutch artists create works of art which give an account of the world; they do not create the ontological relationship between entities in the world and Dasein. The description of entities will not reveal to us their fundamental Being, but this kind of categorization and differentiation is essential for everyday Dasein, which must 'do' with entities in the world as part of its everyday living. We must all reduce the world and our knowledge to make it useful. The mistake is to take this reduction to be characteristic of our primordial relationship to the world. On closer examination the art of the Dutch Republic, through its representation of the everyday, calls forth the entities we encounter as part of our everyday lives and in so doing begins to reveal the underlying ontological structure of the world as Being-in-the-world. Implicitly and obliquely, and in part through the very inauthenticity of the explicit project to make images, they reveal the ground of phenomenology and the onset of the image.

I have tried to show that the explicit enterprise of the artists of the Dutch republic was empirical and yet philosophically speaking phenomenological in its most basic sense. They were trying to show things 'as they are', which amounted to showing them as they appeared. I have shown how this project as a route to knowledge about the entities they depicted is misguided and to that extent futile, in that it can only provide us with knowledge of how things appear rather than what they are for. However in making their attempt they reveal the more primordial ground of our understanding of the everyday. I believe that in the examples that I have chosen, and probably in other works of the period, there are clues to a deeper more hidden truth and knowledge. It seems to me that the constant striving for the perfect image, the act of bringing forth the image, itself eventually reveals a glimpse of ontological structures which make the enterprise of these artists possible in the first place, and allows us to begin to see and to understand not simply the entities we encounter in the world but, more importantly, how we are bound up with these entities and how we can come to know them through this interaction.

In the next chapter I will look widen this discussion to include the appearance of all kinds of places, not just those which have been reproduced but the spaces we all inhabit and which make up our everyday lives. I will attempt this though a return to the work of Sebald and Bachelard.

Notes

[1] Steadman, 2001, *Vermeer's Camera*, makes a good case for the use of optics by Vermeer which pre-dates Hockney's publication.
[2] See, Bailey, 2001 and Brown, 1998.
[3] This artist, reckoned to be Vermeer's teacher, was tragically killed in the explosion of the powder magazine in Delft in 1654.
[4] Alpers, 1983, pp.54-55.
[5] Westerman, 1996, p.76.
[6] Westerman, 1996, p.82.
[7] Westerman, 1996, p.84.

[8] Steadman, 2001, pp.21-23, provides a description and some discussion of these last two pieces of work.

[9] One version of this is in the National Gallery, London.

[10] Alpers, 1983, p.42.

[11] The original is in the Museum Boymans-van Beuningen, Rotterdam.

[12] The original is in the National Gallery, London.

[13] The original is in the National Gallery, London.

[14] Gadamer, 1975, 2004, p.58.

[15] Sebald, 2002, *Vertigo*, p.7.

[16] Sebald, 2002, *Vertigo*, p.7.

[17] McCulloch, 2003, p.101.

[18] Heidegger, 1962, H.53-62.

[19] Heidegger, 1962, H.63-113.

[20] Heidegger, 1962, H.51-52.

[21] Heidegger, 1962, H.50.

[22] Heidegger, 1962, H.55.

[23] Heidegger, 1962, H.86-88.

[24] Heidegger, 1962, H.83.

CHAPTER FIVE

BACHELARD, SEBALD, GADAMER:
DREAMING AND PLAYING

Dreams come before contemplation. Before becoming a conscious sight,
every landscape in an oneiric experience. [1]

In this chapter I want to extend and deepen the ways of thinking being
presented by both Bachelard and Sebald and to try to see where their
thinking can take us both in terms of specific houses and landscapes and
further in terms of spaces in general. I will also use some work by
Gadamer on play and I will suggest that this work can support the kind of
understanding of the world that we get from Sebald and Bachelard. This
will involve not only a more general kind of theorising about how spaces
and places appear and are experienced, but necessarily a closer
examination of how spaces become places, that is how they become
meaningful for an individual consciousness. I think that the value of this
approach is given in the above quote from Bachelard especially in the way
that it begins to layer our experience and to open the way to suggesting
different levels of consciousness. Bachelard is here specifically pointing to
something which seems to pre-figure consciousness, and to come before
we reach the point when we are fully aware of what is there in the sense of
naming our experience. The landscape is something before it is a landscape,
and I will suggest that this dream of a landscape, the oneiric experience, is
crucial to our understanding of how spaces become places.

In attempting to explore what is going on at the onset of the image we
are endeavouring to gain some insight into the everyday before it becomes
fully apparent. The metaphor of the dream provides an opportunity to do
this without directly confronting the work; it provides us with, if not an
eloquent silence, a quiet means of approach which will preserve immediacy
or at least slow the progress of our description and differentiation. The
notion of play provides us with a similarly indirect way of approaching the
world which is also surprisingly fruitful. In addition, and as a direct
complement to Bachelard's oneirism, Sebald's work, by restoring the
sense of uncanny to everyday experience, gives us an opportunity to

transcend mere appearance and to begin to understand a more primordial reality which is too often missed altogether. The ways in which Sebald gets us to stop and think, and the ways that this seems to bring forth the sheer strangeness in the familiar, appears to restore something to our experience rather than detract from it. This focus on the metaphysical interlining or "space between" as Severs has called it shows us something about the appearance that has become lost in differentiation, description, codification and classification. It is as if our conscious appropriation and naming of spaces has removed, rather than provided, any meaning, or as the poet Schiller once put it in his second letter on the aesthetic education of man,

> The very spirit of philosophical enquiry seizes on one province after another from the imagination, and the frontiers of Art are contracted as the boundaries of science are enlarged. (Schiller, 1795, 2004 p.26)

I think that since Schiller's days this incursion has gone far beyond the province of art and now dominates our entire understanding of the world to the extent that we must now engage in an action to recover for the imagination the ground that has been lost. The cost of failure in this enterprise is made clear by Schiller in the sixth letter.

> We know that the sensibility of the mind depends for its degree upon the liveliness of the imagination. Bu the predominance of the analytical faculty must necessarily deprive the fancy of its strength and fire, and a restricted sphere of objects must diminish its wealth. (Schiller, 1795, 2004 p.42)

I will begin with a look at some of Sebald's stories about people and places, then a similar story of my own, I will and then go on to show how Bachelard's more theoretical approach supports my reading of these stories. I can then look at how the things that Gadamer has to say about play complement Bachelard's way of thinking.

Sebald's Places

To begin with; an example from Sebald's first book *Vertigo*. In the second section of this book entitled "All'estero"[2] Sebald describes his own travels in Italy. The whole story of "All'estero" is a story of places, that is spaces or names on the map which have meaning both for the author and the others he encounters on his travels, and indeed for those who have gone before and who form the historical backdrop to Sebald's musings. This is exemplified in his digressions into the histories of characters like

Casanova and Kafka which are injected into the narrative. Particularly striking amongst these journeys are his visits and revisits to Venice, Verona and Milan and his journey on the night train. I am in no position to provide here any kind of substitute for Sebald's remarkable writing and I recommend everyone to go and read "All'estero" (and for that matter the rest of Sebald's work) if they really want to understand what I am trying to say. Only Sebald can recreate his journeys through Italy in 1980 and 1987, and it would be pointless for me to even attempt such an enterprise. I can however give some of the flavour of what is going on here and show how Sebald is doing the kind of thing that Bachelard is talking about.

Sebald describes how his mood becomes strangely altered on arrival in Venice at the end of October 1980 he says,

> I became enveloped by a sense of utter emptiness and never once left my room. It seemed to me then that one could well end one's life simply through thinking and retreating into one's mind, for, although I had closed the windows and the room was warm, my limbs were growing progressively colder and stiffer with my lack of movement, so that when at length the waiter arrived with the red wine and sandwiches that I had ordered, I felt as if I had already been interred or laid out for burial already, silently grateful for the proffered libation but no longer capable of consuming it. (Sebald, 2002, *Vertigo*, p.65)

His setting of such a melancholy, or even morbid, mood at this beginning point of his journey is no accident. Sebald is deliberately trying to detach himself, and us, from the hustle and bustle of everyday life in order to allow something else about the world to appear. This is a device he uses time and time again and one which is usually successful, although the reasons for this success we may leave till later. This mood of solitary detachment stays with him throughout his visit to Italy, he hardly speaks to anyone, and it colours all of his experiences of the places he visits. In characteristic style Sebald creates the kind of dreamlike atmosphere that is so reminiscent of Bachelard's work. It is as if, for Sebald on this trip, the dream of the places he visits precedes his eventual contemplation. This leads him not only to digression (Casanova and Kafka), but to quite irrational speculations about his own safety based on no more than newspaper stories about a series of murders three years earlier. He eventually flees Verona when he begins to fear that two men, who he imagines have been following him, are about to murder him. He leaves the Pizzeria Verona in an irrational panic and rushes to the railway station.[3] Nothing actually happens, or at least nothing tangible, but Sebald gives a vivid account of the mounting fear which results in his eventual flight. The story continues seven years later when, as he puts it,

> I finally yielded to a need I had felt for some time to repeat the journey from Vienna via Venice to Verona, in order to probe my somewhat imprecise recollections of those fraught and hazardous days and perhaps record some of them. (Sebald, 2002, *Vertigo*, p. 81)

He finds that when he revisits these places the memories of what happened to him before go with him and give the places a meaning from which he cannot escape. It is as if on his return journey the shadows of his trip seven years earlier accompany him and lurk in every part of his new experience. In fact the actual events of his second visit are quite different, and, in spite of his fears and misgivings, the places he revisits no longer induce the same terror. This second journey is, of course, affected not so much by the events of the first but by his wild imaginings conjured up in his state of solitary dreaming, but these imaginings have themselves now become part of his present experience. Nothing much of note really happens to him on this second trip to Italy (apart from losing his passport) and when he returns to the Pizzeria Verona it is boarded up. The only thing that remains from his previously terrifying experience at the Pizzeria is a curious image of,

> two men in black silver-buttoned tunics, who were carrying out from a rear courtyard a bier on which lay, under a floral-patterned drape, what was plainly the body of a human being. (Sebald, 2002, *Vertigo*, p.125)

These occasions show how these places and their meaning have changed for him due to his experience of previous visits. The young men who he imagines are following him, the stories of murder, and his own untimely flight, all add layers of meaning to these places which return in memory when he goes back. His state of mind during these travels is often distracted and dreamlike and this seems to give his stories a detachment from his surroundings and, for him, the artifice of a spectatorial point of view. It is not that Sebald sees things that are not there, he simply seems to not see some things that are there in a way that heightens his awareness of what else is there, so instead of merely observing the present reality he is able to remember, and to sometimes imagine, a faded past. In many ways his accounts of the two visits are more like flights of the imagination than descriptions of travel but rather than detracting from it this seems to add to their vivacity.

Further examples are given in the last part of *Vertigo*. "Il ritorno in patria" describes the events of a journey made by the author to his home village of Wertach. During his journey he stops at Krummenbach Chapel[4] which he remembers visiting with his grandfather, and while there he speculates on the history of the building and it decoration and then, by connection, on the journey to the palace at Wurzburg made by Tiepolo and his work there. The Krummenbach Chapel is replete with meaning not only as a result of the author's own remembered visits but from the lingering presence of the artist who painted its Stations of the Cross. When he finally arrives at Wertach the account he gives is reminiscent of the one he provides for Henri Beyle in the first story of *Vertigo*, (the memory of Ivrea).[5] Indeed he says for himself,

> many of the localities I associated with it (Wertach) ...had continually returned in my dreams and daydreams and had become more real to me than they had then, yet the village itself, I reflected, as I arrived at that late hour was more remote from me than any other place I could conceive of (Sebald, 2002, *Vertigo*, p.185)

It is as if the remembered meanings of his home village over the long time of his absence have overtaken the familiarity which he gained, and which he took for granted while he grew up there. Or perhaps the meanings had remained while the simple memories faded or had been replaced, as had Beyle's memory of Ivrea. Whichever, he finds the things he remembers alright, but not quite as he thought they were. Either way it appears that there is something real in his dreams of Wertach, something apart from the physical manifestation of the present day village. Further instances of this kind of awakened dream-like memory occur when he stays in the room in the Engelwirt Inn[6] that was once the living room of his childhood family, and when he remembers seeing films of significant historical events in the large function room at the same Inn.[7] Dreams and reality continually intermingle and produce a rich awareness of the places. In this way Sebald's recollections resemble those of the young Malte in Rilke's novel, and the kinds of experiences he describes echo some of the things that Bachelard says when he is talking about houses. Bachelard's words validate Sebald's musing when he says, "A demonstration of imaginary primitive elements may be based on the entity that is most firmly fixed in our memories: the childhood home."[8], and further,

> To inhabit the house we were born in means no more than to inhabit it in memory; it means living in the house that is gone, the way we used to dream in it. (Bachelard, 1958, 1994, p.16)

Sebald and Rilke are encountering their childhood homes by reawakening their past images and inhabiting their own houses of memory. In both cases the actual houses have disappeared or been altered beyond geometric recognition, but both are still very much alive in the memories of those who once lived there.

Incidentally it is probably no coincidence, because of the way that Sebald so carefully chooses his words, that the play he remembers being performed in the village when he was a boy is *The Robbers* by Schiller.[9] This play is an archetype of the Sturm und Drang movement of late eighteenth century[10] Germany which represented a rebellion against the kind of scientific rationalist encroachment which some felt was bringing with it an impoverishment of our thinking about the world. Sturm und Drang with its own unremitting (and usually clumsy) appeal to imagination and passion is a reaction against this encroachment. In this respect Sturm und Drang was a much earlier attempt to redress the balance between rationalism and dreaming and Sebald's slight reference is notable. This is the kind of clue that Sebald leaves throughout his otherwise apparently trivial musings and rememberings, all of which lead unerringly towards a kind of imaginative and counter-rational approach to understanding the world.

Like "All'estero", "Il ritorno in patria" is the story of a journey through seemingly endless places with apparently limitless meanings; we even have the site of the last skirmish of World War Two at Enge Platt,[11] a place which is marked forever by the events it concluded, and the personal stories of those who were there. In all of these examples the places are more than just physical locations on the map, they are all somewhere for someone.

These are the ways in which Sebald's journeys in "All'estero" and "Il ritorno in patria" show us how places become places; that is how they accrue their meaning. It is because of what happened in these places, both to the author and to others, in the present and in the past, and our knowing and remembering these events, which gives them their meaning. In essence nowhere is nowhere, everywhere is already somewhere, that is, has meaning, and it becomes another somewhere every time we go there. Even places we have not visited will have meaning for us, we can know about them, we can know what happened to others there, and we can imagine what it would be like for us to be there. This makes them all places for us by imbuing them with meaning. Sebald understands this. It is notable in this connection that when he wanders around Milan[12] he lists street names as he goes; the narrative of his walk is given in this listing, a listing of meanings accrued over time and ossified in each street name. He does exactly the same as he walks around London at the end of "Il ritorno in patria".[13] In both of these stories Sebald moves through an historical landscape which is rich in meaning, and his musings illuminate this meaning in ways which others allow to go unnoticed because they become preoccupied with present meaning and involvements. Even his various digressions into the personal stories of his own past and that of others merely reinforce the strength of these meanings and of the meaningfulness itself.

In *The Rings of Saturn* Sebald takes this method on a little further. The whole of the work is constituted as a journey, and the book is made up of the stories of the places he passes through in his walking tour of part of East Anglia. It is in these stories that the meaning of the places is given. This 'passing through' is already an everyday expression that is becoming of interest to us; it is becoming clear now that no-one passes thorough anywhere without leaving some sort of a trace, adding a new part to the meaning, nothing remains untouched as we pass through. A few examples and an illustrative comparison will suffice to show what I mean. Sebald visits Dunwich, or "the town beneath the sea".[14] Dunwich was an important and large medieval town which has now, by coastal erosion, been reduced to a tiny coastal village clinging onto existence in face of the ever encroaching sea. In a way this is a place that has almost gone; the space it occupied has quite literally almost disappeared under the sea. Sebald recognizes this and tries to gives us some impression in his writing of what it might have been like. Once again he gives us a list, he lists the lost parishes of St James, St Leonard, St Martin, St Bartholomew, St Patrick, St Mary, St John, St Peter, St Nicholas and St Felix; as if by naming them he can make them come alive again. He tells us how their churches toppled one by one over the fast receding cliff. Dunwich was a port of international significance in its glorious heyday with links to all of the near continent,[15] a town of merchants and prosperity and now, although the place itself is almost gone (not-there), the meanings it had linger, as it were, in the air of the place, preserved in historical record and testimony, and now witnessed by only a very few remains. In a mirror image of the way that Sebald's home village was intact yet remote to him, Dunwich is gone yet utterly familiar. We can imagine the buildings lost to the sea and the hustle and bustle of a medieval port. We may even imagine the moments of destruction as the sea swept in and destroyed the town. Dunwich is still in some ways the place that it was, even after its almost complete destruction. We could perhaps say that as the familiar can be strange so can the strange be familiar. All of this kind of thinking gives us Dunwich in ways that any other approach will miss.

A second example from *The Rings of Saturn* will further emphasise this point. While in Southwold Sebald visits the Sailors Reading Room, a refuge established for the sailors of Southwold most of who have now gone and, as he says,

> The Reading Room is thus almost always deserted but for one or two of the surviving fishermen and seafarers sitting in silence in the armchairs, whiling the hours away. (Sebald, 2002, *The Rings of Saturn*, p.93)

In addition to the remnants of Southwold's seafaring past the Reading Room contains records and relics of past events related to the sea and to Southwold, the pages of ship log books giving the bare details of events of that past. The place is so evocative that Sebald is driven to astonishment and when reading one such log he says, "I am astounded that a trail that has long since vanished from the air or the water remains visible here on the paper",[16] it is as if we can almost see the trail of a long lost ship as it sails by Southwold. It is in this kind of almost seeing that we understand Southwold's maritime past. The Reading Room is like a museum in miniature, or even the dream of a museum, with its dusty glass cases faded labels, out of date magazines and discoloured documents, all that it requires to bring it to life is our imagining. As a survivor the Sailors Reading Room is redolent with historical memory and feeling. It harks back to a time long gone when many of Southwold's men earned their living and risked their lives at sea, but is a place which has now lost almost all of its purpose and has become an occasional stop off for passing tourists who, Sebald says, leave after taking only a brief look around. The quiet of the place is made apparent when Sebald describes it as somewhere where he can find the peace and quiet he needs to write up his notes from the previous day, and in describing the Reading Room as his "favourite haunt"[17] Sebald sums up the strange quality of this place. The way its meaning clings on, like a haunting, so long after its purpose has faded makes it a place for dreaming. The Sailors Reading Room is now little more than a quaint repository which has remained unspoilt and almost untouched for so long that it is now part of what we call 'heritage', yet it contains all the clues that we need to gain access to places and times long gone by.

The sheer vivacity of Sebald's accounts of these places in Suffolk are brought out when they are contrasted with the descriptions provided by Nikolaus Pevsner in his renowned guide book, *The Buildings of England – Suffolk*. Pevsner visits both Dunwich and Southwold but his descriptions are quite the opposite kind of thing to the accounts that Sebald gives us. In the section on Dunwich Pevsner quotes the Reverend Alfred Suckling, who wrote in 1848,

> Dunwich is so enveloped in the halo of traditionary splendour, that he who ventures to elucidate its history by pursuing the path of topographical enquiry must exercise unusual caution, lest he be misled by imaginary light. For unlike those ruined cities whose fragments attest their former grandeur, Dunwich is wasted, desolate and void. Its palaces and temples are no more, and its very curious present an aspect lonely, stern and wild. (Pevsner, 1961, p.173)

While these are not his own words Pevsner is clearly in agreement as he says of Suckling's account, "There is not much one can add to it.",[18] he then goes on to give us a very brief description of the buildings that remain in present day Dunwich. This compares very poorly with Sebald's much more extensive account of Dunwich in which he succeeds in giving us a highly evocative vision of Dunwich past and present. The clue to the difference between Pevsner and Sebald is given in Suckling's warning that we should not be misled by "imaginary light" in the pursuit of "topographical enquiry". Both Suckling and Pevsner are mistaken in thinking that it is "imaginary light" that will mislead and that "topographical enquiry" is the route to understanding a place. Sebald revels in this "imaginary light" and in so doing makes his enquiry not merely topographical but almost magical as he spreads his thinking across time to give us the real Dunwich of now and of then.. For Suckling, and for Pevsner, Dunwich may be "wasted, desolate and void" but Sebald's account provokes us to image a Dunwich that was vibrant and alive.

This contrast between the methods of Sebald and Pevsner is further exemplified in their accounts of Southwold. We have seen how Sebald gives us an evocation of Southwold in his imagining of the Battle of Sole Bay[19] and in his musing on Southwold's past in the Sailors Reading Room. Pevsner is much more summary and even dismissive in his description of Southwold and gives no mention to the Reading Room. He begins his section on Southwold with a description of the church and a criticism of the water tower, which he thinks is out of place in the skyline alongside the church tower and the lighthouse, he says,

> The church is large, 144 ft. long, and with its tower, 100 ft. tall, imposing from near as well as far. From far, especially the estuary on the south side, the skyline used to be perfect, with the lighthouse as a happy contrast. No-one can call the water tower a happy contrast. It is a crime not to have erected something more transparent in a so important a position. (Pevsner, 1961, p.398)

This does not sound at all like Sebald's Southwold and this is because Pevsner's preoccupation with the empirical and the physically manifest makes his descriptions of places like Southwold no more than a collection of facts about the place. Pevsner is failing to capture the sheer sense of place that we get from Sebald. In his perambulation around Southwold Pevsner notes only a few buildings, he says, "It is a live little town, and it has, at least in its south half hardly a building that is a visual nuisance."[20] He goes on to say,

> The inhabitants appreciate the character of the town. They keep the colours fresh, and the gardens trim. The perambulation is brief, as there are no outstanding buildings and the attraction of the many minor ones eludes description. (Pevsner, 1961, p.400)

Pevsner seems impervious to the charm of the place and to the depth of its history from which this charm emanates. When we compare this to the imaginatively rich account of Southwold given by Sebald the town is hardly recognisable and yet, empirically speaking, it is Sebald's account that is the less complete. Sebald has, by his musing in the Sailors Reading Room and remembering the history of Southwold in the Battle of Sole Bay, given us an account of Southwold that is rich and deep and which stretches out across time to include the maritime history of the town and its place is English history. While we may think that that these two writers are pursuing different aims in their work they are both are trying to tell us about the places they visit in order to inform us, and perhaps to encourage us to visit the same places. It is in their methods of approach that they are so different and it is evident that the more imaginative approach chosen by Sebald gives us more of the place than does Pevsner's rather sterile architectural empiricism. Pevsner tells us about Dunwich and Southwold but Sebald allows us to imagine these places. I hope that it will eventually become clear that the philosophical difference between their approaches, the one collecting facts, and the other using imagination to develop understanding, is not only the key to Sebald's successful evocations but also underlies the way that we can come to know and understand the world.

While we are in East Anglia I will insert my own experience of the Shell Museum in Glandford, North Norfolk.[21] This place is a quaint hangover from times past. Built next to the church by the local squire to house the shell collection accumulated by his mother, I first visited it as a small boy as part of a caravan holiday. The space restrictions of staying in a small family caravan combined with the British summer weather meant that our visits to Glandford were always undertaken in the rain. It was somewhere warm and dry to go when the weather was wet, and there was no entrance fee. The place was a quiet curio when I was a boy, but the strange eclectic contents of the display cabinets, with items found on beaches all around the world, made a lasting impression. It was with surprise that as an adult I discovered that the Shell Museum is still open. I made another visit, once again in the rain, it seemed by now inappropriate to make a visit in fine weather. The place felt smaller although of course this was an illusion due to my having grown in the intervening years. This time the novelty of paying a small entrance charge was rewarded by the recognition that while many of the original artefacts were still there, they have been joined by many new ones from far and wide, sent to Glandford in the intervening years. Nothing much of any real value or significance is to be found in this museum but it preserves the past beach combings of so many people who, when they walked on beaches, remembered the Shell Museum and thought to send their little treasures to Glandford. The Shell Museum at Glandford is not only a repository for my own memories of childhood holidays it also contains the ephemera and memories from the lives of many others who have visited and who have sent back things to add to this collection which now sits silently in a Norfolk backwater. Within the walls of the Shell Museum there is a whole world of memories and experiences just waiting to be noticed.

For a final instance from Sebald on the significance of places I will turn to his last major work *Austerlitz* and a much more complex example. There are many passages in this book which I shall turn to later but for the moment, and in connection with the meaning of places, the recounting of Austerlitz's experience in the disused Ladies Waiting Room at Liverpool Street Station is illustrative of the suggestions that I am making.[22] This room, and the station itself, holds particular significance for Austerlitz. It is his arrival point in England at the age of four and a half years, and the point at which he assumes a new identity leaving behind even his name of Austerlitz, which he re-assumes only some years later. It is like the beginning of a new life for him and the end of an old one. His accounts of the encounters he has at the station and in the Ladies Waiting Room are therefore meaningful, not only in the sense of showing the meaning of places but also in the development and re-discovery of his own identity.

Austerlitz recounts to the narrator his visit to the station as an adult during which he finds the now abandoned and unused Ladies Waiting Room and, while there, sees what can only be described as a vision of a small boy being met by two older people. In this dream of the station Austerlitz witnesses his own arrival and his meeting at the station with the former missionary Emyr Elias and his wife, who were to act as his foster parents for the duration of the war but who eventually looked after him until adulthood. Austerlitz sums up this vision of past life thus,

> I felt, said Austerlitz, that the waiting room where I stood as if dazzled contained all the hours of my past life, all the suppressed and extinguished fears and wishes I have ever entertained, as if the black and white diamond pattern of the stone slabs beneath my feet were the board on which the end game would be played, and it covered the entire plane of time. (Sebald, 2002, *Austerlitz*, pp.192-3)

Obviously there is more going on here than simply the fact of a place giving up its meaning and I will return to the re-creation of the identity of Jacques Austerlitz in Chapter Eight. However it is apparent that there is more to this place, the Ladies Waiting Room at Liverpool Street Station, than just bricks and mortar. The significance which the now abandoned space has for Austerlitz is sufficiently strong for him to re-create, through dreaming, a seminal event in his life and to experience himself as a boy, as it were, spectatorially. His account of this experience given to the narrator is dreamlike and yet utterly convincing as a true narrative of his life. In his visit to the station as an adult, and in particular to the site of the now disused Ladies Waiting Room, Sebald describes how Austerlitz notices the past significance of the place above and beyond its present manifestation as a disused and derelict part of the station. The understanding of his own past that the adult Austerlitz gains from his experience in the Ladies Waiting Room far surpasses any cold rational understanding which he could ever gain from the simple presentation of the facts of his childhood flight from Prague and his traumatic arrival in England. In effect the adult Austerlitz imagines his lost childhood arrival in England,

All of these examples from Sebald, and from my own experience, while obviously different, are suggestive of ways in which spaces gain meaning existentially and so become places. While the experiences of the adult Austerlitz at Liverpool Street Station hark back to a singularly significant event in his life, and my own experience of the Shell Museum is of only minimal significance, both are examples of spaces which have become meaningful through experience. Both of these examples refer to events in the life of a single individual, and while the stories of Dunwich and the Sailors Reading Room refer to many lives, they are all meaningful in the same way. The example of Austerlitz's dream of his past makes this an appropriate point at which to consider Bachelard's approach to spaces, one which understands the oneiric as central to our experience of place.

Bachelard – The Dream of the Everyday

By now, having looked at examples from Sebald, we can see how useful the idea of dreaming is to phenomenology and we can now return to Bachelard in more depth to see how his method of imaginative experiencing extends beyond the description of houses and other geometric entities. For dreaming we can also read daydreaming, we do not need to be asleep to think in the way that Bachelard is suggesting. The nearest visual metaphor we may use would be looking through half closed eyes or seeing with a squint, but this is only a metaphor. Sebald says,

> I suppose it is submerged memories that give to dreams their curious air of hyper-reality. But perhaps there is something else as well, something nebulous, gauze-like, through which everything one sees in a dream seems, paradoxically, much clearer. (Sebald, 2002, *The Rings of Saturn*, pp.79-80)

As we have seen, with reference to the work of both Severs and Rilke, the metaphor of the dream allows us to go beyond simple perception, and to infer imaginings from what we see, or from what we are about to see. This might even at first seem magical or mystical, but we have already begun to see that this is not so. In his works *Air and Dreams*, *Water and Dreams*, and *The Poetics of Space* Bachelard uses the idea of dreaming in the same way that Sebald uses fiction and poetry to get beyond the empirical or geometric appearance of things. He states this clearly, "in philosophic matters only by suggesting fundamental reveries, by providing a means of access from thoughts to dreams can one be convincing."[23] The role of the poet is central for Bachelard as he says,

> Every poet must give us his invitation to journey. Through this invitation, our inner being gets a gentle push which throws us off balance and sets in motion a healthy, really dynamic reverie. (Bachelard, 1943, 2011, p.3)

This sense of vertiginous movement pervades everything that Bachelard says and is highly reminiscent of the works of both Severs and Sebald. As we have seen before,

> When we describe a daydream *objectively* this diminishes and interrupts it. How many dreams told objectively have become nothing but oneirism reduced to dust! In the presence of an image that dreams, it must be taken as an invitation to continue the daydream that created it. (Bachelard, 1958, 1994, p.152)

How true this rings to anyone who has awoken from a pleasant dream or been disturbed in a daydream, but Bachelard wants to emphasise dreaming as a mechanism for understanding reality not for avoiding it. The dream is fragile and Bachelard acknowledges our tendency to reduce and to destroy these seemingly insubstantial products of our imagination as we move to describe, name, and codify our experience. However, as we shall see, it is in the preservation of these ethereal entities that we may begin to gain access to a richer reality. Bachelard recognises the need to preserve immediacy in our encounter with the everyday and dreaming is the device through which this can be achieved. He clearly means more than just the kind of dreaming we experience when sleeping, he is taking dreaming to be a particular imaginative state of mind in which we encounter the world without it coming to our full notice, without our applying the full power of our intellect and reason, without naming it. This is a kind of free roaming formless reverie, thinking in an unsytematised way not governed by the rules of empirical perception or scientific investigation; it is almost not like thinking at all (taking here the full Cartesian notion of thinking) perhaps except in the way that it is also a kind of awareness. The dream is clearly not concerned with reason but with imagination, indeed it is often the opposite of reason that characterises the dream; it is precisely when we dream that we encounter the irrational. Through what Bachelard calls fundamental reveries we gain, and retain, access to something about the entities we come across which does not include differentiation and description, but which gives us immediate access to the phenomena, a kind of access in which image precedes thought, and by which route we can somehow surpass our everyday human condition through a kind of heightened sensitivity. Bachelard believes that this immediacy is available to us through dreaming, and it is in this state that we become receptive to phenomena. Dreaming is thus not simply a reduced state of consciousness but is a state of heightened receptivity to aspects of the entities we encounter and, as he says, "One must be receptive, receptive to the image at the moment it appears".[24] Once again his example of the simple domestic task of polishing a piece of furniture is illustrative of this receptivity and what it can bring.

> The minute we apply a glimmer of consciousness to a mechanical gesture, or practice phenomenology while polishing a piece of old furniture we sense new impressions come into being beneath this familiar domestic duty. For consciousness rejuvenates everything giving a quality of beginning to the most everyday actions. (Bachelard, 1958, 1994, p.67)

This everyday task can pass us by without our noticing anything extraordinary, it is only when we allow our thoughts to wander in a kind of daydream and allow our consciousness to rejuvenate the work that we begin to notice that which is extraordinary in what we are doing. We begin to notice the history of the piece of furniture, and through our rhythmical and repetitive movements as we polish we can reflect on the things that might have happened to the piece over the years. In a moment we have moved from an ordinary everyday task to extraordinary imaginings, we have begun to practice phenomenology. However, consciousness is not the enemy of understanding phenomena in this way; it is consciousness which brings forth the impressions which are at the heart of the appearance, so that,

> Objects that are cherished in this way really are born of an intimate light and they attain to a higher degree of reality than indifferent objects, or those that are defined by geometric reality. (Bachelard, 1958, 1994, p.68)

In simple terms, for any object that we encounter there is more to it than meets the eye. For "Objects" we may read any object of perception, including places and even entire landscapes. In the daydream we see and understand a reality which is destroyed once we begin to differentiate, describe and discuss. Dreaming is then a kind of imagining and,

> The imagination is not …, the facility for forming images of reality; it is the facility for forming images which go beyond reality, which *sing* reality. (Bachelard, 1942, 1982, p.16.)

We must become receptive to this singing, we must be able to hear reality, as it were, above the hubbub of noises which constantly distract our attention, and this is possible in the dream.

For Bachelard then it seems that dreaming (and daydreaming) is a kind of pre-reflective attitude which is not simply a forerunner of awakened consciousness or a kind of pre-encounter with things, it is the way that these very encounters are themselves shaped, it becomes the ground of our understanding of the world. When we awaken from the dream something is lost not gained, description and dissection, the codification of experience, destroys what we had before of the object or place so that.

> Dreams come before contemplation. Before becoming a conscious sight, every landscape is an oneiric experience. (Bachelard, 1942, 1982, p.4)

We are aware before we can codify, name and structure our experience, we are aware before we know. Dreaming is one way in which we can return to this state of simple awareness, and a state through which we can encounter the unstructured complexity of the entities and places we encounter before they are given meaning and structured by our purposive will. Bachelard says,

> When he has returned to his waking state, man rationalises his dreams using concepts form his everyday life. He has a vague recollection of the dream images, and already distorts them by expressing them in the language of his waking life. (Bachelard, 1943, 2011, p.26)

Even the application of concepts from the language of everyday life is enough to dispel our delicate imaginings and to destroy the fragile image. The application of purpose drives away the multiple possibilities of the entities we encounter and enables them to become useful for us, but these multiple possibilities must remain and are awakened when we return to them in the dream so that, "We must give ourselves over to an elemental life, that is to our own particular elemental imagination."[25] Bachelard is proposing a complete reversal, and the radical nature of his thinking about the world is given when he says,

> The dream is not a product of waking life. It is the fundamental subjective state. A metaphysician can see a *kind of Copernican revolution of the imagination* at work here. In fact images can no longer be understood by their objective *traits* but by their subjective meaning. (Bachelard, 1943, 2011, p.101)

A Copernican revolution completely reverses our approach to the world, the imagination is no longer a secondary activity which follows our discovery of the world; it is now made the primary activity through which we make this discovery. This reversal of the imaginative and the objective is exemplified in his discussion of the blue sky when referring to a passage by Paul Eluard where he says,

> If, as I believe, the meditating being is first of all the dreaming being, a whole metaphysics of aerial reverie can derive its inspiration from Eluard's passage. Here reverie is integrated into its rightful place, i.e. before representation. There, the imagined world takes its rightful place before the represented world; the universe takes its rightful place before the object. As is only right, the poetic knowledge of the world precedes rational knowledge of objects. The world is beautiful before being true. The world

is admired before being verified. Every primitive condition is pure
oneirism. Bachelard, 1943, 2011, p.166)

Bachelard is restoring primacy to the imagination and taking it away from
objective rationalisation which, though it remains necessary for our
everyday existing, is a secondary movement which is grounded in our
imagining. The contrast between these two is made very clear when he
says,

> It is widely assumed that utility is an unmistakeable concept and that its
> value was always surely and immediately obvious. Now useful knowledge
> is knowledge that has already been rationalized. Conversely to conceive of
> a *primitive idea* as a *useful idea* is to fall into a *rationalization* which is all
> the more specious since today utility is an integral part of the framework of
> a very complete, very homogenous, very material, very definitely closed
> utilitarianism. (Bachelard, 1942, 1982, p.73)

Bachelard recognizes that this kind of utilitarian thinking is embedded in
our present understanding of knowledge, and while this is necessary for
our day-to-day living in the world, he is showing us that this way of
thinking about the world is not fundamental, and in fact that the
epistemological polarity must be reversed if we are to reveal the true
nature of the world and our position in it. The consequences of failure in
this respect are clear because,

> A long imaginative evolution leads us from fundamental reverie to a
> discursive understanding of the beauty of forms. A metaphysics of
> utilitarian understanding explains man as a mass of conditioned reflexes. It
> leaves the dreaming man, the dreamer outside of its inquiry. (Bachelard,
> 1943, 2011, p.167)

And, as he says elsewhere, "Man, alas, is not so reasonable as all that!"[26]
Bachelard brings the dreamer back into the inquiry and places him at
the centre. In this connection we can see that the similarities between
Sebald's musings and Bachelard's theories are striking. Bachelard
encourages us to see more than is apparently there and wants us to allow
ourselves to dream in ways that are reminiscent of Sebald's thinking about
both the world he is in, and worlds that have passed. Straightaway we can
hear resonances from Sebald's story of his visit to Wertach in Bachelard's
words when he says,

> Indeed at times dreams go back far into an undefined, dateless past that
> clear memories of our childhood home appear to be detached from us.

> Such dreams unsettle our daydreaming and we reach a point where we begin to doubt that we ever lived where we lived. Our past is situated elsewhere and both time and place are impregnated with a sense of unreality. It is though we sojourned in a limbo of being. (Bachelard, 1958, 1994, pp.57-58)

Sebald feels this detachment when he visits Wertach and in his account of his remembered childhood gives us the dream which is all that he can have, since as Bachelard reminds us,

> We are unable to relive duration that has been destroyed. We can only think of it in the line of an abstract time that is deprived of all thickness. (Bachelard, 1958, 1994, p.9)

Bachelard's point also applies significantly to the experience of the disused Ladies Waiting Room recounted by Austerlitz, indeed Austerlitz is not even quite sure himself whether the scenes he dreams are real memories or just an apparition. It is only later that he is able to rationalize his extraordinary vision. The imaginings of Austerlitz at Liverpool Street lead him to discover the objective reality of his journey to England.

For Bachelard dreaming and imagining are intimately connected, just as imagining goes beyond the simple image that we see, so dreaming represents a free roaming kind of thinking without form, he says,

> Reverie merely takes us elsewhere, without our really being able to live the images we encounter along the way. The dreamer is set adrift. (Bachelard, 1943, 2011, p.3)

This is because (otherwise),

> we fail to de-objectify objects and deform forms—a process which allows us see the matter beneath the object—the world is strewn with unrelated things, immobile and inert solids, objects foreign to our nature. (Bachelard, 1942, 1982, p.2)

So that,

> At least we must feel that the oneiric life is purer the more it frees us from the tyranny of forms and restores us to substances and to the life of our own element. (Bachelard, 1943, 2011, p.26)

While at first it might seem that the language of 'formlessness' and 'setting adrift' portray a deficient kind of awareness I am arguing that the reverse is the case. Lack of form and drifting consciousness gives thinking a freedom to roam which disappears as the dream dissipates. It is as if in dreaming and imagining we are not so much lost to the world as able to see it anew in its multiplicity and complexity, undifferentiated by any purpose. Description, differentiation, discussion and dissection all lead to a loss of this world which becomes enveloped in what Bachelard calls a tyranny of forms and which I shall consider to be the consequences of our necessarily instrumental individual purpose and engagement with the world. Bachelard wants us to escape from this to gain a more primordial understanding of our being and of the world, an understanding which precedes purpose. He explicitly identifies this escape route with the art of poetry but I think that this only points us towards the many kinds of ways in which we can become newly and more deeply aware, we might call this a broad spectrum poetic engagement with the world.

At this point critics will be thinking that all of this dreaming seems all very well but must risk a steady descent into a kind of airy mysticism which I agree must be avoided. To gain the full import of what Bachelard is attempting with his poetic method and to acquit his work from a charge of mysticism we must attend carefully and slowly to the things he says. In the foreword to *Air and Dreams* he says that he is going to "school us in slowness".[27] We must try to understand what Bachelard means by this and although it may first appear that he is trying to turn us away from our accepted, even traditional, mode of seeing and understanding the world— towards a more imaginative and poetic mode of understanding—this is not simply the case. Bachelard is emphasising the oneiric but only as a re-emphasis of an approach which, though not completely lost, has suffered a loss of prominence in our thinking. To this extent only may Bachelard's enterprise be seen as looking backwards to a more poetic and mystical way of understanding the world. However his task is much greater, and much more sophisticated, in seeking to provide an understanding of the richness and complexity of the world, one which could not be provided by naïve rationalism. It is not his aim to eliminate our rational approach to the world but to enhance it, to succeed in this Bachelard must therefore connect imagination with reality. Near the beginning of *Air and Dreams* Bachelard says,

> Imagination allows us to leave the ordinary course of things. Perceiving and imagining are as antithetical as absence and presence. To imagine is to absent oneself, to launch out towards a new life. (Bachelard, 1943, 2011, p.3)

The absenting, which is also a launching out, gives us the clue to the real relation between perceiving and imagining. If we take Bachelard to mean by "perceiving" the whole complex of activities that we automatically undertake when we see, hear, touch, smell or taste something, the categorization and description (or pigeon-holeing as Severs would call it) of our experience, then we can understand this activity in opposition to imagining. The real relationship between perceiving and imagining is dialectical, that is the meanings of the terms are intertwined and interdependent and it is their synthesis that we can call experience. Imagining and perception must come together in true experience, neither can have any real meaning without the counterpose of the other. In this way it becomes clear that neither perceiving nor imagining alone can be sufficient to provide us with access to the world, to allow the world to appear we need both. The imaginary lacks reality and perception reduces reality, it is only when they come together that we can begin to speak of experience. Bachelard is showing us, "how the imaginary is immanent in the real, how a *continuous* path leads from the real to the imaginary."[28] He is emphasising the continuity between the imaginary and the real, a continuity which is essential if we are not to fall permanently into sterile rationalism or hopeless mysticism, he says,

> In point of fact I see no solid basis for natural direct elemental rationality. Rational knowledge is not acquired all at once, nor is the right perspective on fundamental images reached in the first attempt. Rationalist? That is what we are trying to *become,* not only in our learning generally but also in the details of our thinking and the specific organization of our familiar images. (Bachelard, 1942, 1982, p.7)

This places a rationalist approach in context and suggests that we can move from an imaginative approach to rationalism along a path from the imaginary to the real. The antithetically opposed activities of perceiving and imagining are at opposite ends of this same path; this is the path along which we must travel in order to fully realize our engagement with the world and to have it appear to us as it does, and as it must. Bachelard is no mystic; he is simply trying to redress a balance that has been lost. This is the same loss of balance that Schiller laments.[29]

The same dialectical pair are re-presented throughout Bachelard's work, we have the useful and the agreeable, sleeping and awakening, thought and dreams, and, from Sebald, the strange and the familiar. With the dialectic of perceiving and imagining Bachelard is freeing us from the tyranny of forms and helping us to "get as close to the essential experience as we can".[30] In this way we can nullify the "problem of description"[31] by forestalling it so that,

> In order to enter into the essence of an oneiric reality as clear cut as flight, we must, in my opinion, refrain from bringing in visual images... the wing is already a rationalization. (Bachelard, 1943, 2011, pp.26-27)

Bachelard, like Sebald, is providing us with a reason to pause or "schooling us in slowness", but although our progress is slowed it is more certain and we will, as a result, arrive at the real with our appreciation of the imaginary intact, and at the same time gain an understanding of the real that is complex and rich. Bachelard wants to chart a course back from dreaming to a more concrete notion of reality. His task in this can be more easily grounded if we move away from the areas of explicit art and poetry and into simple everyday experience. With direct and pregnant reference again to Rilke and with clear resonances of Sebald, Bachelard says,

> Every object that is contemplated, every exalted name that is whispered is the starting point for a dream and a poem; it is a creative linguistic movement. How many times, at the edges of a well with its old stone covered with wild sorrel and fern, have I murmured the names of distant waters, the name of a world buries in water ... And how many times has that world suddenly answered me ... O my things! What conversations we have had! (Bachelard, 1943, 2011, p.5)

This echoes both Rilke's account of the end wall of the house and many of Sebald's musings about place and time in, for example, *The Rings of Saturn*. While it is the phenomenon of poetry that demonstrates the existence of the world beyond our mere perception, we do not necessarily need poetry to make this world accessible. We can hear the singing of reality once we allow ourselves to hear, free from the distractions and purposes of our everyday dealings. It is in the purposelessness and formlessness of dreaming that we can begin to understand phenomenology as the onset of the image. The ordinary can be extraordinary and the familiar can be strange, it is for us to see it and to create our own dream of the everyday. It is not enough that we can escape the tyranny of forms and individual purpose through poetry and explicitly poetic images. In a significant sense there is a kind of poetry in all that we encounter. It is for us to see the poetic in the world, and in particular in the everyday, and to do this we must each create our own dream of the everyday. So that when Bachelard says, "For being is before all else an awakening, and it awakens in the awareness of an extraordinary impression"[32] we need look no further than our ordinary everyday experience, which is a kind of not-noticing, and notice what is extraordinary about the ordinary. Like Sebald we need to recognise the strange in the familiar. To this extent we may call Sebald's and Sever's work poetic, but this would both stretch a point and, more importantly miss out on the sheer significance locked up in our everyday experience which Sebald in particular is trying to show us.

But after the dream we will and must awaken. Having understood the world in its complexity and possibility we return to our own purposive activity in a way which limits these possibilities. While we may stand at the site of an ancient battle we do not have to duck to avoid the flying arrows. Our understanding of places is deepened when we understand the significance which makes these spaces into places, this significance may be rich and multi-layered, but our own everyday behaviour is conditioned by everyday circumstances. We accept the meaning of places while at the same time making new meanings. So, for example, when Sebald visits his former home he understands the events of the past which have given this place meaning, but in addition the account of Wertach as he finds it now, as an adult, adds a further layer of meaning to this place as a home re-visited. Sebald cannot escape the past nor can he escape making the present into a new past. We cannot just pass through spaces and leave no trace, in this way everywhere becomes somewhere the moment we arrive, or even when we set off. What Sebald and Bachelard do is to help us to understand more about the places we visit than may at first be apparent so that when we awaken from the dream and pursue our individual projects we do so with a deeper understanding, not only of what others have done to make spaces places, but of what we ourselves are now doing in the same way. We are thus able to apply our own purpose to places replete with meaning but we are able to do so with an understanding of how these spaces became places, we may not even remember our dream of the everyday but its effects stay with us.

Gadamer and Play

In *Truth and Method* Gadamer discusses play in relation to the work of art. I will suggest that the process that he describes is also effective in the same way as Bachelard's oneirism and Sebald's musings are in giving us access to the world in its richness and complexity, and without the radical reduction that other ways of understanding can entail. I suggest that this is effective because the things that Gadamer says about aesthetic consciousness and its relation to art are also true of all consciousness and its relation to world. Gadamer quickly notices the apparent purposelessness of play when he says,

> in playing, all those purposive relations that determine active and caring existence have not simply disappeared but are curiously suspended. The player himself knows that play is only play and that it exists in a world determined by seriousness of purpose. But he does not know this in such a way that, as a player, actually *intends* this relation to seriousness. Play fulfils its purpose only if the player loses himself in play. (Gadamer, 1975, 2004, p.102-3)

We may take Gadamer to mean by "caring" the fundamental relation of our being to the world as inevitably and inextricably involved. In playing these involvements are temporarily suspended but already this is a knowing suspension. It is an imaginative act in which we self consciously free ourselves and allow ourselves to be taken in by the playing. We can all recognize the kind of absorption that Gadamer notices.

> In our concept of play the difference between belief and pretence is dissolved. (and...) The structure of play absorbs the player into itself, and this frees him from the burden of taking the initiative, which constitutes the strain of existence. (Gadamer, 2004, pp.102-3)

In the context of the work of art and its relation to play this means that,

> The work of art is not an object that stands over and against a subject for itself. Instead the work of art has its true being in the fact that it changes the person who experiences it. (Gadamer, 1975, 2004, p.103)

It is as if by allowing ourselves to be taken in, by allowing ourselves the freedom to play, we allow that which we experience, in this case the work of art, to change us. I suggest that this is not only true of our aesthetic experience but the same is true for all of our experience. Once we allow ourselves to encounter the world freely, as we do in play, we can experience the world without purpose. In the same way that Bachelard invites us to dream Gadamer asks us to come and play. We have seen in Sebald how even the apparently most insignificant occurrence or encounter with the world that we might have can be significant in illuminating the world, and in changing us just as we change it. In the same way that art changes those who experience it, and thereby gains its true being, so the world gains its true being by changing those who experience it. The play exists independently of the player but is brought to presentation in being played, in the same way the world exists independently of the subject but is brought to presentation by being experienced or to put it another way, by being played with.

It is not the case that play is completely without purpose but that its purpose is contained within the play. This means that the player, while divorced from the serious purposes of the world, is fully engaged in the purposes of play. As Gadamer points out,

> Seriousness is not merely something that calls us away from play; rather seriousness in playing is necessary to make the play wholly play. Someone who does not take the game seriously is a spoilsport. The mode of being of play does not allow the player to behave towards play as if it were an object. The player knows very well what play is, and that what he is doing is 'only a game'; but he does not know what exactly he "knows" in knowing that. (Gadamer, 1975, 2004, p.103)

Playing makes us aware of the serious world by detaching us from it. Play provides us with a perspective by temporarily removing us from this world. The rules we play by are the rules of the game not the rules of the serious world, and we play by these rules in the full knowledge that they are only the rules of a game and to this extent not 'real'. This knowing detachment is a kind of knowing that knows it is detached, but knows also that this detachment is imaginary and therefore temporary. It is not any kind of mysticism, it is the kind of perspective that Sebald strives for and the dream like state that Bachelard encourages us to cultivate, it also the state we freely adopt in play. It is the kind of playing that Sever's encouraged the viewers of his house to engage in so that they might understand the history of the place that he had created. We are encouraged to play with the world and in doing so, to bring it to presentation and understanding in a very specific kind of way.

As players we play and we play seriously, in so doing we become temporarily disengaged from the world of caring and in this disconnection, while absorbed in the play, we reveal something of ourselves, as well as instantiating the play itself.

> The self presentation of human play depends on the players conduct being tied to the make-believe goals of the game, but the "meaning" of these goals does not in fact depend on their being achieved. Rather in spending oneself on the task of the game, one is in fact playing oneself out. The self presentation of the game involves the player achieving, as it were, his own self presentation by playing—i.e. presenting—something. (Gadamer, 1975, 2004, p.108)

Gadamer succeeds in freeing the concept of play from the subjective meaning that it has previously had and which he says has dominated modern aesthetics and the philosophy of man. This is necessary to prevent both the play and the world from becoming the creature of subjectivity. He achieves this by making a clear distinction between play and the behaviour of the player so that "our question concerning the nature of play itself cannot therefore find an answer if we look for it in the players subjective reflection."[33] And so,

> Play is not to be understood as something a person does. As far as language is concerned the actual subject of play is obviously not the subjectivity of an individual who among other activities also plays, but instead the play itself. (Gadamer, 1975, 2004, p.102-3)

Although Gadamer is here referring to play as the clue to the ontological explanation of the work of art his words are reminiscent of those of Heidegger when he says,

> It is not the case that man "is" and then has, by way of an extra, a relationship-of-Being towards the "world"—a world with which he provides himself occasionally. (Heidegger, 1962, H.57)

Which means that

> The perceiving of what is known is not a process of returning with one's booty to the 'cabinet' of consciousness after one has gone out and grasped it. (Heidegger, 1962, H.62)

In these cases Heidegger is affirming the unity of being and world and rejecting both solipsism and dualism in the same way that Gadamer rejects these in his conception of play. Just as we do not provide ourselves with a relation to the world and thereby instantiate the world, in play we do not create the play. Just as play does not need players to exist but is brought to presentation by the players the world exists and is brought to presentation (appearance) by consciousness. Gadamer goes on to say, "In being presented in play, what is emerges. It produces and brings to light what is otherwise constantly hidden and withdrawn."[34] I suggest it is the case that in all experience, not only aesthetic experience, the same process takes place and through our experience of the world we bring the world to presentation. Sebald, for example, is inviting us to play with the world in order to discover what is there and in order to provoke the emergence of what is.

Play, and the act of playing, provides the artifice of a spectatorial point of view by temporarily suspending our involvement in the world of seriousness, a kind of detachment from the world in which the imagination has free play. This is the kind of free play which Sebald shows us in "All'estero" and "Il ritorno in patria". It is also the kind of detachment which Bachelard is describing in *Air and Dreams* and *Water and Dreams*, and it is the position from which we can come to appreciate the everyday before it is reduced through our necessarily active engagement with the serious world.

Next Steps

So far so good, but as with any philosophical project of this nature, it is always necessary to move deeper into the problem, and its solution, and to seek a more profound understanding. Both Sebald and Bachelard (and to some extent Severs) have shown what happens when we experience spaces and places, both of them have made us stop and think and see more than we first thought was there, all of them have brought forward aspects of our experience and the world which seem to have gone unnoticed. Gadamer has shown how play gives us a temporary release from purposive thinking and frees the imagination. The question remains however as to how this is possible, what makes it happen? What is it about the world and ourselves that means that this is the way in which we experience? To begin even the most tentative approach to this question will require recourse to some further philosophical reflections which may appear to take us further from, rather than closer to, our phenomenological purpose. In the next chapter I will therefore look more closely at memory and how this affects our understanding of the world and the ways in which it may shape the images we encounter. Following that will be a chapter on history which will also include the notions of tradition and culture which I think constitute a kind of collective or shared memory.

Notes

[1] Bachelard, 1942, 1982, p.4.
[2] Sebald, 2002, *Vertigo*, pp.31-137.
[3] Sebald, 2002, *Vertigo*, pp. 78-81.
[4] Sebald, 2002, *Vertigo*, pp.178-80.
[5] Sebald, 2002, *Vertigo*, pp.6-8.
[6] Sebald, 2002, *Vertigo*, pp.191-6.
[7] Sebald, 2002, *Vertigo*, p.187.

[8] Bachelard, 1958, 1994, p.30.
[9] Sebald, 2002, *Vertigo*, pp.187-90.
[10] *The Robbers* was written in 1780 at the end of the Sturm und Drang period but in style it belongs to this movement.
[11] Sebald, 2002, *Vertigo*, p.181.
[12] Sebald, 2002, *Vertigo*, p.115.
[13] Sebald, 2002, *Vertigo*, p.258.
[14] Sebald, 2002, *The Rings of Saturn*, pp.154-161.
[15] Of course Sebald lists these places *The Rings of Saturn*, p.157.
[16] Sebald, 2002, *The Rings of Saturn*, p.93.
[17] Sebald, 2002, *The Rings of Saturn*, p.93.
[18] Pevsner, 1961, p.173.
[19] Given in Chapter Three.
[20] Pevsner, 1961, p.400.
[21] www.shellmuseum.org.uk
[22] Sebald, 2002, *Austerlitz*, pp.180-95.
[23] Bachelard, 1942, 1982, p.3.
[24] Bachelard, 1958, 1994, p.xv.
[25] Bachelard, 1943, 2011, p.26.
[26] Bachelard, 1942, 1982, p.73.
[27] Bachelard, 1943, 2011, p.vii.
[28] Bachelard, 1943, 2011, p.4.
[29] Schiller, 1795, 2004, p.26.
[30] Bachelard, 1943, 2011, p.26.
[31] Bachelard, 1958, 1994, p.6.
[32] Bachelard, 1942, 1982, p.7.
[33] Gadamer, 1975, 2004, p.103.
[34] Gadamer, 1975, 2004, p.112.

CHAPTER SIX

MEMORY:
REMEMBERING AND UNFORGETTING

This chapter is concerned with the notion of memory and the ways that it contributes to the construction of our experience of the world as appearance. The complementary notions of remembering and unforgetting are closely associated with the idea of memory and all three will require some preliminary definitions and clarification before we can proceed with the investigation. In simple parlance memory is the faculty of recalling past events and experiences, essentially a looking back at what was, or, as we have already seen in the case of Henri Beyle, what we think was. Sebald makes many references to memory including this one from Ambros Adelwarth at the end of the diary of his travels with Cosmo Solomon in *The Emigrants*; it will suffice as a working definition,

> Memory, he added as a postscript, often strikes me as a kind of dumbness. It makes ones head heavy and giddy, as if one were not looking back down the receding perspective of time but rather down on the earth from a great height, from one of those towers whose tops are lost from view in the clouds. (Sebald, 2002, *The Emigrants*, p.145)

This seems to capture both the simple aspect of looking back as well as the indistinct image of the past that memory can give us. We see the past through a haze of clouds as if from the tops of tall towers. However it also includes the sense of sheer vertigo that we can experience when looking back. The past, which has gone away from us, seems to draw us back and we fear looking back in the same way that we fear looking down from a great height. It is as if we are reminded of that which we cannot change and that which will always be with us. In horror we turn away and look to the future which presents itself as a field of open possibilities from which we seem free to choose. The vertiginous nature of remembering gives a crucial pointer to its role in constructing experience. Gadamer considers the connection between experience and memory when he says,

> An experience is no longer just something that flows past quickly in the
> stream of conscious life; it is meant as a unity and thus attains a new mode
> of being one. (Gadamer, 1975, 2004. p.58)

So that,

> What can be called experience constitutes it self as memory. By calling it
> such we are referring to the lasting meaning that an experience has for the
> person who has it. (Gadamer, 1975, 2004, p.58)

Memory becomes experience that stays with us, and it stays with us as an
individual, memory is an intensely personal phenomenon. Remembering is
then, the act of recall, a re-assembling of our past experience, but before
this can be understood we must consider unforgetting. It is obviously true
that we cannot remember anything that we have not already forgotten, for
unless it has been forgotten it cannot be re-membered. This means that our
experience must go through a complex process of mediation in which we
first come to experience the phenomena and then forget what we have seen
and heard. Remembering is the resurrection of these forgotten experiences
which is why I have chosen to call this 'unforgetting', a term which
preserves the ordering and continuity of events; experience – forgetting –
unforgetting (remembering), and their dynamic and connected quality.
Unforgetting is the act of bringing back to mind that which not only has
passed but which we had forgotten, or somehow lost, misplaced in our
consciousness, but forgetting is not simply misplacing, it something much
more significant. As Heidegger puts it when he is writing about
temporality and everydayness,

> This forgetting is not nothing, nor is it just a failure to remember; it is
> rather a 'positive' ecstatical mode of one's having been—a mode with a
> character of its own. (Heidegger, 1962, H.339)

Most of the time we live with this "forgetting", it is a way of leaving
behind that which has gone but in a way that retains the experience
through the possibility of recall and unforgetting, or again in Heidegger's
words,

> Just as expecting is possible only on the basis of awaiting, remembering is
> possible only on that of forgetting, and not vice versa; for in the mode of
> having-forgotten, one's having-been 'discloses' primarily the horizon into
> which a Dasein lost in the 'superficiality' of its object of concern, can
> bring itself by remembering. (Heidegger, 1962, H.339)

Forgetting is our way of retaining our past while being in the present and pre-occupied, as we must be, with our everyday concerns.

Memory is not simply and straightforwardly the re-gaining of phenomenal experience that has past. In remembering, and in unforgetting, we do not experience again what we once did. Memory does not take us back in time, we cannot re-live only remember. Memory, as we know, is selective and we mis-remember almost at least as often as we remember. The past is in a strong sense gone, and unforgetting merely brings back the shadow of what once was, but a shadow from which we can never rid ourselves and which must always be there whether we choose to notice it or not. I will return to Heidegger and the temporality of the everyday at a later stage but for now the simple recognition of forgetting as something more than just a failure to remember will be sufficient to inform the discussion that follows. I hope that the implications of this, and its full meaning for the notion of memory and how it contributes to phenomenal experience, will become clear as the discussion progresses. I will now begin the process of examining how memory, and particularly unforgetting, contributes to the construction of our experience. I will begin with some reflection on the perceptive and lively writing of David Hockney along with brief reference to the work of Gadamer; this will be followed by some examples from Sebald of the ways in which memory contributes to our experience of the world. After that I will take a look at the role of photographs and gravestones in the work of memory and remembering. Eventually I will return in more detail to Heidegger to show how memory, remembering and unforgetting are part of the temporal structures of the everyday.

Hockney and Memory - Gadamer and Bildung

David Hockney notices that memory has a key role to play in phenomenal experience when he says,

> Because each of us has a different memory this proves to me that objective vision cannot be. When you look at this, you remember that you've seen things like it before. Your memory comes in and forms part of it. (Hockney, 1999, p.56)

Hockney's consideration of memory is naturally specific to his work as a visual artist but his reflections contain the seeds of more profound features of memory and point to the ways in which memory contributes significantly to world that we experience and the ways in which we experience it. For Hockney this is the central problem of depiction, that is;

what he and every other artist like him is doing is not re-creating what they see but giving an account of what they see. Although we have seen some of this kind of distinction in the study of the Dutch painters who painted what they knew to be there, as opposed to simply what they could see, Hockney is saying something more. While we might say that the Dutch painters, in their limited way, were trying to provide scientific or objective representations of the things that they knew to be present, Hockney wants to make a distinction between this objective presentation and what he calls artistic presentation. He says, "There's a difference between scientific representation and artistic presentation, and that difference is the hand."[1] I will argue that in the wider fields of perception and phenomenology Hockney's hand is the individual consciousness and that a large part of the seeing of this individual is determined by the memories that this individual has accumulated. We will return to this distinction between scientific or objective representation, and artistic or individual representation later in a discussion of the way photographs portray the world, but for the moment we can just acknowledge Hockney's insight into the way that memory is inextricably enmeshed into the way we see the world. While the issues of objective vision and their re-creation as works of art are, at least for Hockney, initially technical problems, I think that he is also aware of their deeper significance as philosophical problems which affect not only the artist in consideration of his subject, but all of us in our encounters with the phenomena that make up our world. No-one comes to the world with nothing, we all carry with us the sum of all of our experiences, some explicit and prominent in our consciousness, some half-remembered as in a dream, and even some that we have forgotten. All of them are a part of, and contribute to, the onset of each new image.

    This more extensive interpretation of what Hockney is describing is supported by Gadamer's notion of Bildung as set out in *Truth and Method*. Bildung, though usually translated as culture, contains not only the explicit manifestations of culture but also deeper meanings and memories which we all acquire and carry as part of our membership of a particular society. It encompasses not only our language but the structure of our thinking, as Gadamer says, "In Bildung... that by which and through which one is formed becomes completely one's own.",[2] and,

> Every single individual who raises himself out of his natural being to the spiritual finds in the language, customs, and institutions of his people a pre-given body of material which, as in learning to speak, he has to make his own. Thus every individual is always engaged in the process of Bildung and in getting beyond his naturalness, inasmuch as the world into

which he is growing is one that is humanly constituted through language and custom. (Gadamer, 1975, 2004, p.10)

Bildung is thus an environment and a process. It is a process of learning and of making the world our own which is essential to self-realisation. Central to this process of learning and self-realisation is keeping oneself open to new ideas and more universal points of view. It is the process of coming to understand ourselves as part of the world we all inhabit through the reconciliation of world, which is Other, and our own individual consciousness. Bachelard introduces something similar when he speaks of culture complexes in *Water and Dreams*. He calls these, "prereflective attitudes that govern the very process of reflection"[3] and I take him to be stalking the same territory as Gadamer in respect of the way that our way of thinking is governed by the world in which we exist. Memory plays a key role in Bildung, and as Gadamer goes on to say,

> Moreover the nature of memory is not rightly understood if it is regarded as merely a general talent or capacity. Keeping in mind, forgetting and recalling belong to the historical constitution of man and are themselves part of his history and his Bildung. Whoever uses his memory as a mere faculty ... does not possess it as something that is absolutely his own. (Gadamer, 1975, 2004, p.14)

It is not simply that the kind of objective vision that Hockney is referring to is elusive, it is not simply that memories get in the way of objective vision. Bildung is inescapable and, even more, is the only route through which self-realization is possible. Bildung is the only avenue we have for our inescapable participation in the world and memory is one of the ways we make the world our own because, "Memory must be formed, for memory is not memory for anything and everything".[4] We may choose the kind of participation that we have but not the fact of participation itself. Memory thus plays its part in our becoming what we are. As Gadamer says the essence of Bildung is the return to our own self, and is "the element in which the educated man moves".[5] A more complete explanation of the idea of Bildung is not required to support the argument here, we have already seen enough to show that the truth of the apparent unavailability of objective vision noticed by Hockney lies in the fact of Bildung, and it is also clear that memory is much more than a simple faculty of recall. In an echo of Heidegger's words Gadamer says,

> Only by forgetting does the mind have the possibility of total renewal, the capacity to see everything with fresh eyes, so that what is long familiar

fuses with the new into a many levelled unity. (Gadamer, 1975, 2004, p.14)

Our own personal development is made up of this constant swirl of new experiences combined with past memories within a context of customs language and ways of thinking which we get from the world we live in.

Before moving on from Hockney and Gadamer there is one further point to consider. For the artist Hockney the problem of objective vision "leads to the central problem of depiction: that is it not an attempt to re-create something, but an account of seeing it".[6] I want to take this "account of seeing it" as the witnessing of the onset of the image, that is; what the artist is doing in the act of depiction is reporting their own experience of phenomena, and not just painting what they are seeing. We have seen how this is important specifically in the case of the Dutch artists, but its significance goes much further into any exploration of the onset of the image and phenomenology. We must be careful at this point not to fall into the dualist error of separating that which we see from that which is there. Once we allow anyone, artists included, to say that the image is only their account of what they saw, rather than a phenomenon directly related to some entity in the world, we are committed to an inner world of perception which will betray the power of phenomenology. The artists are not copying into their pictures the pictures that they already have in their minds. We must not allow any room for a theory in which phenomena bar access to the world, rather we should understand phenomena as constitutive of the world as we know it. This is true of the work of art as it is of anything else; once again Gadamer is firm on this when he says,

> The essence of imitation consists precisely in the recognition of the represented in the representation. A representation intends to be so true and convincing that we do not advert to the fact that what is so represented is not "real". Recognition as cognition of the true occurs through an act of identification in which we do not differentiate between the representation and the represented (Gadamer, 1986, p.59)

In the acts of recognition and identification we close the gap between the image and what is represented. This is reminiscent of the portrait painters of the Renaissance and their attempt to create the illusion of presence,[7] not the presence itself but certainly the very best illusion possible. This does not mean that a picture of something is the same as the thing pictured, but it does mean that the picture only has meaning in that it is a picture of something which is itself real, and that the picture in some way partakes of this reality.

The key notions that I will now take forward from Hockney are the idea that, in the widest sense, memory comes in and forms a part of what we see, and the idea that depiction, in its widest sense, is not a matter of re-creating our experience but of giving an account of our experience and an account which can be constitutive of both the world and of our selves.

Sebald

I want to argue in this section that Sebald's work illustrates how memory is part of how we construct the account of all of our experience of the world, and not just in the sense of the visual. In this way memory is central to phenomenology in that it is always present at the onset of the image and helps to determine this process itself. Sebald makes many references to memory including the one from Ambros Adelwarth that I have already given, however as Gadamer has indicated,[8] memory is not simply and straightforwardly the re-gaining of experience that has past. In remembering and in unforgetting we do not experience again what we once did, but our unforgetting does frame our present and new experiences.

We have already seen how memory plays us false in Sebald's account of Beyle and the prospect of Ivrea. In this case the memory of the time Beyle first went there was replaced by an image in an engraving which he saw later. We may assume that Beyle would only be able to remember what he really saw if he were to have gone back to Ivrea, but even in this eventuality both he himself and the prospect he first saw would have been changed and essentially would have disappeared, for memory is not a recreation of experience but merely the recall of an account of experiencing. The case of Beyle in Ivrea is not so much a case of memory constructing the account of experience but a failure of memory, a forgetting, and one in which his subsequent unforgetting is disrupted by the memory he has of the engraving of Ivrea. At the same time it shows that memory is playing a part in our understanding of the world. When Beyle finds the engraving of Ivrea many years later he realises that he has forgotten what he actually saw, and that he can no longer recall what it might have looked like when he was there, this new knowing now becomes part of his experience of Ivrea. The next step would be for him to somehow remember, or unforget, and to retrieve his original memory. Whether this might be possible is the subject I will turn to next.

We have seen earlier in the discussion of places how Sebald writes about his return to his home village in "Il ritorno in patria".[9] His account

of this homecoming is so full of memories it is sometimes hard to tell what
is present and what is past. This blurring of the distinction is exactly what
Sebald is attempting to achieve. In recollecting the memories of his
childhood in Wertach the accounts of his early experiences overlay his
present experience and are now given to us in the book as an account of
his visit home, a memory with memories embedded in it, and as he says,

> over the years I had puzzled out a good deal in my own mind, but in spite
> of that, far from becoming clearer, things now appeared to me more
> incomprehensible than ever. The more images I gathered from the past, I
> said, the more unlikely it seemed to me that the past had actually happened
> in that way, for nothing about it could be called normal: most of it was
> absurd, and if not absurd, then appalling (Sebald,2002, *Vertigo*, p.212)

Past and present have become mixed, past becomes part of present and
helps to form it. The first lesson, it appears, is that if just as in the case of
places, everywhere is already somewhere, then, in the case of our
consideration of memory it seems that everything is already something.
Even new experiences of phenomena never encountered before are
mediated through the memories we have of things that have gone before,
be they similar or just reminiscent of what we come across now. In this
way Sebald describes a process of unforgetting but it is a process which is
to a degree unreliable, making it barely possible to distinguish which of
what appears as memories are just that, and which may be constructions
we now place on our recollections as part of our renewed experience.

In *The Rings of Saturn* Sebald is even more explicit about the vital role
of memory in the actual construction of our experience in his telling of the
story of Vicomte Chateaubriand and Charlotte Ives.[10] The story of the love
of the French diplomat for the English girl, which concludes with their
parting on his regretful return to France, is a tale of what might have been.
It is told from the point of view of his recollections as an old man of a time
long ago, when his life might have taken a very different turn but did not.
Chateaubriand remembers his time in England fondly and, as he writes,
ponders what happened to the extent that in recalling he fears a repetition.
When writing he thinks, "As I did so I was troubled by the question of
whether in the writing I should once again betray and lose Charlotte Ives,
and this time forever".[11] It is a as if his memory is so powerful that
remembering would be as painful as the actual experience of leaving
Charlotte. There is also a fear that by awakening the memory, by
unforgetting, he will allow the memory to dissipate and lose her again. The
memory and the pain are further reinforced by his unexpected meeting
with Charlotte years later who, as a married woman with children, comes

to him to seek a favour. He goes on to say, "Memories lie slumbering within us for months and years, quietly proliferating, until they are woken by some trifle and in some strange way blind us to life".[12] This is the nature of unforgetting, it comes upon us sometimes when we least expect it like an awakening, Proust and his madeleines spring immediately to mind, although we can all probably think of occasions when a seemingly disconnected instance has triggered a memory we thought we had lost. But memory is even more important than this, Chateaubriand goes on to say,

> And yet what would we be without memory? We would not be capable of ordering even the simplest thoughts, the most sensitive heart would lose the ability to show affection, our existence would be a mere never ending chain of meaningless moments, and there would not be the faintest trace of a past. (Sebald, 2002, *The Rings of Saturn*, p.255)

So, in spite of the pain it brings him, he finds that memory is not only unavoidable but essential to any kind of coherence in his experience. Memory provides the initial context of all of our experience; it is the frame through which we view the world and that which gives meaning to our existence. In this sense, by giving meaning, memory makes our experience as we know it possible, for as both Chateaubriand and Sebald point out, without memory we have nothing more than a "chain of meaningless moments", and no past at all.

It would be remiss at this stage to fail to at least refer to probably the most powerful example of unforgetting in Sebald's work; that is the gradually emerging account of Austerlitz recovering his past. I will return to this example once again when specifically considering identity but one particular instance will also serve as an example of unforgetting. While watching a porter at work cleaning Liverpool Street Station Austerlitz is somehow prompted to remember his first arrival as a little boy at the same station. The account is given in a haunting passage, somewhere between a daydream, an apparition, and a memory, during which he seems to see himself meeting with those who will act as his parents for the rest of his childhood.

> And I not only saw the minister and his wife, said Austerlitz, I also saw the boy they had come to meet. He was sitting by himself on a bench over to one side. His legs, in white knee-length socks, did not reach the floor, and but for the small rucksack he was holding on his lap I don't think I would have known him, said Austerlitz. As it was I recognized him by that rucksack of his, and for the first time in as far back as I can remember I recollected myself as a small child, at the moment when I realized that it

must have been to this same waiting room I had come on my arrival in
England over half a century ago. (Sebald, 2002, *Austerlitz*, p.193)

This memory had lain slumbering and forgotten for many years and had
suddenly emerged as Austerlitz contemplated the past of the station, the
former uses of the site and the many passengers and others who had
passed through. Austerlitz has no idea why this unforgetting occurs, he
says "To this day I cannot explain what made me follow him",[13] (the
porter) but as a result of this simple and seemingly disconnected act he
recovers the memory in the most vivid fashion, and in so doing gives
meaning to another small but significant part of his life. Without this act of
unforgetting, in some sense, it is as if Austerlitz never arrived at Liverpool
Street and never left his home in the east. No amount of being told about
his past by his school headmaster can match his own remembering. He
needs his own memories to give meaning to this part of his life; a part
which helped to make him what he is as we find him now. This is but one
of a number of instances of unforgetting throughout the story of Austerlitz
through which he pieces together the shreds of his life as he unforgets his
life before the Kindertransport and the journey from this life to another in
Bala and beyond.

All of these examples serve, once again, to show how memory
significantly helps to construct our experience, and how without our own
memories we remain somehow incomplete, even if someone else tells us
what happened to us. In the example of Austerlitz at Liverpool Street we
have an instance of unforgetting bringing back memories which begin to
change Austerlitz's own perception of himself, and which subsequently
help him to address the nagging discomfort about his origins which have
plagued him throughout his life. In this case re-membering begins reconstruction. Having seen how important memory and unforgetting can be
I now want to take a look at two of the most common mechanisms through
which unforgetting takes place by looking at the way in which photographs
and gravestones can apparently bring back memories.

Relics - Photographs and Gravestones

I have chosen to discuss photographs and gravestones because these
are ways in which our memory can be instantiated and preserved. Both of
these memorialize our experience and a discussion of them will suggest
the part that memory plays in our experience, and what it says about our
relationship with the world. Photographs and gravestones bring back
memories because they are relics. They are survivors from an age that has

passed, but more than that they are survivors that bring with them a record of that age. They are a means of transmission in that they try to bring us back to the past, and the past back to us, as Sontag says, "Photographs show people being so irrefutably there and at a specific age in their lives",[14] and even more,

> A photograph passes for incontrovertible proof that a given thing happened. The picture may distort; but there is always a presumption that something exists, or did exist which is like what is in the picture. (Sontag, 1979, p.5)

The mechanism through which this proof is achieved is the mechanism of unforgetting, or the bringing back to us the shadows of experiences that we once had, things that once happened and people that we once knew. The extent to which photographs and gravestones are successful in evoking past times shows both how unforgetting works and how it can fails us.

Photographs

To begin with photographs are images and usually representations. They are images of people, places and things and are usually constituted as an attempt to represent these entities. To this extent at least they are like memories in that they evoke the thing, person, or place represented, but they are not the actual object in question. A photograph of a man is not the man himself, just as the memory we have of an absent relative is not the same as their presence in person. On this basis I will consider three kinds of photograph and some key points about the phenomenological nature of photography. The three kinds of photographs are; fully referenced photographs, these are the photographs for which we have meaningful names, places and dates. Next there are partly referenced photographs, these may have names on them but these names are not to known to us and the places and times they were taken are indeterminate. Finally there are photographs with no apparent referential context, no names, no places and no dates, these are anonymous photographs.

First of all let us be quite clear that it does not matter in the least that there may be photographs which do not fit into this categorization. The fact that at least some photographs are images and representations is quite sufficient for my argument. In fact it would be a mistake to read this and to take me to be trying to say something about photographs, I am using photographs as a means to an end, an example of a kind of phenomena, in order to say something simple but fundamental about phenomena and remembering.

Most of the photographs which we all have are images which represent people places and things in our lives, or at least things relevant to our lives. They are pictures of something, someplace or somebody. We know who, where, and what they show. In this sense they are fully referenced and we view them not as images but as meaningful representations of a whole something-or-other. We remember when and where they were taken and who and what is in them. We do not distinguish at all between the different levels of image, representation, context, and meaning, all of these are thrown together in, for example, the family wedding photograph, or the holiday snap. All of the meaning is given to us at once, and the context, which provides this meaning, is submerged or taken for granted, being already part of our relationship with the photograph. In this way we can learn little about the make-up of their meaning from these wholly meaningful images. It is only when we begin to strip away some of the things we know about the photograph that we begin to appreciate what should be there when it is not there and thus to discover what makes it meaningful, and what it is that makes it memorable.

We have all probably seen or possessed photographs in which we see people and places we think we know and recognize but cannot quite put a name to. For example the old black and white holiday snap on which someone forgot to write the date. We think we know where it is, and it might be Aunty June and Uncle Jim at Clacton but we cannot be sure, in the same way that Austerlitz once thinks he has a picture of his mother but is in fact mistaken.[15] Looking in a wider context we can be sure that these familiar people in the photograph are part of our family group simply because the photographs came out of a box in the house of a member of our family, moreover on the box is written 'Holiday Photos 1949-55'. In this case we have some referential context and the photographs can begin to evoke some memories, and from this we can begin to build meaning sufficient for our purpose of fixing the memory and unforgetting the past. Typically in these cases we begin to add context, like writing who we think it is on the back of the photograph or putting it in a new album with a new label. All of this in an attempt to prevent the further decay of context and loss of meaning, after all what is the point of a photograph of someone we don't know? Once we have unforgotten we strive, often in vain, to stop ourselves forgetting again. In these cases we already have some understanding of the images and representations we find, but this is not a complete unforgetting and the meaning is not complete. We notice what is missing and try, either to put it back or to reconstruct what we see as missing from the context that remains (where they were found, the writing on the box etc.). These kinds of photographs are more troublesome and problematic than the fully referenced kind, but they fit into a kind of continuum and take their place in terms of the understood phenomena which make up our experienced life.

Finally, consider the album full of photographs found in the charity shop; an anonymous green album with the word 'Photographs' written in gold letters on the front. Inside there are black pages stuck with small black and white photographs of people, some singly, some in groups, some recurring, and set against a variety of backgrounds. There are no apparent clues to the origins of these photographs nor is there any indication as to who they are and where they were taken. They are images representing people and places, but whom and where we know not. They are literally meaningless and they bring back no memories. We can strive to attach meaning by surmise or by inventing context. We may closely examine the style of their clothes and make a guess at date, or look at the buildings pictured and try to tie them down to a place or even just a particular country, but all of these attempts are really no more than vain efforts to give meaning to the meaningless. There is certain sadness in this album of photographs. Once they had context and meaning, someone took them and knew who and where they were, someone once went to considerable trouble and stuck them in the album not thinking to attach any further marks of recognition, presumably because at the time it was not required. Perhaps they once reminded someone of happy times now passed. Originally these photographs were as fully referenced as our own treasured family photographs, but now that their context is gone and so is their meaning, it is utterly lost and they are now no more than faded images representing unknown people and unrecognized places. The world in which they had meaning has passed and they evoke no power of memory to bring back even the shadow of this world. In the terms of this discussion they are images and representations but they lack context and meaning. We can understand, by noticing what is missing from these anonymous photographs, what it is that makes our own fully referenced photographs meaningful and therefore how they bring back the memories and help us to unforget. It is, of course, their context; that complex of relationships and environment in which they are set, and which both we and they are a part of, which gives them their evocative power. Once they slip out of context they lose almost everything. The anonymous photographs may remain but their world has gone forever.

From consideration of these three kinds of photographs we can see how they gain their meaning and their power to evoke memories. The photographs are meaningful if we know who, when and where they represent. As mere unreferenced images, without context, they are literally meaningless, as in the case of the anonymous album. When the context is missing or very sparse, we strive to create context in an effort to create meaning by building on what we have in the way of references to bring forth more meaning, but we can stare for ever and a day at a photograph without getting any closer to its meaning. This is because as Sontag says,

> Despite the illusion of giving understanding, what seeing through photographs really invites is an acquisitive relation to the world that nourishes aesthetic awareness and promotes emotional detachment (Sontag, 1979, p.111)

I think that this emotional detachment is also an ontological detachment or dislocation in our encounter with reality, this conclusion is reinforced by Sontag when she says,

> Photography implies that we know about the world if we accept it as the camera records it. But this is the opposite of understanding, which starts from not accepting the world as it looks. All possibility of understanding is rooted in the ability to say no. (Sontag, 1979, p.23)

The photograph tries to make voyeurs out of all of us by radically separating us from the world and by making our experience a process of collecting of images. The photograph gives us a kind of pseudo-presence so that "Ultimately, having an experience becomes identical with taking a photograph of it."[16] However, because we can now manipulate images to show almost anything we want, and because from time to time we are thus deceived, we are aware that all of these images may have been altered, they are artificial and an abstraction. The fact that some photographs and digital images are patently false brings forth the truth that all of these images, altered or not, are false to the extent that they cannot show us the real world at all. Meaning, if there is any, is not to be found by a closer and closer examination of the photographs themselves but by a reference beyond. We discover the meaning of the photograph not in the photograph but in the environment (world) in which it exists or has its being. As Sontag says "The photograph is, always, an object in context."[17] The connections between the photograph and the world that surrounds it make it what it is. Meaning is given in context and this is meaning in the sense of that which makes possible, for the meaningless photograph is left with a shadow or fugitive existence, sadly lacking meaning and quickly drifting back into the almost non-existence of a mere image. That which makes the photograph possible as photograph and as relic is its context, its connection to us and to our world. While we have come to accept that photography provides us with a more or less accurate view of the world we forget that,

> All that photography's program of realism actually implies is the belief that reality is hidden. And, being hidden, it is something to be unveiled." (Sontag, 1979, p.120)

If we allow this photographic view of the world to persist and to become ingrained on the way we see the world, we will be plunged into a helpless dualism as we continually strive to look for meaning and reality behind the veil of our senses. The reality of the world is not to be found in the photograph, we must learn to look about us and not at the pictures we are given. I will discuss this at greater length below with reference to Heidegger's ontology.

From this we can say that where a photograph awakens a memory and precipitates an instance of unforgetting, it does so as a result of the memory itself. If we have no memory then we cannot unforget and the photograph remains meaningless. The photograph itself has no meaning except that which we are able to give it through our recall of its representation of an event in our experience, an event which has now passed. The photograph is a trigger but nothing more. Moreover, because our own memory is exclusive, this single trigger may precipitate different unforgetting in different subjects. I may remember one thing as a result of seeing the photograph while you may remember another or none at all. The same photograph can mean different things to different people. The photograph itself does not belong to experience it is just a brief record of something we might once have seen and it has no meaning outside our experience. Photographs cannot be meaningful in themselves and we construct memories out of them at our peril. If we rely on photographs to provide us with memory we can even deprive ourselves of true memory altogether as did Beyle with the engraving of Ivrea. In an age where image making is ubiquitous and where simply looking, without recording or trying to record permanently in one form or another, is becoming idiosyncratic we stand in danger of our memories being supplanted by the pictures we choose to take. Like Beyle at Ivrea we will lose the true nature of our lived experience.

Drawing and Photography

At this point a small digression will serve to further emphasize the vital component of context if we pause to consider the relationship and difference between drawing and photography. Hockney bring this out very clearly in his book, *That's the way I See It*, when he explains that drawing is a mode of expressing and communicating what we see, while photography is not, and is simply a flat representation of a world that is anything but flat. Hockney goes so far as to say that the only true use of photography, that is use which does not deceive, is to take pictures of pictures themselves. In this way the photograph represents as a flat surface another flat surface and provides no distortion of the world.[18] This means that, by comparison with the act of drawing, the taking of a photograph decontextualises the subject by placing it in a confined frame and removing it as an image from the environment in which it exists. In a way our labeling of photographs to give them context is no more or less than an act of trying to restore context to an image that we have seen and then attempted to preserve in the photograph. This act of restoration is necessary not only for the sake of posterity but in order that we may have a photograph the meaning of which can be communicated through the context which we have added back. As Hockney says, "We do not look at the world from a distance, we are in it, and that's how we feel."[19] This means that if we try to escape from the world, or extract an individual entity from the world, we lose more than just a point of view; in fact we begin to try to see the world as a series of pictures from which we are detached, instead of a continuous lived experience in which we are submerged. Hockney believes that this detachment is not a consequence of drawing which preserves the subject in connection with the image through the action of the hand. The invisible hand represents the subject in the finished image because it chose not simply the view as represented by the frame of the viewfinder and photograph but also the way in which the elements of the picture are represented and connected, their juxtaposition and their lighting. In this way Hockney asserts that the drawing represents a more personal and precise depiction of the scene and thereby provides us with a more accurate and more evocative memory of the scene and the events depicted. We may remember not only the scene itself but the time it took to do the drawing, the sounds, smells and sights of the occasion of the drawing and how difficult or easy it was to draw. Most importantly the drawing retains a connection with the hand which is lost in the unthinking act of photography. In philosophical terms, and going on from Hockney, I will argue that photography provides a representation of a decontextualised world isolating the subject and reinforcing its primacy, while drawing achieves deeper meaning through communicating experiences and characterizes the inescapable involvement of authentic being-in-the-world. Attempts to ignore context always sacrifice meaning and photographs themselves, as attempts to render a view of the world as it is, or at least as we suppose it to be, can never capture the full richness of the meaning of our experience.

Gravestones

Before going on to examine in more detail the philosophical background to the ways that we understand photographs I will briefly look at gravestones as another example of the importance of context to the meaning of images and representations. As with photographs we can consider three kinds of gravestone. First, the gravestone of a close relative, inscribed with their dates and places of birth and death. This is probably the grave of someone we knew well and we may even have been at the funeral. The gravestone, like the family photograph, is fully referenced and set into a context that is rich with meaning as it stands sentinel to the life of the person buried beneath. In a sense the stone represents the dead individual by commemorating their life and we do not think twice about the source or ground of its meaning. A strange inversion of this kind of example is the case of the philosopher Berkeley who was Bishop of Cloyne in County Cork, Ireland. After his death a magnificent memorial consisting of an enormous marble effigy of the Bishop was put in the cathedral at Cloyne. It has every appearance of a tomb being set upon a large high plinth, which one would assume contains the body of the deceased. However all is not what it seems. Berkeley is actually buried at Christ Church in Oxford where he died so the edifice at Cloyne is a mere memorial a representation of Berkeley without substance. Paradoxically, in this case, because it is fashioned in the way of an effigy it perhaps provides a better representation of the Bishop than would an actual grave with no effigy.

Second, we come across a gravestone in a country churchyard while on holiday. The name of the occupant of the grave and their dates and places of birth and death are more or less discernible on the stone, but for us these have only incidental meaning. We understand the words, we know where the place is and the dates may have coincidental relevance to our own lives, but we are not able to fill in the details of the life of the deceased. In this case what is written is all we have and we have no access to the fuller context to which these inscriptions apply. There may or may not be others for whom the stone means more, but this meaning is greater only because they are more fully immersed in the context, which is constituted by their knowledge of life and times of the person buried. This representation has incomplete context for us and we can only guess and imagine at what it might really mean.

Finally consider an uninscribed plain gravestone or a stone on which no information remains, perhaps in an abandoned churchyard. The stone may even be as basic as a simple piece of native rock placed at the head of the grave by whoever buried the body. This has the same flavour of sadness as the album of anonymous photographs. Clearly someone once knew who was buried there, knew who they had been and what they had done, perhaps they were related and had erected the stone to remind themselves of the person who had died. However, by now, and with the passage of time, the abandonment of the graveyard and the lack of any inscription this entire context is lost. We can tell that we have a grave and a stone marking the grave, the outward signs are clear, but no more. Once again we can only guess at meaning in the absence of any context. The representation is without meaning and we can only surmise who may be buried there and what they were. Although we are able to identify the site of the grave and know that it is a grave, this is nowhere near enough to give it meaning or to evoke memory. This will be even more acutely the case where gravestones have been moved from their original gravesite and now merely indicate the fact that someone was once buried somewhere. The connections between the person buried, their grave, and the world beyond have gone, and with these connections the meaning of the grave itself has evaporated. The same process is going on here as with the photographs, both these relics of a bygone age rely on their meaning, and their power to evoke meaning on the context of their existence, their mere survival as physical artifacts is insufficient to make them meaningful and to enable them to continue to fulfill their original purpose of evoking memories.

Phenomenology and Beyond

All of this may be interesting, perhaps even moving, but not necessarily illuminating. The story of photographs and gravestones may be no more than musings on the curiosities of life and imagination. However I believe that a more detailed philosophical, and in particular phenomenological, investigation of the examples I have set out will reveal more, not only about the nature of photographs and gravestones as representations, but also about the way we understand and interpret the world around us. From this we can begin to say some more things about the nature of memory and what makes our thinking about photographs and gravestones possible in the first place. These conclusions can, by analogy, give access to the more fundamental aspects of being. First a re-visit to something about the way we perceive the world,

> The perceiving of what is known is not a process of returning with one's booty to the 'cabinet' of consciousness after one has gone out and grasped it. (Heidegger, 1962, H.62)

The sense of this position is more radical than it first appears. It is a direct challenge to the notion that we see things as things and can separate them from the matrix of phenomena in which they exist, a matrix in which we are also included. This apparent separation is just what we cannot do, although we may imagine it to be done when we regard an image. I think we are all the more susceptible to this form of radical separation when we take a photograph than when we simply look at the scene before us. This futile attempt at decontextualisation which is attempted here we may call 'the epistemological project' and it is the target of much of Heidegger's criticism of traditional philosophy.[20] It is the attempt to seize on an individual entity and dissect its meaning as thing-in-itself apart from any relation it may have to other entities in space or time, to deliberately isolate it from its context in the belief that this is the route to understanding and meaning. In the case of relics like photographs and gravestones, which as we have seen gain their power to evoke from precisely this context, this approach must always be fatal. The chemical make up of the photograph or the electronic means of its production and reproduction tell us nothing about the meaning of the photograph, just as knowing the rock from which a gravestone is made from tells us nothing of its purpose. The epistemological project is grounded in a search for what is called unconditional meaning but fails because it mislocates meaning and misunderstands the nature of Being. Meaning, as we have seen in the case of photographs and gravestones, is never unconditional; in fact the meaning acquired by these entities is highly conditional depending on the consciousness which is considering them as phenomena. Heidegger's position is that the attempt to separate entities from their links with the environment in which they exist is the way to make them meaningless. Since it is meaning which makes possible or supports being, the entities thus lose the foundation of their being. Without context we are unable to answer and maybe even unable to ask the question, "What it is for?" This means that the entities are literally not possible as what they are outside their context. The existence of gravestones and photographs as relics of bygone times depends on both their temporal context and our own conscious apprehension of them as what they are now in relation to other entities. From another angle we may say that this position takes as primary to the existence of all entities, their relations to other entities and phenomena in the world around them, this is why, as we have already seen, Heidegger is able to say,

> What we 'first' hear is never noises or complexes of sounds, but the creaking wagon, the motorcycle. We hear the column on the march, the north wind, the woodpecker tapping, the fire crackling. (Heidegger, 1962, H.164)

All of these things are only what they are, not because that is how we apprehend them, but how we encounter them in the world, our world. Moreover there is no other way, no other environment in which this encounter can take place. We are unable even to gesture towards a world in which our encounter with entities could take place in another way because this is the way that both we and they are.

This means that the way in which context is fundamental to meaning is much deeper than the idea that we need to know the 'who' and the 'where' and the 'when' of a photograph or gravestone. Who, when and where are exactly, only, and already what these photographs and gravestones really are. All phenomena come to us already in context and not as separate items of perception. We may indeed decontexualise these phenomena but this process is secondary and a function of what we ourselves bring along after the fact. The context gives us our only access to the being of entities in a way that means that we cannot know them for what they are without the context. The photograph would remain a mere slip of coloured paper and the gravestone a piece of rock unless we have the outward signs of the uses that these entities have been put to. It appears thus that our need for context to provide meaning to the photographs and gravestones that we come across is grounded in the fundamental way in which we must encounter the world. The being of these entities is wrapped inextricably into the phenomenal matrix in which we encounter them and this includes not only our present experience but our memories. Into this we can now bring fully the distinction that Hockney makes between drawing and photography as means of engaging with the phenomena (appearance) of the world. Drawing is a mode of expressing what we see; it sets entities, places and events into their context and gives them meaning, and this context includes the consciousness of the artist. These meanings are grounded in the actual experience, past and present, of the artist and the drawing becomes a means by which these experiences are transmitted and shared. On the other hand photography represents de-contextualising; by imposing a frame on the image and viewing the world as it were through a keyhole, and by the attempt to freeze a moment in time. The photographer is attempting to create a permanently external memory. Paradoxically it is the borders of the photograph that become important as the limits to our vision rather than the content or subject. In the photograph, space, the border, is defined beforehand and the description of the entity is necessarily limited. As Hockney says in a criticism of one view of painting and with reference to the photograph,

> The argument that painting is about itself, that it does not need to concern itself with the description or appearance of the visible world, rests on the idea that this can be achieved much better by photography—which is like saying, we know what the world looks like; it looks like a photograph. This seems to me to make the world a duller place. I don't think that we fully know what the world looks like, because I think you begin to realize that whatever you're looking at, what you experience, is, after all, through your own consciousness. So you realize, it is not possible to separate what you're looking at from yourself. (Hockney, 1993, p.127)

Apart from reminding us that we are ourselves an inextricable part of the perceived world as active participants rather than observers, this is a recognition, by one undoubtedly skilled in the representation of the world, that keeping the context is the only way to preserve meaning. The fundamental involvement of the artist in the world is central to the successful representation of meaningful entities; this immersion is expressed in the act of drawing. In philosophical terms the world is the sum of that which can be encountered and individual Dasein is that entity which can approach and be approached, the individual being that perceives and understands, remembers and projects. Hockney's insight shows that there is more than one possible representation of the world and this allows for a number of meanings, depending on the precise context, for each person experiencing the world. The world is not a dull place at all. The dislocation that photography engages us in leads to a loss of context and loss of meaning, if we create external photographic memories we will lose our connection with past times as our own memory is obliterated. This conclusion is reinforced by consideration of the experiential difference between handling an original drawing by a famous artist and handling a photograph of the same work. The former brings us close to the experience of the artist in seeing the subject of the drawing and it subsequent representation, while the latter is unexceptional and probably draws no more than comment on the techniques used to obtain the image.

If this is the case then contextuality goes to the root not only of our understanding of the world and entities in it, like photographs and gravestones, but also of our own being. Consequently an attempt to withdraw from context or to remove entities from context will not only rob us of any possibility of gaining meaning in the sense of understanding, but will also fatally misinterpret the nature of our own being. Whether we like it or not we are all active participants, partaking of and being a part of the context, a context created by own our aims and ambitions and those of the others like us. In this way context provides meaning. Without it we are, like the anonymous photographs and unmarked gravestones, that is, without meaning. We can have no being beyond this involvement. Simply put, "For the Dasein there is no outside for which reason it is also absurd to talk about an inside".[21] Involvement is not a relationship with which we can choose to provide ourselves with or not, it is the very stuff of our being. In the specific case of memory the context is both spatial and temporal. Our memories give us an awareness of times which have passed and the objects of memory, like photographs and gravestones, which have come down to us from these times, seem to bring some of those times with them. It is in this way that we can say that they memorialize our experience.

In order to understand how it is that things can 'come down to us' we must also look briefly into the temporality of our everyday experience, Heidegger begins from the simple fact of involvement and proceeds directly to the temporal stretch of this involvement.

> Letting something be involved is implied in the simplest handling of an item of equipment. That which we let it be involved in has the character of a "towards-which"; with regard to this, the equipment is either usable or in use. The understanding of the "towards-which"—that is, the understanding of what the equipment is involved in—has the temporal structure of awaiting. In awaiting the "towards-which", concern can at the same time come back by itself to the sort of thing in which it is involved. The awaiting of what it is involved in, and—together with this awaiting—the retaining of that which is thus involved, make possible in its ecstatical unity the specifically manipulative way in which equipment is made present. (Heidegger, 1962, H.353)

This sounds more complicated that it needs to. The simple point that Heidegger wants to make is that our involvement or engagement with the world although it may seem momentary; a series of individual moments or instances, is in fact temporally structured whatever we do. We are all always aiming towards an end based on a concern or aim, and using knowledge that we have accumulated, and all this is taking place now in the present, and this is true whatever the circumstance. We think and act intentionally and therefore temporally. In terms of memory this means that,

> If, when one circumspectively lets something be involved, one were not 'from the outset' awaiting the objects of ones concern, and if such awaiting did not temporalize itself as a unity with a making present , then Dasein could never 'find' that something is missing. (Heidegger, 1962, H.407)

Heidegger's language is again difficult here but if we take him to mean that unless we understand our actions, this letting something be involved, as a temporal whole with a beginning, middle and an end we would never be in a position to notice that the piece of equipment which we needed was not there. We have to know already what we want to do and what we need to do before anything can become equipment, that is, something that we may use. Similarly we have to remember the use that each piece of equipment has before we can consider using it. The connectedness of Dasein to the world applies not only to the present spatial world but also and essentially to the temporal stretch of the world so that,

> Even if concern remains restricted to the urgency of everyday needs, it is never a pure making-present, but arises from a retention which awaits; on the basis of such a retention, or as such a 'basis', Dasein exists in a world. (Heidegger, 1962, H.356)

This temporality is so ingrained in everything that we do we do not even notice it or think of it most of the time, this is because,

> When in one's concern, one lets something be involved, one's doing so is founded on temporality, and amounts to an altogether pre-ontological and non-thematic way of understanding involvement and readiness-to-hand. (Heidegger, 1962, H.356)

It is this structure to our activity which makes memory possible and, as we have seen, it is memory that makes the understanding of our experience possible, for without memory we cannot make any sense of the events of our lives. Chateaubriand was right; it is memory which gives our experience some meaning. Just as being-in-the-world is constitutive of Dasein and not simply a relationship which we can take or leave, so the temporality of Dasein is equally constitutive. We can no more step outside time than we can step outside the world. Sebald is showing us this through his examples of the working of memory by showing us how we are tied to our own past whether we like it or not, and by making it clear that without memory our lives would be no more than a series of disconnected events.

Heidegger puts it more technically when he says, "Dasein's constitution and its ways to be are possible ontologically only on the basis of temporality",[22] but I think he means much the same and this is certainly sufficient for our purposes to this point. We will consider Heidegger's work on temporality in more detail when we come to history in the next chapter.

Summary

The consideration of memory shows that this phenomenon is essential to our understanding of experience and is also suggestive of underlying features of the ways in which our own being and the world itself are structured. The examples of photographs and gravestones show how the entities we choose to memorialize our experience are themselves dependent for their meaning on the context in which they are placed and found and that, in extreme cases, photographs in particular can replace our memories. We can begin our remembering with a simple image, which then represents, but this representation can only have meaning in the matrix of the context in which all of our encounters and engagements with entities can take place. Without this engagement there can be no meaning, and thus representation, unsupported, falls back into mere image. Photographs and gravestones are examples of actual entities which can exhibit degrees of meaning and an initial superficial discussion of how they have their meaning provides an analogy for the way in which we experience the phenomenal world. However at a much deeper level we can see that the being of these phenomena rests on a much more fundamental and, as Heidegger would say, primordial, relationship between ourselves as Dasein, and the phenomena which make up the world which can be encountered. At the level of everyday phenomenal experience we need context, both spatial and temporal, to provide meaning to the entities (like photographs and gravestones) which we encounter, but at the more primordial ontological level this context has already become an absolute requirement for our continuing experience of the world of phenomena. Without it we are nothing, and we are nowhere. In the next chapter I want to broaden the discussion of memory into a discussion of history. These two are inevitably connected and rest on similar if not the same ground. If memory is the attempt to recall our own individual past then we might see history as the attempt to record and recall a more collective past.

Notes

[1] Hockney, 1999, p.56.
[2] Gadamer, 1975, 2004, p.10.
[3] Bachelard, 1942, 1982, p.17.
[4] Gadamer, 1975, 2004, p.14.
[5] Gadamer, 1975, 2004, p.13.
[6] Hockney, 2008, p.58.
[7] See Buck, 1999, p 56.
[8] Gadamer, 1975, 2004, p.14.
[9] Sebald, 2002, *Vertigo*, pp.171-263.
[10] Sebald, 2002, *The Rings of Saturn*, pp.250-8.
[11] Sebald, 2002, *The Rings of Saturn*, p.255.
[12] Sebald, 2002, *The Rings of Saturn*, p.255.
[13] Sebald, 2002, *Austerlitz*, p.189.
[14] Sontag, 1979, p.70.
[15] Sebald, 2002, *Austerlitz*, pp. 350-3.
[16] Sontag, 1979, p.24.
[17] Sontag, 1979, p.100.
[18] Hockney, 1993, p.89.
[19] Hockney, 1993, p.102.
[20] Heidegger, 1962, H.10, H.59.
[21] Heidegger, 1988, p.56.
[22] Heidegger, 1962, H.367.

CHAPTER SEVEN

HISTORY:
GONE BUT STILL HERE

In this chapter I am moving on from the idea of personal memory to history. This move is ostensibly a move from personal past experience to collective or group memory, but one which will tell us more about the onset of the image and our relationship with the world. Having seen how our own memories frame and help to construct our present experience, we can now look at how our collective past experience comes to influence both our individual and our collective response to present experience. History is the way in which the past appears or shows itself to us. Once again we can turn to Sebald for a beginning.

Sebald

Sebald's work is suffused with a sense of history and of the past. It is not simply the fact that everywhere is already somewhere in terms of place, but, even further, everywhere is already lots of places, the one that it is now and all those that went before. Although history forms a constant backdrop to Sebald's work there are many instances in which he shows this process explicitly in operation and I will summarise below a few of the most illustrative.

The first of these is Sebald's description of his visit to Orford Ness in *Rings of Saturn*.[1] The site, opposite the village of Orford, is at the end of a long shingle spit stretching eleven miles down the Suffolk coast, and had for many years been the location of a secret military research establishment with strictly restricted access. Now abandoned, we can take a boat across the short stretch of water to the strange ruins leftover from its military past and examine the remaining structures at closer quarters. This is a place with a sense of history and anyone who has even stood on the quay at Orford opposite the site can feel the weight of this history. The strange buildings left on the site, eerily visible across the water, provide echoes of a past use which has now gone altogether. This is perhaps made easier to imagine because the site is now abandoned and there is no present human activity to distract us from the ghosts of the past. Orford Ness in now a nature reserve but its history lingers in the remains of what it once was. This means that our experience of Orford Ness is at least twofold, the present bleak shingle spit with the constant wind in the rigging of the small boats in the harbour, alongside our imaginings of what used to go on there and to what purpose, a purpose that we will never know.

Perhaps the nearest Sebald comes to giving us any kind of definition of history is when Austerlitz is telling him of how the teacher Hilary used to recount the details of the Battle of Austerlitz. He says,

> Our concern with history … is a concern with pre-formed images already imprinted on our brains, images at which we keep staring while the truth lies elsewhere, away from it all, somewhere as yet undiscovered. (Sebald, 2002, *Austerlitz*, p.101)

As in the case of simple photographs we cannot find the meaning by focusing on the images of history that we are given. The meaning of history is not to be found in the contemplation of a single historical event but more in the ripples it makes which come through to us now. Again, like photographs, these descriptions of isolated events do not tell the whole story. Austerlitz remembers that although his history teacher could talk for hours about the battle it was his opinion that he could never recount all of the details and that,

> All of us, even when we think we have noted every tiny detail, resort to set pieces, often enough by others. We try to reproduce the reality, but the harder we try, the more we find the pictures that make up the stock-in-trade of the spectacle of history forcing themselves upon us. (Sebald, 2002, *Austerlitz*, p.101)

This rings true to our experience of recounting history and is reminiscent of Beyle's experience with the engraving of Ivrea. Our received idea of what happened combines with the sheer impossibility of even gathering, never mind recounting, every detail. This leaves any account we might attempt of any historical event fundamentally incomplete. This means that while history will profoundly affect the way in which we encounter the world, it is never the whole story, nor even need it be the same story that someone else has. Even the same story may affect each individual in a different way and history will mean different things to different people. It seems that the way in which history appears to us is at least problematic, if not paradoxical. We can neither escape it nor can we wholly encompass it.

In its totality it remains beyond our experience but it provides the backdrop to our present experience of the world and the ways in which that world appears to us.

When Austerlitz visits Terezin in the search for his parents and his own origins he sees the town with eyes which understand the personal tragedy of the Jews who were held there. While Terezin is now, and has been for many years, an "ordinary town",[2] for Austerlitz it will always be where his mother was imprisoned along with many others, most of whom will not have survived their imprisonment. His account of the town as he finds it is eerie and haunting and could only be given by someone who knew of its history. The account of Terezin is not simply an account of what Austerlitz is seeing, there is more to it than that, and by de-populating the town (there are no people to be seen) Sebald allows the ghosts of the past to make their presence felt. We cannot help thinking, as we read the story of the ghetto of Theresienstadt and the bizarre dressing up of the place before the visit of the Red Cross Commission, how all of this recorded history makes the town of Terezin more a part of the past even than its own present. It is as if the history of Terezin is more present, and certainly more famous, than its present manifestation.

In *The Rings of Saturn* the Battle of Sole Bay, which took place off the coast near Southwold, plays a similar but much more muted part in the history of the town.[3] It is hard to imagine now the battle of so many years ago raging off the coast, when we stand on the Gun Hill of today. There are memorials around the town reminding us of the battle but these go largely unnoticed as the daily business of Southwold continues, as if the town of the present is too busy and too distracting to allow the past to break thorough. No such memorials are mentioned or needed in Terezin but the past is still there in both places.

In *Austerlitz* the narrator's visit to Breendonk fortress[4] provides more illustrations of the presence of history. This is a fort first built for defence of Belgium and then occupied by the Nazis who used it as a penal camp. Significantly he encounters no other visitors while he is there and he is able to imagine both the prisoners and their guards going about their daily round, including the horrors of torture, forced labour and execution, alongside the mundane playing of cards and letter writing of the SS guards. The fort is now a museum and memorial to the Belgian resistance and is thus explicitly historical in its present day purpose. However it is with forgotten history that Sebald is finally taken when he says,

> I think how little we can hold in mind, how everything is constantly
> lapsing into oblivion with every extinguished life, how the world is, as it
> were, draining itself, in that the history of countless places and objects

which themselves have no power of memory is never heard, never
described or passed on. (Sebald, 2002, *Austerlitz*, pp.30-31)

History is not just the history of world changing events, even little things
have history and often these little events and their little objects are lost
without anyone noticing. Once again Sebald reveals the incompleteness of
history and the way that what is passed down is not always, or even
usually, a complete account of what really happened. These ways, in
which Sebald shows how places and people are affected by history, may
seem obvious and even trite, but they open the way to apparently more
tenuous but equally valid ways in which history is part of our present
encounter with the world, and the ways in which different and often
distant histories can connect in surprising ways. Sebald is a master of this
kind of almost surreal conjunction and I will now look at a couple of
examples in which he illustrates just this kind of relationship.

In *The Rings of Saturn* Sebald visits Southwold and walks from the
harbour to the bridge which crosses the River Blyth. The bridge once
carried a light railway which has long since been closed. What now
remains is an isolated river crossing with no vehicle access. The point of
the bridge has gone it serves almost no purpose, especially since there is a
now a ferry which crosses the river between the harbour and the village of
Walberswick on the other side. However, instead of reflecting on the
history of the bridge or speculating about the people and things that may
have crossed it in the past, Sebald is instead drawn to an unlikely legend
about the trains that once used the bridge. He says, "According to local
historians, the train that ran on it had originally been built for the Emperor
of China."[5] As we have already noted in Chapter Three, while there is no
real substantiation of this apart from some painted out heraldic dragons on
the carriages, this single eccentric piece of barely-history leads Sebald into
a long discourse about Imperial China and its history through the
nineteenth century. Suddenly from the bridge on the River Blyth we are
transported to the orient and given a detailed account of Chinese history.
Sebald is showing us how apparently unconnected events, which took
place far apart and long ago, can be brought back to life from even the
most unpromising sources. History it seems is there in the background of
all of our experience, and this is not just the history we may imagine every
day, not just more details about our present experience, but the whole
breadth of world history.

This is given again and even more obliquely in *The Rings of Saturn*
when Sebald is staying at the Crown Hotel in Southwold.[6] As a
consequence of simply falling asleep in front of the television he gives us
an account of the lives of two significant historical figures, Roger

Casement and Joseph Conrad, and then, from this, he moves to a discussion of the evils of the Belgian Congo and some explicitly historical musings on the battle of Waterloo. We are transported from a mundane scene in which Sebald falls asleep in front of the television in his hotel room to a world of colonialism, war, adventure, and the intricacies which entwined the lives of these two men. What Sebald is showing is that it appears that we are never far from history, or perhaps it is never far from us.

It is notable that for his examples of history Sebald seems always, or almost always, to choose tragic and violent events from history, battles at Austerlitz, Sole Bay and Waterloo, the horrors of the Belgian Congo, the gruesome histories of Terezin and Breendonk. Why this is so is not made clear by Sebald but we can speculate. Maybe it is simply that these are the events that come to mind, but that would be too much of a coincidence. Maybe it is these kinds of events that linger longer in our minds and are remembered long after our memories of happier times have faded. More likely, and in view of the way in which Sebald is always so precise in his use of words and images, we are tempted to conclude that Sebald uses these kinds of events in illustrating history because it is these kinds of stories which do the job he is trying to do best of all. If, as we may imagine, Sebald is trying to show us that history is not simply that which has passed but that which lingers from the past, then perhaps the strong collective memory we have of these awful events is powerful enough to break through the immediate appearance of the present, a present which Sebald has so obligingly cleared of people. We certainly find that tragic and violent events in history are more often well recorded than are other events, and this inevitably gives them a greater resonance in the present. Perhaps the bigger lesson of Sebald's work on history is that he is showing us how absence is just another form of presence. So, by choosing events from the past which involve the deaths of many people, the ghosts of whom he is then able to evoke in his descriptions of the places where these events took place, he is able to show us that the people who died, and who are therefore no longer present, are still conspicuous by their absence and in this way present to us. In this sense history, that which has passed and gone, is given a place in our present experience of the world and is thereby made part of that world of appearances. This may seem an unusual way of speaking, but philosophically we understand something as absent when it is not present and present when it is not absent. The two notions, absence and presence, co-exist and the one without the other loses meaning. In Sebald's writings on the nature of history he shows us that, that which has gone (our history) supports our present experience of the world, and without this support present experience loses at least some of its structure and meaning. Similarly if we were not here in the present there would be no history. Once again we seem to have some curious and thought provoking speculations which may appear to offer little more than intellectual diversion; however, as with memory, I think that Sebald's work provides a path into the discussion of a much more fundamental way of understanding history and our place in it.

Irene Nemirovsky

In Irene Nemirovsky's work *Storm in June* we have another example of history coming alive in the present. *Storm in June* (the first part of her book *Suite Francaise*) is more directly a work of fiction in the way that Sebald's work is not. It takes the form of a novel describing the fall of France in 1940 and the flight from Paris of an assemblage of disparate and unconnected characters, some of whom survive and some of whom do not. This breathtaking novel shows us the tide of unstoppable history and contains intense and personal descriptions of the disruption and, in some cases destruction, of the lives of the characters. Nemirovsky was herself caught up in these events and, even though the work is not explicitly biographical, her account of the fall of France is an account of events in which she was taking part. It is contemporary in the most vivid sense. Through her prose we are plunged into the lives of her characters as if we were reading contemporary news reports of events unfolding as we read. Taken in its original context *Storm in June* could almost be a work of journalism, but because of an unlikely happenstance it has come to us as a work of historical fiction.

Storm in June is both an account of the events of June 1940 in France and an example of what it is like to be caught up in history. Nemirovsky's work provides analogies which show the living process of history, the process of the dislocation of French society as a whole and of the dislocation of the lives of her characters. The world is turned topsy-turvy as the German Army advances, seemingly in pursuit of her characters. The quiet law abiding couple who work in the bank are left destitute and the opportunistic dancer uses her low cunning to survive, everyone is in turmoil and is carried along on the tide of history. Nemirovsky fictionalises her own experience of the momentous changes going on around her as they happen and, in reading *Storm in June*, we are taken into the maelstrom of invasion, defeat, conquest, fear, and headlong flight as the characters are taken out of their mundane everyday existence and propelled through history. This alone would make *Storm in June* a defining work on history as a living process, but the power of this work as an historical account is enhanced by its strange and almost accidental emergence over sixty years after the events depicted, and the time when it was written. The manuscripts of the two parts of *Suite Francaise* could not be published when they were written. The papers were carried by Nemirovsky's daughters throughout the war years and then lay untouched and undiscovered until 2004 when they were eventually published. Nemirovsky's witnessing of the events in France in 1940 only became an act of historical witness with the passage of time, and the sudden emergence of *Suite Francaise* over sixty years later gave her work added poignancy. *Storm in June* was never the contemporary novel that the author had intended. In spite of its contemporary origins it suddenly emerged into the public view as an historical account of events now long past, and as the lost work of a known author. The story of *Suite Francaise* from its creation to publication is an historical process in itself and we come to know its story now only when the events it portrays have passed into history. The awful inescapability of historicality in the story of *Suite Francaise* is even further reinforced when we learn that Nemirovsky herself fell victim to history and died in Auschwitz in 1942. The rest of *Suite Francaise* was left unwritten and Irene Nemirovsky became part of the history we now know as the Holocaust. In *Storm in June* Nemirovsky has given us an outstanding piece of historical witness, and even though her work is entirely fictional, the book is an expression of her own bearing witness to events that were all too real. *Storm in June* tells us about history in three ways, first as an account of events which adds to our understanding of what actually happened, second as an example of historical survival and third, in the way that the author herself fell victim to the tide if history it shows us how we are all historical. I will now use the work of two explicitly philosophical writers, Heidegger and Gadamer, to take further both the phenomenon of *Storm in June* and Sebald's writing on history.

The Living Process

Gadamer appears to support the view of history that emerges from Sebald's work when he says,

> For the structure of the historical world is not based on facts taken from experience which then acquire a value relation, but rather on the inner historicity that belongs to experience itself. What we call experience and acquire through experience is a living historical process; and its paradigm

> is not the discovery of facts but the peculiar fusion of memory and
> expectation into a whole (Gadamer, 1975, 2004, p.217)

And,

> Every part expresses something of the whole of life—i.e. has significance
> for the whole—just as its own significance is determined by the whole.
> (Gadamer, 1975, 2004 p.218)

This means that we cannot see history as a string or collection of historical
facts which stand opposed to our own existence, and the existence of other
facts. Historicity belongs to experience itself, that is; our experience is
inextricably and unavoidably historical in nature. Each experience cannot
be isolated from the memories we have of previous experience, or the
wider frame of reference for the world that we have already developed and
which constitutes our expectations. Neither can we come to the world as
new or separate. What Sebald and Nemirovsky are describing is this living
process of history. They are not trying, or even pretending to provide us
with an objective history. They are not gathering and presenting facts,
quite the reverse. Nemirovsky is writing contemporary fiction, and while
some of what Sebald says might be true, the detail of its truth is strangely
irrelevant. It really does not matter, for example, even whether Sebald ever
went on a walking tour of Suffolk; the things he says about the places and
their history retain their meaning. Gadamer criticises so called objective
historical science, not on the grounds of its inevitable failure to gather all
of the facts, but on the grounds that what we might call the scientific view
of history is itself mistaken in pursuing the kind of objectivity it seeks.
The basis of Gadamer's method is set out when he says,

> The context of world history—in which appears the true meaning of all the
> individual objects, large or small, of historical research—is itself a whole,
> in terms of which the meaning of every particular is to be fully understood,
> and which in turn can be fully understood only in terms of these
> particulars. (Gadamer, 1975, 2004, p.178)

This hermeneutic approach will run through everything Gadamer has to
say about history like the name of a seaside town through a stick of rock,
he says, "the foundation for the study of history is hermeneutics"[7] and he
describes it like this, "Hermeneutics is an *art* not a mechanical process.
Thus it brings its work, understanding, to completion like a work of art."[8]
This is why the collection of facts about the past does not give us the
meaning of history. Austerlitz's teacher is right when he says that no
matter how many facts about the battle (any battle) are collected the

account will remain incomplete.[9] History is not a collection of disconnected or even connected facts, to understand history we must understand fundamental historicality itself. This is the processes that both Sebald and Nemirovsky are engaged in, and is also reminiscent of Severs work on 18 Folgate Street. It means that the work of revealing and understanding history is not a simple or even an explicit empirical process; it is a process in which history is allowed to appear. For those of us who study history Gadamer reminds us that,

> History is not only not at its end but we as interpreters are situated within it, as a conditioned and finite link in a continuing chain. (Gadamer, 1975, 2004, p.97)

As observers and interpreters of history we ourselves are part of the story.

Gadamer is highly critical of those historians who have tried to divorce themselves from the historical process. The neglect of tradition and the disowning of prejudice, in the sense of our preconceptions and previously understood knowledge, the kind of thing that Heidegger would call fore-having, has in Gadamer's view impoverished the study of history and given us a view of the past which is entirely divorced from our own experience. While he recognizes that prejudice will, and must, colour our view of history the answer to this is not to try to disregard our predispositions but to acknowledge and to understand them in order to be able to follow them or to reject them freely. Otherwise, as he points out, they will persist in the background of all our accounts of history and continue without being questioned or criticised, so that,

> The overcoming of all prejudices, this global demand of the Enlightenment, will itself prove to be a prejudice, and removing it opens the way to an appropriate understanding of the finitude which dominates not only our humanity but also our historical consciousness. (Gadamer, 1975, 2004, p.217)

This domination is grounded on our own historicality which is inescapable. He says, (that)

> we study history only so far as we are ourselves "historical" (this) means that the historicity of human Dasein in its expectancy and its forgetting is the condition of our being able to re-present the past. (Gadamer, 1975, 2004, p.252)

Thus emphasising the way that the things that we have remembered and those we have forgotten, together create the expectations which provide the frame for our understanding of history. This is the frame through which we must see all history. Whether we acknowledge it or not Gadamer reminds us that we all belong to a tradition and that,

> belonging to a tradition belongs just as originally and essentially to the historical finitude of Dasein as does its prejudices towards future possibilities of itself. (Gadamer, 1975, 2004, p.252)

For Gadamer tradition is essentially preservation and as such it "is an act of reason, though an inconspicuous one".[10] Our own prejudices and the influence, often unwitting, of tradition condition the way we see the world, and the way in which we understand our own lives and the lives of others, or 'history'. They condition the choices we make about what we do and thereby condition the development of our own selves. This is not a frame which we can discard but one which changes with the choices we make in our lives. The attempt to untangle ourselves from prejudices and tradition not only destroys whatever chance we may have had of understanding history, it is also futile since this kind of belonging is part of what makes us what we are, and any denial amounts to a denial of self. It is in this sense that Gadamer can say that it is not history that belongs to us but we who belong to history.[11] However this does not mean that we must be creatures of our tradition and Gadamer show how the authority of tradition and our own prejudices can be rehabilitated in the serious business of historical interpretation. While we can accept that the conclusions of prejudice and tradition may not appear to be gained thought the free exercise of reason, this does not mean that these conclusions are necessarily untrue, the point is that their truth or untruth cannot be determined by their basis in the authority of tradition. Furthermore our prejudices and the tradition to which we belong are neither unacknowledged nor separate from us, provided as Gadamer has already said, that we acknowledge the inevitable bias that we bring to the question of history. We are free to accept or reject both prejudice and tradition wherever and whenever we choose. In the same way that we grant authority to others when our reason tells us that that they know better, we follow tradition when we accept its superior understanding and reasons, based on the cultivation and affirmation of the tradition by those who have gone before. We reject tradition when our reason tells us the opposite.

The antithesis offered by both the scientific and romantic schools between rejection and acceptance of tradition is false. Tradition is not fixed, it is not something to be continually and necessarily copied and recreated in a form fixed for all time. To survive a tradition needs to be embraced and cultivated, to be continually affirmed and adapted otherwise it will die out. This means that we must continually and freely exercise our reason and choose tradition for it to be able to continue its influence; alternatively we reject a tradition and form a new set of behaviours in its place, a new tradition. In this way following tradition means following the dictates of reason and Gadamer is thus able to say that it, "is an act of reason, though an inconspicuous one."[12]

Gadamer is equally critical of those romantics who elevate tradition for its own sake and bow to its authority whatever the context in the same way as their opponents bow to the apparent power of present reason whatever it is that tradition suggests. Both reify their positions and neither can allow that other is true, but this is a false objectification which leads to a false antithesis as Gadamer says,

> We are always situated within tradition, and this is no objectifying process—i.e. we do not conceive of what tradition says as something other, something alien. It is always part of us, a model or exemplar, a kind of cognizance that our later historical judgements would hardly regard as a kind of knowledge but as the most ingenuous affinity with tradition. (Gadamer, 1975, 2004, p.283)

The fluidity of tradition and our part in it means that rather than have us surrender to our prejudices and give up on the use of reason in the critical study of history, which is what the demands of the romantics amount to, Gadamer wants us to participate actively in the creation and maintenance of tradition as a means of understanding history so that,

> *Understanding is to be thought of less as a subjective act than as a participating in an event of tradition*, a process of transmission in which past and present are constantly mediated. This is what must be validated by hermeneutic theory, which is far too dominated by the idea of a procedure, a method. (Gadamer, 1975, 2004, p.291)

This view of history and tradition is the kind of thinking which provides space for the musings of Sebald and those like him, space which we might not recognize as empirical or scientific, but a space in which history can appear. It shows how Sebald and Nemirovsky contribute to a kind of knowledge that is not gained directly from reason but which certainly gives us what we know of history. In particular Sebald's way of saying without quite saying allows the past to appear without trying to codify or objectify. By simply and quietly putting himself and his characters in the places where significant events occurred in the past, and by providing a few relevant facts, Sebald then relies on nothing more than his own and, our own, historicality to bring these events into focus, and in so doing gives us an understanding of history itself. Similarly Nemirovsky's fictional account of the fall of France informs our view of this period of history in ways that a more objective approach could not, and yet she does this in a way that is equally valid. We may know the historical facts regarding the fall of France in 1940, these events have marked our tradition and our thinking about European history, yet it is in reading Nemirovsky's account that we come to understand what it could have been like to experience these events.

As I have already said, Sebald is not trying to be objective in his use and interpretation of history; this is why it does not matter if everything he says is not always true. He is trying to re-emphasise the role of our own prejudices, in the sense of preconceptions, and the tradition in which we live and think, as contributing significant elements to what we understand by history. Rather than being mistaken in this we can see that he is correct in showing how objective knowledge of the past is not only incomplete but is also inadequate unless it is considered alongside tradition and prejudice. This is because we are historical beings. Gadamer makes it clear that if we try to divorce our understanding of history from preconception and tradition we will not only be unsuccessful, and bring them with us anyway, but we will also lose the sense and meaning of history. The hermeneutic process is circular thus,

> The circle ... describes understanding as the interplay of the movement of tradition and the movement of the interpreter. The anticipation of meaning that governs our understanding of a text is not an act of subjectivity but proceeds from the commonality that binds us in the tradition. But this commonality is constantly being formed in our relation to the tradition (Gadamer, 1975, 2004, p.293)

We have already seen that our relation to the tradition is one governed by reason; we assent or dissent, and in so doing either freely and rationally accede to the tradition, or reject it and begin to frame a new tradition. Tradition cannot therefore be equated with mysticism or irrationality; neither can it be avoided because we ourselves are historical. The power of the works of Sebald and Nemirovsky in the ways they portray history originates in this historicality.

Historically Effected Consciousness

Gadamer finally brings together understanding and experience in his setting out the notion of historically effected consciousness. He says that,

We must regard as one-sided the principle that experience should be
evaluated only teleologically by the degree to which it ends in knowledge.
(Gadamer, 1975, 2004, p.344)

And then,

The dialectic of experience has its proper fulfilment not in a definitive
knowledge but as the openness to experience that is made possible by
experience itself... Experience in this sense belongs to the historical nature
of man. (Gadamer, 1975, 2004, p.350)

This is an outright rejection of the notion that experience is merely a
process of gathering information which then accumulates into what we call
knowledge. This kind of empirical teleology close off the possibilities of
experience and in so doing closes off the possibility we have of
understanding the world as a whole. It also brings us back both to the
inadequacy, or one-sidedness, of the scientific approach to history which
attempts to deny both the inevitability of prejudice, and the importance of
a living and changing tradition in our interpretation of history. But the role
of tradition is not passive as Gadamer affirms.

I must allow traditions claims to validity, not in the sense of simply
acknowledging the past in its otherness, but is such a way that it has
something to say to me. (Gadamer, 1975, 2004 p.351)

Sebald's work and the way in which he presents history is an invitation
to us to listen to tradition and to allow it to speak to us. This is the way in
which Sebald's rather strange and often attenuated accounts of historical
events go beyond the simply curious and quaint. To merely acknowledge
tradition is superficial and leads to the quaint, but by listening to the
tradition and by allowing it to speak to us we can begin to understand our
own historicity as beings in time. Sebald takes this step beyond simple
curiosity by the way that he invites us to linger and to contemplate.
Gadamer puts the same point another way when he says, "This is precisely
what we have to keep in mind in analyzing historically effected
consciousness: it has the structure of experience."[13] The consequences of
failing to allowing tradition to speak are severe,

A person who reflects himself out of a living relationship to tradition
destroys the true meaning of the tradition.... (and) To be situated within a
tradition does not limit the freedom of knowledge but makes it possible.
(Gadamer, 1975, 2004, p.354)

The clear implication is that when we divorce ourselves from tradition we divorce ourselves from the possibility of knowledge. We are not, and cannot be, spectators on history. Sebald, by his careful choice of subjects, his idiosyncratic take on the apparently familiar, and the way he lets his thoughts wander, allows this living process to show itself through the hubbub of everyday appearances. The historical nature of our experience becomes apparent when we read Sebald's work. We are able, when we see with Sebald's eyes, to see the strange in the familiar and the uncanny in the everyday, strange and uncanny because we appear to experience the past emerging into the present. The source of this historicity is our own consciousness which exists as our living experience such that, "We are concerned here with knowledge of the historical world, and that is always a world constituted and formed by the human mind."[14] This means of course that,

> The first condition of a possibility of a science of history is that I myself am a historical being, that the person studying history is the person making history. (Gadamer, 1975, 2004 p.217)[15]

This is not only highly reminiscent of Nemirovsky's writing and her fate, it also reminds us of Sebald's process in that, as he passes through the sites of historical events these sites, and these events, become part of the new history that Sebald is creating. As we read and perhaps visit the places that Sebald describes, we too become part of the history of the place and of the event. While it is clear that our passage through the site of a significant historical event will not be as significant as the event itself, this is not important since history is not necessarily the story of earth shattering or epoch making events. Our own visit becomes historical in itself by nature of its recounting; we make history through our experience of the world. The 'living process' is never ending and inescapable.

Gadamer's example of the festival is illustrative of the way that traditions show us this living process and the stretching out of being in time. By festival Gadamer is referring to celebrations that recur in time,

> It is in the nature of periodic festivals, al least, to be repeated. We call that the return of the festival. But the festival that comes round again is neither another festival nor a mere remembrance of the one that was originally celebrated. (Gadamer, 1975, 2004, p.121)

The celebration of the festival marks our participation in the tradition but there is apparently a paradox at the heart of each celebration for, "The festival changes from one time to the next."[16] This is not simply resolved by accepting that the festival changes and yet remains the same, as Gadamer says,

> However this (historical) perspective does not cover the characteristic of festival time that comes from its being celebrated. For the essence of the festival, its historical connections are secondary. As a festival it is not an identity like a historical event, but neither is it determined by its origin so that there was once the real festival—as distinct from the way it later came to be celebrated. From its inception—whether instituted in a single act or introduced gradually—the nature of a festival is to be celebrated regularly. (Gadamer, 1975, 2004, p.121)

The festival has no substantial existence, it is not like a relic which is handed down and preserved. It seems that each time the festival ends it disappears, only to be renewed on the next occasion of its celebration, but the festival somehow remains with us in between the periodic celebrations. It survives and is brought back to the foreground once again at the next celebration. The very being of the festival, and the only being that it can have, can only be found in the regular repetition of the festival which, although different and distinct every time, is no less the same festival. A festival is a kind of being which has no other being than being-in-time; it has no substance apart from temporality. By understanding this we understand history and time in a distinctive way, not in the way that science could ever give us but in a way that we can only experience for ourselves. The insubstantiality of the festival allows its temporality to emerge, or as Gadamer puts it,

> Thus its own essence is always to be something different. An entity that exists only by always being something different is temporal in a more radical sense than everything else that belongs to history. It has its being only in becoming and returns (Gadamer, 1975, 2004, p.121)

The tradition of the festival comes down to us from the past and we give it back its being every time we celebrate the festival, this is possible only because we are historical as the festival is historical. We both partake of the same temporality and this is made explicit every time we celebrate the festival.

While these examples begin to be more or less satisfactory in explaining our own progress through known history it leaves at least two questions unanswered and unaddressed, as Gadamer says, "The question is how the individual's experience and the knowledge of it comes to be historical experience".[17], that is the process by which the making of history takes place, and even more,

The real historical problem, as we have seen, is less how coherence is generally experienced and known than how coherence that no-one has experienced can be known. (Gadamer, 1975, 2004, p.219)

This is the difficult problem of how there comes to be history when there was no-one there to see it .We may have answered the first question as to how experience comes to be historical, but we now face the problem of how to stop history becoming entirely subjective, a creature of our own individual and collective memories and recollections (accurate or not) framed within our own prejudices and the dispositions given to us by tradition. We want to acknowledge, and even to understand the continuity of history and even pre-history, events that occurred before there was someone there to experience them or events which no-one witnessed. We must do this without making history a distant, or any other kind of, object. Both of these questions have at their root the temporality of our own existence and the way in which this temporality makes history. To even begin to address these questions, and to deepen the analysis even further, we must turn to some of Heidegger's work on history.

Dasein and History

Heidegger conducts a specific discussion with regard to history and Dasein in *Being and Time*. He begins by saying of history,

At bottom, even in the ordinary way of taking the 'connectedness of life', one does not think of this as a framework drawn tense 'outside' of Dasein and spanning it round, but one rightly seeks this connectedness in Dasein itself... Dasein does not fill up a track or stretch 'of life'—one which is somehow present-at-hand—with the phases of its momentary actualities. It stretches *itself* along in such a way that its own Being is constituted in advance as a stretching along. The 'between' which relates to birth and death already lies *in the Being* of Dasein. (Heidegger, 1962, H.374)

This places the being of Dasein firmly in temporality and means that history is not like a river running past as we watch helplessly. A more accurate analogy maybe more like a river in which we are adrift and being carried along by the current. The problem with even this analogy is that, if it is in any way apposite, it is equally impossible, since if we are adrift in this river we would have no view of its end or its beginning, or even a view of the banks of the river, and without this we could have no idea of the river at all. As ever, spatial metaphors fail to do justice to Heidegger's thinking, history is not a river that we ever jumped, or were pushed, into, we find ourselves in history in such a way that we can have no idea of not being part of it. This means that "As Care Dasein *is* the 'between'[18], that is, it is our own very living, doing, and existing that makes us historical and the source of history. Dasein itself is historical; it is part of what we are, or as Heidegger puts it,

> As long as Dasein factically exists, both the 'ends' and their 'between' *are*, and they *are* in the only way which it is possible on the basis of Dasein's being as *care*. Thrownness and that being towards death in which one either flees it or anticipates it, form a unity; and in this unity birth and death are 'connected' in a manner characteristic of Dasein. As care, Dasein *is* the 'between'. (Heidegger, 1962, H.374)

Dasein exists as care because our involvement in the world is inescapable. Care denotes this inevitable relationship, and because our involvements themselves are temporally structured, they are made up of projecting, awaiting and retaining; this means that Dasein itself is inescapably temporal. The structure of Dasein's Being-in-the-world as thrown and projecting is the basis of historicality. We exist as beings that have a past and look towards a future while living in the present, and, without this perspective there can be no history, and similarly there can be no Dasein. Dasein and history cannot be separated and any attempt to do so will only produce an impoverished notion of both. With clear and direct relevance to the work of Sebald Heidegger goes on to say,

> 'the past' has a remarkable double meaning; the past belongs irretrievably to an earlier time; it belonged to the events of that time, and in spite of that, it still can be present-at-hand 'now'—for instance, the remains of a Greek temple. With the temple a bit of the past is still 'in the present'. (Heidegger, 1962, H.379)

This is the way in which we have seen Sebald bring the past back to life on his visits to sites of significant historical events. The apparent way that the past seems to reappear time after time in Sebald's work is possible because of this connectedness and the unity of the temporality of Dasein. Like Gadamer, Heidegger criticizes the attempt by those he calls historiologists to separate out the events of the past and to make history an object of science in order to achieve epistemological clarification. This process not only fragments the unity of history and breaks our connection with these events, but misses altogether the real point which is,

> How history can become a possible *object* for historiology is something that may be gathered only for the kind of Being which belongs to the

historical—from historicality, and from the way it is rooted in temporality. (Heidegger, 1962, H.375)

Although, as I have said, Sebald tends to choose events of some historical consequence, battles, wars and the like, it is now emerging that the same applies to all past events, however minor, and to the past of each and every one of us. It is the temporality of Dasein which makes all history possible in the first place. History is no objective edifice standing apart from Dasein to which Dasein may be made subject. Dasein makes history because Dasein is historical itself, and this will apply even to the events which happened before there was any Dasein. It is when we call these events historical that they become what we call history. It is not only the case that without Dasein there can be no science of history, Dasein must have a history because Dasein is itself historical and it cannot help making all the events it considers 'historical'. It is from this ground that all discussion of history must begin. This position is reinforced when we consider antiquities, which are defined by their past. Their existing as antiquities is only possible on the basis of Dasein's existing. The entities we now consider to be antiquities are no more than equipment, that is, things that were used by others in a context (world) which is no more. The people who used them have gone and the things themselves may even have become broken or obsolete, or may have been used for another purpose entirely. They were involved in a world that has passed but they were engaged with Dasein existing at that time so that,

> the historical character of the antiquities that are still preserved is grounded in the 'past' of that Dasein to whose world they belonged". (Heidegger, 1962, H.380)

Heidegger goes on to say,

> The antiquities which are still present-at-hand have a character of 'the past' and of history by reason of the fact that they have belonged as equipment to a world that has been—the world of a Dasein that has been there—and that they have been derived from that world. (Heidegger, 1962, H.380-1)

This coming down to us is much more than just a change of location so that,

> When, for instance a ring gets 'handed over' to someone and 'worn', this is a kind of being in which it does not simply suffer change of location. The movement of historizing in which something 'happens to something' is not

to be grasped in terms of motion as change of location. (Heidegger, 1962, H.389)

In a sense it is not the antiquities that have moved at all, it is that world to which they belonged which has gone, they are left behind and survive to bring a bit of the past down to us. The movement is thus not spatial but temporal. Heidegger puts it like this,

> What is 'past'? Nothing else than that *world* within which they belonged to a context of equipment and were encountered as ready-to-hand and used by a concernful Dasein who was in-the-world. That world is no longer. (Heidegger, 1962, H.380)

This shows us the way in which objects from the past (antiquities) give a specific access to the past. This access is provided because these entities were used by Dasein as part of its projects. This use, or involvement, is more than accidental or coincidental, it gives the entities their meaning, their 'for-the-sake-of-which'. This is highly reminiscent of the way that Bachelard speaks of polishing furniture and doing what he calls practicing phenomenology.[19] Whoever used these things knew what they were for. They formed part of the context or work of the Dasein, a context which has now passed, and thereby provide us with an intimate and ontologically significant connection with that Dasein. It is not simply that we are handling and sensing objects that have been handled and sensed before us by others, but that when we use these objects, because we and those who have gone have their meaning in what they do, we share in the *existing* (verb not noun) of the Dasein that used them previously. We can connect not simply with the physically present Dasein of the past but with the ontological Being of this Dasein through our connection to its own projects and thrownness. We are connecting with what made those who were in the past what they were, their willing, active and living being. This is a very intimate and primordial connection and one which is all too easily obscured once we allow our experience to be mediated and analyzed, but if we allow it to appear then the beings of the past will also appear, just in the way that Severs got the Gervais family to appear in 18 Folgate Street. The way that these things appear to us is the way that it is because of the way that Dasein is historical in itself. It is also the very basis on which mediation and analysis are possible. It is because we are also living Dasein that we can understand, analyze, and live, in the world, and this is a world with history. We are able in this way to connect with the very Being of Dasein that has passed at the level of its fundamental constitution.

On a broader scale we can now see that this is not only true of the objects which were equipment for those who have gone before. In Gadamer's terms by participating in the traditions that come down to us we are choosing patterns of behaviour which were developed by those who preceded us. We use these in the same way that we use equipment and in so doing modify them for our own ends. Tradition is a system of handed down ways of doing things based on the experience of others, and by participating we connect ourselves with these others. This means that when we consider what are termed pre-historic artefacts, or even geological specimens, we interpret these in the manner we have come to accept as part of the tradition which we inhabit, and it is through this process that they become historical.

Heidegger is committing himself here to a notion of history and of temporality which is unified, not splintered, and which can only be understood as a unity rather than a phenomenon which is broken into parts (past, present and future). This is essentially a repeat of the form of argument against the spectatorial perspective on the spatial world. In the same way as we are not outsiders looking in on a world of things, we do not stand outside time and watch it go by, we experience ourselves as temporal. This is because Heidegger believes that,

> Temporalizing does not signify that ecstases come in a 'succession'. The future is *not later* than having been, and having been is *not earlier* than the Present. Temporality temporalises itself as a future which makes present in the process of having been. (Heidegger, 1962, H.350)

And,

> The ecstatical unity of temporality—that is the unity of the 'outside-of-itself in the raptures of the future, of what has been and of the Present—is the condition for the possibility that there can be an entity which exists as its "there". (Heidegger, 1962, H.350)

Totality and hermeneutics again, and the primordiality of the unified notion of temporality out of which we then construct the fractured clock-time by which we live our everyday lives. The unity of temporality becomes the basis for the existing of entities. Dasein exists as thrown and projecting being-in-the-world; that is, its Being is made up of a fundamental unity of past, future and present, which is only later fragmented by the practical necessity to organize our everyday lives. This structure is revealed to Dasein through a three-fold unity, past, (or having-been), projecting (future, or for-the-sake-of-which) and being-alongside (present), or as Heidegger puts it.

> With one's factical being-there, a potentiality-for-being is in each case projected in the horizon of the future, one's 'Being already' is disclosed in the horizon of having been, and that with which one concerns oneself is discovered in the horizon of the Present. (Heidegger, 1962, H.365)

In the end "Dasein's constitution and its ways to be are possible ontologically only on the basis of temporality".[20] This is the basis on which we must understand history.

Summary

History is only possible because Dasein itself is ontologically structured as temporality, as thrown and projecting being-in-the-world. This goes a long way towards showing how the past appears to us as part of the present. It is because of the way that we exist as historical, as a living process, that everything that has gone, that is, all of history, remains with us as a part of what we have become and what we are. Sebald shows us, in the way that he conjures up the ghostly apparitions of the past, that this kind approach to history and temporality is not the preserve of idle and often obscure theorising, but it is part of how we all experience and understand the world. The paradox of the apparent appearance of the world that has passed is not explained away by this kind of reasoning it is simply shown to be the way that we are.

In the next chapter I will consider the notion of personal identity and show how this often tricky question can be illuminated by the kind of thinking that I have already applied to the subjects of each of the chapters so far.

Notes

[1] Sebald, 2002, *The Rings of Saturn*, pp.232-7.
[2] Sebald, 2002, *Austerlitz*, p.166.
[3] Sebald, 2002, *The Rings of Saturn*, pp.75-80.
[4] Sebald, 2002, *Austerlitz*, pp.23-34.
[5] Sebald, 2002, *The Rings of Saturn*, p.38.
[6] Sebald, 2002, *The Rings of Saturn*, pp.103-34.
[7] Gadamer, 1975, 2004 p.197.
[8] Gadamer, 1975, 2004 p.190.
[9] Sebald, 2002, *Austerlitz*, pp.98-102.

[10] Gadamer, 1975, 2004 p.282.
[11] Gadamer, 1975, 2004 p.278.
[12] Gadamer, 1975, 2004 p.282.
[13] Gadamer, 1975, 2004 p.341.
[14] Gadamer, 1975, 2004 p.217.
[15] Quoting Dilthey.
[16] Gadamer, 1975, 2004 p.121.
[17] Gadamer, 1975, 2004 p. 217.
[18] Heidegger, 1962, H.374.
[19] Bachelard, 1958, 1994, p.67.
[20] Heidegger, 1962, H.367.

CHAPTER EIGHT

IDENTITY AND APPEARANCE

In this chapter I want to address the question of the appearance of the self. This presents its own particular problems when it comes to phenomenological discussion, not least that in this discussion it is we ourselves who are both the object of discussion and the investigating agent. The sheer enigma of the question of the appearance of the self means that, of all the phenomena I have so far considered, it is this one which requires the most oblique approach in order that we may escape from the morass of philosophical problems which have surrounded our notion of personal identity. I will make this approach along a circuitous route which will first use some of Sebald's work relating to identity, this will set the tone for the rest of the discussion. I will then set out two modern controversies concerning the appearance of faces as ciphers for identity which will throw some light on the importance of our appearance to our idea of personal identity. Following that, in order to deepen the analysis of the idea of personal identity, and continuing with the theme of faces and their appearance, I will consider some aspects of portraits and self portraits as appearances of faces, and of individuals. At appropriate points I will use philosophical insights from Descartes, Hume, Hegel, Sartre and Heidegger which I hope will throw light on the discussion where it is most needed. By the end of this chapter I hope to have given not so much as a clear definition of personal identity, but more to have defined the territory which this notion inhabits.

Sebald

The notion of personal identity is one of the most important ideas that Sebald is trying to get us to think about in his works, and there are many instances in all of the books which give us insights into this notion. I will select and describe a few which I think summarise his thoughts on identity and which point towards some interesting and difficult problems with this most personal of notions.

The first, and apparently unremarkable, example occurs in the second part of *Vertigo*, entitled "All'estero" in which the narrator travels through Italy. During this journey he stays at a rather strange Hotel Sole in Limone. To his consternation when the time comes for him to depart his passport, which had been stored in a locker at the reception desk, had "gone astray".[1] Eventually it is discovered that his passport has been given, by mistake, to another German guest at the hotel, and that he has already left He is now cast adrift in a foreign country with no means of proving who he is, as he says,

> The question was now how I was to be provided with provisional papers proving my identity, in the absence of a passport, so that I could continue my journey and leave Italy. (Sebald, 2002, *Vertigo*, p.100)

This simple example shows both the importance and fragility of identity. Without the documents to prove who he is, he is formally without identity. The simple error of the hotel clerk has deprived him of the means to show who he is in the eyes of the world. The importance of being able to prove who he is is emphasised by the fact that he cannot leave Italy without these documents. Without his passport he is stranded. In effect he has lost the ability to be formally recognized. The mere possession of this recognizable image of himself, with the accompanying information, would be enough to confirm his identity. Fortunately his loss of identity is temporary and short lived and he is issued with documents sufficient to restore his identity and to allow him to travel. Some of the characters in his other works are not so fortunate, as I will now describe.

In *The Emigrants* the teacher Paul Bereyter commits suicide at the age of seventy-four. On learning of this Sebald notes that,

> Almost by way of an aside, the obituary added, with no further explanation, that during the Third Reich Paul Bereyter had been prevented from practising his chosen profession. (Sebald, 2002, *The Emigrants*, p.27)

Sebald is then driven to take up the story of this teacher and to throw light on the life that he chose to end himself. Paul Bereyter wanted to do nothing else but to teach children and when, just after beginning his career, he was prevented from doing so his whole world collapsed. Sebald even notes his physical diminution in the photograph on page 49 where Paul is "so terribly thin that he seems almost to have reached a physical vanishing point".[2] This is a man who is a teacher or he is nothing. After dismissal by the Nazis he finds a post as a house tutor in France in a desperate attempt to continue his vocation. While he is away from his home his parents perish and their house is sold. It is as if the foundations of his being have been cut away and he is left with nothing. Even after the war, when he could return to teaching, he could not recover from the twelve years and the family that he had lost. In effect, by being prevented from teaching, and with the untimely deaths of his parents, he is robbed of his identity to the extent that after the war he is a hollow man with nothing to live for.

The story of Henry Selwyn[3] is the story of another man sundered from his origins, this time in Lithuania. He arrives in England as an almost accidental immigrant when his family disembark at London when they had intended to go to New York. At the beginning of the story Henry is already an old man and introduces himself as "merely a dweller in the garden, a kind of ornamental hermit."[4] By this stage of his life he is presented to us as a mere adjunct of his wife's life, it is she who owns the house, it is she who we suppose is quite wealthy, and it is she who they must see about renting the flat. It is only later in the story that his past is revealed and we find that he has changed his name from Hersch Seweryn to Henry Selwyn. He is to all intents a lost soul, disconnected from his past and seemingly unable to recover from the loss of the friend of his youth Johannes Naegeli on the Aare glacier many years before. The sheer pointlessness of his life is overwhelming, he is no-one and it is no surprise for us to hear that he has shot himself with the elephant gun that he has fired only once before.

In the story of Ambros Adelwarth[5] we have not quite another case of suicide but a similar episode of loss of meaning and identity which leaves Ambros unable to carry on. Ambros Adelwarth pursues a career in service and from humble beginnings eventually become the companion to Cosmo Solomon, the rich son of a rich man. They travel the world together and through the sharing of good and bad times a close intimacy arises between them. Eventually Cosmo dies and, while Ambros is financially secure, he has nothing more to do once his life of serving others is over. Towards the end of his life he admits himself to a kind of mental hospital and apparently wastes away. In this case it seems that so much of his life and his identity have been invested in serving others, and in particular in the service of Cosmo Solomon, that once Cosmo is dead and the world through which Ambros had moved with him has passed, the meaning of his life had gone too. His mental collapse is the result of this loss of meaning and his death is unremarkable. After living for an Other all his life once that Other is dead his identity becomes unsustainable. In all three of these stories from *The Emigrants* Sebald describes men who have lost something, their origins, their meaning in life, their soul mate. In so doing they have lost something which they feel makes them what they are. They have lost their identity and, while all three continue for a while after this loss, their existence has become meaningless and their extinction a mere formality.

By way of contrast, Sebald's last major work, *Austerlitz*, is perhaps best read as the story of a man reconstructing his identity and I will now revisit some episodes from this book. Sebald's device of setting out the work as a series of meetings and conversations between the narrator (who we take to be Sebald) and the fictional character, Austerlitz, allows us to accompany Austerlitz on his journey to fill in the gaps in his life and to reconstruct his identity. We are drawn through the book like it is a detective story, always wanting to find out not what will happen, but what had happened. From the first point at which he discovers that his name is not Dafydd Elias but Jacques Austerlitz,[6] Austerlitz is impelled by the trauma of the destruction of his childhood identity to try to rediscover who he really was and who he is now. Austerlitz is driven to distraction by his lack of identity, he says,

> I came to realize how isolated I was and always have been, among the Welsh as much as among the English and French. It never occurred to me to wonder about my true origins, said Austerlitz, nor did I ever feel that I belonged to a certain social class, professional group or religious confession. (Sebald, 2002, *Austerlitz*, p.177)

This sense of isolation eventually precipitates a mental breakdown and sometime afterwards, as part of his nocturnal ramblings, he finds himself at Liverpool Street Station. This is where perhaps his most significant moment in the unforgetting of who he is takes place, in the now disused Ladies Waiting Room. As we have already seen he recounts his dream like hallucination,

> I felt, said Austerlitz, that the waiting–room where I stood as if dazzled contained all the hours of my past life, all the suppressed and extinguished fears and wishes I had ever entertained, as if the black and white diamond pattern of the stone slabs beneath my feet were the board on which the endgame would be played, and it covered the entire plane of time. (Sebald, 2002, *Austerlitz*, p.193)

This is a graphic expression of his encounter with his own life and times, and he goes on to say,

> Perhaps that is why, in the gloomy light of the waiting room, I also saw two middle aged people dressed in the style of the thirties, a woman in a light gabardine coat with a hat at an angle on her head, and a thin man

beside her wearing a dark suit and a dog collar. And I not only saw the minister and his wife, said Austerlitz, I also saw the boy they had come to meet ... I recognized him by that rucksack of his and for the first time as far back as I can remember I recollected myself as a small child (Sebald, 2002, *Austerlitz*,. p.193)

It is at this moment, many years after his true identity has been revealed to him at school, that Austerlitz really begins to find himself. Until this revelation he cannot think of himself as a small child, his identity has no ground on which to stand. Although he, as we all do, knows that he must once have been a child, up until this moment that part of his former existence is a void. After this revelation he can set off on his journey to Prague and begin the reconstruction of his origins.

When he has Austerlitz travel to Prague Sebald uses the device of Austerlitz finding his nurse Vera to fill in more of the gaps and to continue the tale. The story of the visit to his Czech homeland is more conventional than the revelations at Liverpool Street. He walks the streets his mother would have walked along and he visits Terezin where she was imprisoned. He searches for a picture of her on an old Nazi film. He is eventually able to accept the fact of her death by finding out from Vera at least some of what happened. There is however one rather more strange occurrence in his conversations with Vera; he appears to regain an understanding of the Czech language. He is, "like a deaf man whose hearing has been miraculously restored".[7] This is Sebald's metaphor for the recovery of his identity, the language of his forgotten childhood comes back to him, and through it he is able to listen to and understand Vera as she tells him about his parents. It is as if the restoration of his original Czech becomes the ground on which his personal identity can be restored. Finally Austerlitz is able to confront the picture of the small boy in fancy dress and accept it as a picture himself, even so, as he says,

Yet hard as I tried in me both that evening and later, I could not recollect myself in the part. I did recognize the unusual hairline running at a slant over the forehead, but otherwise all memory was extinguished by the long years that had passed. (Sebald, 2002, *Austerlitz*, p.259)

Austerlitz now knows that this is a picture of him as a little boy and this fact is important to him as part of the reconstruction of his identity, yet he has no memory of the events, places and times surrounding this photograph. It is a vital link in the continuous chain which forms his idea of himself but he cannot remember it. In spite of his acceptance of the photograph he is left with a lingering unease as if, without a memory, the photograph and the little boy in fancy dress still remain to some extent external to his identity. The simple fact of knowing that this is a picture of himself as a small boy is insufficient to make it part of his real identity.

Clearly the notion of personal identity is not simple and even at the end of *Austerlitz* Sebald's character is still searching, this time for the history of his father. His story is still incomplete. Writing about Sebald's work Mark McCulloch says,

> In Sebald, consciousness is a theatre that blends meaning, hallucination, counterfeit memory, dream, soliloquy and the unending stream of immediate perceptions. The possessor of that inner theatre is at once actor, audience and playwright. (McCulloch, 2003, p.25)

This seems as close as we can come to a explanation of personal identity in Sebald's work and is reminiscent of Hume's writing on identity when he says,

> The mind is a kind of theatre, where several perceptions successively make their appearances; pass, repass, glide away and mingle in an infinite variety of postures and situations." (Hume, 1959, Vol. 1, pp.239-40)

But as Hume goes on to point out there are problems with this metaphor. While we can see and demonstrate the existence of the contents of the theatre, the theatre itself remains a metaphor, a metaphor for our own consciousness which is never present to us. It is as if every time we try to look we slip away just before we come into view. While others can be present to us we cannot be present to ourselves as viewer and viewed. The problem becomes acute when we consider the problem of the continuity of our own self with ourselves at other times. We are clearly not the same people we were when we were children, or even perhaps last week, but we want to be. We want to say that we are the same but different. Sebald's work contains the clues to help us escape from this apparent dilemma. If he says anything Sebald says that we should not look within ourselves if we want to find our identity. Sebald is inviting us to use our imagination in our search for identity. He points us outwards towards the connections and relationships we have with people and with the world. We are, to that extent, what we do and what we make ourselves by our choices in life. It seems that the self cannot be some self-contained self-supporting entity which we preserve within ourselves, it is more like that dynamic ever changing process in which we are all involved and from which we can never escape. For Sebald's characters identity is all the things that have happened to them, all the things that are happening to them and all the things that will happen to them, and the same is true for all of us. It is in this way that we are connected to our own selves throughout our lives and Sebald describes this continuity.

I now want to change the focus of the discussion completely and consider two additional examples drawn from recent history which reflect on our notion of identity and which point towards the kind of conclusions to which Sebald's work suggests. These are the lively debates about face transplants and the wearing of veils.

Face Transplants

The public discussion over recent years about the acceptability of face transplants demonstrates an abiding fascination with faces and their appearance. Aside from the purely functional issues of eating, breathing and being able to see properly, we are most concerned with the questions of appearance, identity and mutual recognition.

Isabelle Dinoire became the first recipient of a partial face transplant in 2006. In her case facial deformity and malfunction had been caused by accident. She had been attacked by a dog, and the transplant was carried in out in the first instance to restore functionality, to help her to eat and breathe more easily, but also to stop people looking, and to give her back the kind of anonymity we all enjoy when out in the crowd. In contrast the publicity surrounding the release of the news of the operation concentrated almost wholly on what were called the ethical aspects of the case concerning her appearance and that of the donor. Her face was not changed to make it distinctive or to enhance her identity, this was not the kind of plastic surgery that increasing numbers of people indulge in to make themselves more attractive. This surgery was therapeutic in the strictest sense, but the reaction of public and medical establishment went much further and was strangely ironic as the surgeon's intention had been to make her less, not more, distinctive and less noticeable, to make her look more ordinary, just a face in the crowd. It seemed that somehow, as a result of the attack by the dog and because of her deformity, she was not being recognised as an individual and giving her back her face became an attempt to restore both her identity and her anonymity.

As Peter Butler, a specialist surgeon in this area said, "I soon realised that your face is seen as your true distinguishing mark, your identity, the window to your soul.", and "Hands, feet legs – you can live with losing them but if you lose your face it can destroy your life."[8] This means that while the transplantation of a face from donor to recipient is a surgical and clinical challenge, the greatest challenge is psychological, for both the relatives of the donor and for the recipient. So potent is the way that we appear to others that the relatives of donors are concerned that by allowing a face transplant they give away the identity of the donor, and will risk running into their dead relative in the street. Recipients themselves are concerned that they will be taking on an entirely new identity. These are concerns which do not seem to be at the forefront when people are considering other organ transplants. However they are very real concerns in spite of the fact that it is unlikely that, after transplantation, the recipient will even look much like the donor, since distinctiveness in facial features is founded on the structure of facial bones rather than the envelope of muscle and skin. Even with this reassurance face transplant still attracts controversy in ways not seen before in the cases of other kinds of transplants. Hearts, kidneys, corneas, lungs and livers, and now even hands are transplanted without these widespread concerns over personal identity. It seems that the way we appear to others through our faces is a significant constituent of what we call our identity.

The plain reality of facial transplant is clearly not to give someone the identity of another but to restore to functionality, and to some semblance of normal appearance, people who have either been damaged or who have been born with some kind of deformity, as Peter Butler says, "You have it (a face transplant) because you want the simple pleasure of reacting with the world without seeing people recoil as you walk down the street".[9] From this it is clear that the appearance of the face is the key visual representation of our individuality. Faces are what we look at when we walk down the street and faces are what we remember and recognize about those we meet. It is as if without a face we do not have an identity and cannot be recognized as another individual by our fellows. This in turn has meant that the psychological aspects of face transplantation have dominated the discussion, and the most important things have been to select the right patients and to engage in a philosophical debate. It is as if the face were the unique property of the donor in ways that do not apply to other organs that might be transplanted. We have only to see the tragic cases of parents who bury and rebury their dead children as organs removed for the purposes of 'research' turn up years later, to be aware of the need for completeness as a constituent of what we are.[10] But while all organs are seen to belong to the donor, and in some way constitute their totality, it is our faces which most definitely constitute identity and the ethics of face transplants become quite different from those of heart or kidney, or even cornea transplants. Somewhere, underlying the psychological impact, there is a powerful belief that having someone else's face makes us another person and not ourselves. The change in the appearance of this part of our body has a significant impact on our idea of our own identity. In short we would not make such a fuss about face transplants unless faces themselves are much more than just the site of sensory organs.

Veils

It is purely coincidental that the fuss and furore about the wearing in public of full face veils by Muslim women arose at the same time as the ethical discussion about face transplants, and I am in no way concerned to engage in the discussion of the rights and wrongs of this practice. My only interest is in the ways in which the fact that there is such a debate says something about faces, and about identity, which can contribute to our understanding. The fact that this debate is probably correctly construed as a clash of cultural norms does not detract from any philosophical conclusions about identity that might emerge. The layer of understanding that I am concerned with in this enquiry goes much deeper than cultural relevance, and anyway I think it will eventually become clear that the same phenomenology underlies the attitude towards faces and identity in both cultures. The controversy began in October 2006 when Member of Parliament Jack Straw said that he would ask Muslim women attending his constituency surgery in Blackburn to remove their veils in order for him to be able to communicate adequately with them, and to enable him to be of maximum assistance to them with whatever problem they were bringing. This caused a predictable uproar amongst both Muslims and well meaning non-Muslim libertarians. The political and religious dispute still rumbles on, with arguments about the rights of members of different cultures to stick to their own customs, along with often conflicting views on multiculturalism and integration. After the initial controversy the case of Aishah Azmi, a Teaching Assistant in Dewsbury, was given lots of publicity.[11] She was asked to remove her veil in class even when there were men present and was dismissed from her employment when she refused. In this case the central issue appears to have been the ability to communicate adequately in order to support children in the classroom. While much was made of the muffling effect of the veil, which it was claimed made it difficult for the children to hear what she was saying, a purely practical difficulty; this was clearly underlain by a discomfort with regard to the recognition of her as an individual by her pupils. Communication, particularly in the classroom, is more than merely verbal, and the supportive relationship between Teachers and Teaching Assistants, and their pupils depends, in part, on the recognition of the individuality of all those involved. The almost unspoken presumption was that a Teaching Assistant wearing a veil would not be able to relate to children in a way that supported their learning. Recognition, trust, and relation to the Other, all seem bound up with the face to face encounter. It seems that for some people a Teaching Assistant wearing a veil is in some way not fully present. By concealing her face she is denying part of herself and, it is argued, a crucial part in her encounter with the children. This accords with the origins of veil wearing in Islam where the veil is intended to allow women out in public without showing themselves to men in ways which might be construed as sexually provocative, it is a form of denial of access. Even in this very different culture the face is definitive of identity, so that by obscuring it individuals cannot really meet.

As I have said I do not wish engage in the ongoing and often acrimonious debate about the rights and wrongs of veiling. What does seem to me significant is the very fact of this debate, and whether the participants are motivated by religion, politics, bigotry or liberalism all of the arguments are made possible by the potent but, in this debate, unrecognised, phenomenology of the face, and the way that it serves as a cipher for personal identity. The philosophical task is to uncover the ground for this debate. The then Bishop of Rochester, Nazir Ali, perhaps came closest to identifying this in his December 2006 statement[12] in which he suggested that banning the veiling of women in public would improve security and *cohesion*. The question of security is merely a practical problem of recognition, although it is based on the fact that recognition of individuals is largely based on recognition of facial features. Cohesion brings to the fore the very basis of the relationship we have with the Other. Social cohesion is based on mutual recognition by different individual identities, and faces it seems are crucial to this recognition. Covering faces therefore prevents recognition, inhibits cohesion and can dislocate society. It is ironic that the wearing of the veil by Muslim women is designed to isolate them from the male population by making them indistinct when the same veiling in another culture makes them stand out, but once again it shows how important the face is to human recognition and integration, and to personal identity.

The Other

At this point some philosophy from Sartre may help to clarify what is really going on. In *Being and Nothingness*, his *Essay on Phenomenological Ontology*, Sartre is concerned, in part, with a demonstration of the existence of Others.[13] Sartre's problem with the existence of the Other, like everyone who went before, is the uncertainty of the veracity and reliability of the evidence of the senses. When questioned we have to admit that, at least sometimes, our senses play us false. If we admit this then we also admit that we have no way of telling the difference between a true perception and one that is erroneous, and this includes perceptions of the appearance of Others. Once the evidence of our senses is brought into doubt then, apparently, we have no means by which we can trust that the things we see, hear, touch etc. are really what they seem to be. We appear to exist behind a 'veil of the senses' which is impenetrable, and which denies us access to the things and beings beyond ourselves. As a result Sartre's enterprise, set out at the beginning of "The Look" in *Being and Nothingness,* [14] is as follows,

> My apprehension of the Other as an object essentially refers me to a fundamental apprehension of the Other in which he will not be revealed to me as an object but as a 'presence in person'. (Sartre, 1956, p.253)

What this means is that Sartre is avoiding the problem of knowing the Other through the doubtful evidence of the senses and picking another route so that,

> If the Other is to be a probable object and not a dream of an object, then his objectness must of necessity refer not to an original solitude beyond my reach but to a fundamental connection in which the Other is manifested in some way other than through the knowledge I have of him. (Sartre, 1956, p.253)

Sartre wants to demonstrate the certain existence of Others by linking this existence inextricably to the certain existence of his own self given in the Cartesian cogito (I think, therefore I am). This connection is to be made through 'the look'. Sartre's description of himself looking through a keyhole, suddenly surprised by footsteps coming along the corridor is vivid.[15] His description of the shame he feels strikes a chord. From the simple orientation of himself (as a subject) looking at the world (as an object), to the transformation of the situation by the look of an Other, and his discomfiture under this look, the movement is inexorable, but may say less than he hopes. Sartre claims to be saying more than something like simply; 'I feel shame, I cannot feel such a thing alone in the world, and therefore there must be Others for me to be ashamed before'. Such a deduction would be unworthy of Sartre and would miss the point of his entire project. What Sartre wishes to say is that, in shame, I actually and immediately experience the Other within my very being, and in a way as if he were me or part of me. This is a kind of way of knowing the Other which is quite different from being told about an Other, or even the experience or simply seeing someone else. It is a kind of knowing that we must feel for ourselves. However it is not clear that the simple example of shame achieves all of this as the notion of shame itself already involves the necessary existence of others. Rather less emotionally compelling, and more useful philosophically, is his description of objects he sees in the park in their primary relation to him as a subject, and the way in which this description is radically re-orientated when he becomes conscious of the look of the Other. As he says, "suddenly an object has appeared which has stolen the world from me".[16] Another subject (not me) now orientates the world and I feel this presence uncannily *within my own self.* In this example we do get a sense of the otherness of the Other which is different from the sense we get from mere observation. In "The Look" Sartre demonstrates the existence of Others with a description of certain self evident psychological facts, or states of mind, which we experience, and through which we gain an immediate apprehension of the Other. "The Look" is essentially a piece of philosophy concerned with *relation* and this proves to be the foundation not only of our own being but also the being of Others. Sartre is most insistent that no space is left for inference between my own self and the Other, my apprehension of the Other is *immediate.*[17] The only way in which Sartre can be certain of the existence of the Other is to experience the Other as subject, and for this to happen a radical, and necessarily alarming, conversion must take place in which object becomes subject and subject becomes object. Sartre argues that this is what takes place in "The Look", and that, far from being a contradiction it is a satisfactory explanation of everyday conscious experience. Suddenly from the commanding heights of my own subjectivity, seeing the world and organizing its elements in my own way, I am subjected to the look of an Other under which the world, including me, undergoes a re-organization in such a way that it escapes from my control and I become an object for another subject. Sartre eloquently describes the theft of my world by the Other.

> The Other is first the permanent flight of things towards a goal which I apprehend as an object at a certain distance from me but which escapes me inasmuch as it unfolds about itself its own distances. (Sartre, 1956, p. 255)

And "In experiencing the look ... I experience the inapprehensible subjectivity of the Other directly and within my being".[18] In the same way that in Descartes *cogito* I apprehend my own consciousness, (I think therefore I am) so in the look of the Other I apprehend the Other. Apart from anything else this means that Sartre is actually experiencing the Other not as object but as subject, and is experiencing a radical transformation not only of the world of objects, which is re-orientated towards the Other, but a transformation of his own self, which is also re-orientated under the look of the Other. If Sartre's demonstration is successful then the place of 'the look' in our understanding of our relation to Others like ourselves cannot be underestimated, to the extent that, "in order for me to be what I am, it suffices merely that the Other look at me",[19] and,

> I am possessed by the Other; the Other's look fashions my body in its nakedness, causes it to be born, sculptures it, produces it as it *is*, sees it as I shall never see it (Sartre, 1956, p.364)

In this way, just as I experience the Other not as an object of knowledge but as a subject in the look of the Other, I am given my own self as an object as well as being a self conscious subject. In the look the Other recognizes me for what I am. It seems then that looking at the face of another, or being looked at by someone else, is much more than a simple matter of perception. Seeing the faces of Others shows us their Otherness at the same time as their looking upon us gives us ourselves, and both in ways which are beyond doubt and which tie us into an inescapable, fundamental, and constitutive relationship to the Other, as Sartre puts it,

> If the Other-as-object is defined in connection with the world as the object which sees what I see, then my fundamental connection with the Other-as-subject must be able to be referred back to my *permanent* possibility of being seen by the Other. (Sartre, 1956, p.256) (my italics)

Sartre's method in "The Look" is highly imaginative, his departure from the empirical, made necessary by the problem of the 'veil of the senses', means that he is left appealing to our imagination to do the work of understanding our own selves and the otherness of Others. The key importance of faces which is publicly manifest in the controversies concerning face transplants and the wearing of veils rests on this ontological foundation. In short, the faces of Others bring us up short in our own being. The grateful miracle of facial reconstruction and the discomfort in the denial of the look by the wearing of a veil are both grounded in this structure of looking and counter-looking.

Portraits – The Illusion of Presence

The consideration of portraits and self-portraits in this section is a device to overcome the identity between the object of investigation and the investigating agent. I am going to use this discussion to provide a metaphorical space in which we can consider aspects of the appearance of the self—but this space really is only metaphorical—and we must never forget the dilemma of identity given in Hume's analogy of the mind as a kind of theatre.[20] Within these limits a consideration of portraits and self portraits as appearances may still be able to illuminate some of what we mean by personal identity. Put simply a portrait is a likeness of a specific person at one moment.[21] We can fill this out a bit with the apparently obvious but significant fact that portraits are always pictures of faces. It is important to remember throughout this discussion that for conventional portraiture, that is excluding sculpture and sophisticated modern electronic imaging, all portraits are two dimensional renderings of three dimensional subjects. We must never forget, first the skill of the artist who is doing his or her level best to make us see in three dimensions, and second the distortion of reality that must necessarily arise from this exercise of skill. In a portrait what we have before us is an illusion, a representation and not the 'real thing'. The ways in which the portrayal has been executed can therefore tell us something about the artists intentions and, if the portrait is a good one, something about the sitter. This is important; already we are thinking of a good portrait as one which tells more than what is visually available. This is because, in the very act of representing, the artist selects items and features to portray and ways in which to portray them. In this way the portrait is a very different entity to the image of a person we get when we see them, it is an image which may tell us more us less, but certainly different, about the individual in question, and probably something about their identity. A portrait is an invitation to imagine what the person in the picture is really like, a bit like the way that Sebald's accounts of his travels are invitations to imagine what the places he visits are really like.

If we consider the portrait as an illusion we may say that what makes a good portrait is the 'illusion of presence'. As Erasmus once said of the work of Hans Holbein portrait painter to Henry VIII,

> The highest value that a portrait could attain, that of being able to conjure up absent friends so vividly that the desire to see them in person was almost satisfied. (Buck, 1999, p 56)

This is similar to the inscription made by the artist himself on the portrait of Bonifacius Amerbach[22] which says,

> Although a painted face, I am not second to the living face; I am the gentleman's equal and I am distinguished by correct lines... thorough me this work of art depicts with diligence what belongs to nature (Buck, 1999, p.24)

And again on the portrait of Derich Born,[23]

> If you could add the voice Derich is here in person, so that you will doubt whether the painter or the creator made him. (Buck, 1999, p.96)

These inscriptions invite us to take the visual appearance further and to imagine what it would be like to meet the real person that they bring to mind. Portraits that do not meet the single condition of recognisability are not really portraits at all. Recognizability is central, but not simply visual recognizability. While the intention of those being painted and paying the bill was to have created an image of themselves which would both serve them in life by showing their importance, standing etc., and remember them in death as a kind of eternal living, the intention of the artist is to bring the subject to life by provoking our imagination. It is ironic that portraits are now more often known not by the name of the sitter but the artist, and it is they who have gone down to posterity.

There are many reasons why people had their portraits painted. Paintings of significant figures in society were made to show status, in the case of royalty to cement a dynasty or to tout for a prospective marriage partner. With the rise of the European bourgeoisie more people had themselves painted to show how much they had come up in the world. Just as royalty sometimes had themselves painted alongside religious or even godly figures, so these newly wealthy and important people wanted to show that they too now stood on a par with their supposed betters. Portraits of those who excelled in some field of arts, science and business illustrated a life well lived. Most of all people had their portraits painted as way of showing off. They saw these images of themselves passing down through history and taking with them something of themselves. The portrait was an affirmation of their identity, as well as the depiction of their appearance at a particular point in their lifetime. It seems that by the two dimensional representation of a face something more of the individual is revealed, and not simply a mere representation of the surface features more or less accurate and recognizable. Portraits go beyond realism. While they can only provide a two dimensional image of the three dimensional face they can also convey something of the sitter which may not be apparent from the immediate image we have when we see them 'in person'. A good portrait simply looks like the sitter while a great portrait both looks like and says something of their individual self and life, it speaks of identity. We have now come some way from the portrait as simple visual likeness and begun to consider the nature of portrayal, and therefore the nature of individual identity itself. Just as personal proximity is much more than mere spatial closeness so the power of portraiture is more than the illusion of simple visual presence. To get closer to what is going on we need to broaden our notion of presence and to take individuality well beyond visual appearance. Foister explains how Holbein's portraits "are given a sense of presence and vitality by the way in which Holbein positions the direction of eyes".[24] This notion, that something of the inner person is to be understood, if not directly perceived, through their eyes is familiar. As Eichler says of Durer's self portrait in a fur collared robe of about 1500,[25]

> The eye is particularly significant, being the painters second "tool" after his hand. Hence a small window is reflected in the portrayed artist's iris, and this should be viewed not as a naturalistic depiction of the workshop window but as an expression of the classical topos... "the eye as the window of the soul". (Eichler, 1999, p.62)

And for Holbein, "he challenges the viewer to take a close look at the face and therefore explore the personality of the sitter."[26] This challenge is the challenge to use our imagination.

Portraits and Phenomenology – Hegel and Heidegger

To understand portraits as a depiction of the person is uncontroversial but further clarification is needed when we start to use terms like 'individual', 'presence' and indeed 'soul'. This is more than the mere depiction of recognisable physical form and requires our imagination for its impact and success. When Erasmus recommended Holbein as producing the 'illusion of presence' he meant more than mere visual identity between sitter and portrait. Seeing the portrait is something like seeing the individual, particularly an individual that it personally known to the one viewing the portrait. It brings them to mind in a way that is more or less complete, with the character traits and vital facets of individuality that we have got to know through direct acquaintance. In giving us the Other in this way a great portrait can also give us ourselves. Hegel elegantly demonstrates the importance of this process when he describes the "Interdependence and dependence of self-consciousness: Lordship and Bondage." in the *Phenomenology of Spirit*. He says, "Self-consciousness exists in and for itself when, and by the fact that, it so exists for another; that is, it exists only in being acknowledged."[27] But this relationship has two sides so that,

> Each sees the other do the same as it does; each does itself what it demands of the other, and therefore also does what it does only in so far as the other does the same. Action by one side only would be useless because what is to happen can only be brought about by both. (Hegel, 1977, p.112)

In simple terms only recognition by another self consciousness can validate our own identity as a self consciousness ourselves, so the relationship we have with the other must be mutual and reciprocal. We can only affirm the identity of the other if we recognize them as another like ourselves, but we must also be recognized by an other in order to be able to achieve this act of recognition, thus validating the identity of the other at the same time as they validate our own identity. We can never be ourselves alone because if we try to isolate ourselves we deny our own self-conscious identity. This means that recognition by others is a vital part of who we are and constitutes at least some of what we call our identity. While we expect the portrait to be visibly recognizable (though this may not always be so in modern portraiture) we are looking for more than just a temporary visual likeness. The portrait presents to us another individual like ourselves, an illusion of presence, but a presence all the same, and one which can validate our own identity as a self-conscious being. It is in this that the power of a great portrait lies. The great portrait shows us not only what the individual looks like but also something of their character, their past achievements and their future potential. It shows us the stretching out of their existence over time through the marks on the faces of those who are portrayed; above all it provokes our imagination in our attempt to know something about the person portrayed, and in so doing it shows us another one like ourselves. The illusion of presence created by the portrait painter is an illusion not of singular or momentary presence but of the continuing presence of another subject like ourselves. In this way we gain the illusion of being looked at by another self consciousness in simultaneously recognizing the painted face as another like ourselves.

Heidegger provides his own radically alternative idea of self and personal identity which takes further the insights of both Sartre and Hegel.[28] For Heidegger the self is precisely not the substantial being of the post-Cartesian world but is an active and self creating be-ing (verb not noun). Heidegger's self is not the isolated individual subject but a *being-*

with (Mitsein).[29] This is most important in emphasizing the public nature of our being. We see and are seen in ways which makes us part of a shared world. We do not simply look out across a void from an isolated or monadic self at Others who we suppose to be like ourselves. The looks we exchange are constitutive of our selves and without them we cannot be what we are. This means that how we appear to Others matters more than just in the ways that it makes us feel, phenomenology makes our face into the manifestation of our self. Any attempt to avoid this publicness denies us our selfhood. The facially deformed are restored to themselves by transplant, those who wear the veil deny their publicness and being-with, and the portrait provides an enduring image which is looked at forever and gives the sitter a kind of immortality beyond the preservation of image. It is because we are in a world with Others like ourselves that faces have their meaning and their being; to put it another way, we have faces which work in this way because we are fundamentally and inescapably in a world with Others like ourselves. As I have said, faces are not just the site of our sensory organs. Sartre shows us how the look works but it is not our face which makes the looking possible. We have faces because we are looking beings, so that it is looking that makes faces possible as the appearance of our selves. Our looking is the way we are.

I will now briefly discuss the special case of self portraits in order to illustrate a particular facet of personal identity which they illuminate before going on to summarise what we have found out about the appearance of our own selves.

Look Me! – The Special Case of Self Portraits

In the case of self portraits there is complete identity between sitter and painter and the representation is a specific reflection of the subject who creates the image. The representation of characteristics beyond visual appearance is therefore specially privileged in the case of the self-portrait. In painting a portrait the artist may deduce what she can about the sitter and this may or may not be accurate, the rest is down to the skill of the artist in representing what she finds. In self-portraiture the artist has no deduction to make, her own subject is most intimately known, and while it is notable that some self-portraits, particularly in the modern era can, bear scant visual resemblance to their subjects, it is still simply a case of representing what is already known to the artist. This self-reflecting makes self-portraiture a form of self presentation and, I will argue, self-affirmation. I proposed to approach this through Descartes classic affirmation of his own indubitable existence.

Descartes famous pronouncement *cogito ergo sum*[30] has been interpreted in many ways but remains both compelling and enigmatic. For the purposes of this discussion I will take one of the more controversial interpretations of the *cogito* which has been propounded by Hintikka.[31] Hintikka argues that the truth of the *cogito* can only be given in its performance, or at least that Descartes proof of the certainty of his own existence is performatory in nature. That is, the statements 'I exist' and, 'I think' verify themselves through their performance. Every time I say, 'I am', or for that matter, 'I think', I demonstrate my own existence. This interpretation is radical and has certainly not been central to Cartesian scholarship but I think it contains within it at least the way forward in showing how the *cogito* really works. The *cogito* is not a syllogistic sort of proof nor is it *merely* self-evident; however I believe that the fact that the *cogito* is self-evident indicates that it is also an act of self-affirmation. In truth it is a primary act of self-affirmation and, as this, it tells us much about our idea of personal identity.

I want to argue that being and identity are about doing; active and not passive, changing and not essential, and that an interpretation of the *cogito* along these lines is needed to show its real power. I want to say that when I say 'I am' I am *demonstrating* my own existing, my own be-ing. This takes Hintikka's ideas a little further and makes available a more fruitful interpretation of the *cogito*. It is an interpretation that is very much in tune with the very act of self-portraiture and reinforces the theory that being is fundamentally doing, an active existing rather than a static essence. Once we move from a static, and fundamentally essentialist conception of the self, to an active self-creating and self-sustaining notion of selfhood then the *cogito* becomes the performance of being at its most basic level, that is, it represents the most fundamental sort of doing, which is the awareness of my own being.

Hintikka says that there is an existential presupposition in the *cogito* in that 'I think' presupposes 'I am', however it seems to me that the case is much more like 'I am thinking' presupposes 'I am existing' because existing is itself the performance of being, and for being its meaning is in this performance. This takes us a vital step further and changes the sense of 'being' from the passive noun to the active verb. It goes beyond Hintikka's position by emphasising the performatory nature of the cogito to the extent that it stops being anything like the subject at all and becomes the performance itself, and as Gadamer once said the real meaning and being of the play is in the performance.[32]

In essence Descartes has shown that if he stops thinking he stops existing, or, in existential terms if he loses the ability to think (perform) he loses his existence. This may be a weaker formulation of the *cogito* than if it were construed as a logical proof and it places a significant weight on thinking, but it means that thinking, or awareness, as performance, is inextricably linked to existing and to being, and constitutes the ultimate strength of the *cogito*. Descartes proof of his own existence is not an analytical or a logical proof, nor is it simply a performatory truth. It is an existential demonstration; that is, it is all about the way that I am, or the way that I find myself. No proof at all is ever going to be available because it is not necessary. We delude ourselves that a proof of our existence is needed and when we ourselves sit down to muse on the problem, our own identity must be already apparent. The process which Descartes describes, particularly in the First and Second Meditations, is the defining example of consciousness at the work of working itself out. This is the being which can question itself in its own being and the process that Descartes is engaged in is just this questioning. As Hintikka says,

> Descartes in effect says that one cannot think that one doubts anything without thereby demonstrating to oneself that one exists. (Hintikka, 1968, p.134)

Or as Kenny puts it, "Consciousness carries with it indubitabiltiy".[33] This means that the fundamental act of self demonstration is also singular because this kind of existential performance can only be singular. Although we may say that everyone thinks, so everyone exists (by deduction) the demonstration of self hood is not like this, we can only do it for ourselves. However we must not be misled into thinking that this kind of thinking leads us to the isolated subject of the Cartesian tradition as Williams says,

> In a solipsistic universe in which nothing and no-one exists except in me and "for me", what function can it fulfil? None, for the 'I' is ubiquitous. There is nothing, nor can there be anything, from which it is to be distinguished. Yet it is in this way that the world appears to Descartes at the crucial point at which the *cogito* is situated. (Williams, 1968, p.106)

It is from this solipsistic universe that we must escape and the way out is to change our understanding of being from essential thing to active self fashioning being, and to re-remember our fundamental and inescapable being-in-the-world. Only in this way, at the crucial point, can we avoid isolation. This brings us to a very different notion of the self, more like Heidegger's *Dasein* than Descartes thinking being, but a notion that is much more in tune with the way we appear to live our lives. Heidegger says,

> The idea of a subject which has intentional experiences merely inside its own sphere and is not yet outside it but encapsulated within itself is an absurdity which misconstrues the basic ontological structures of the being which we ourselves are. (Heidegger, 1988, p 64)

And, "For the Dasein there is no outside for which reason it is also absurd to talk about an inside."[34] Heidegger moves the thinking from the isolated Cartesian subject to the active, engaged, and essentially involved self which finds its being beyond the confines of its own consciousness. Our identity is not simply what we *are*, be that thinking being or physical body. Our identity is to found in what we *do*, beginning with the act of self-affirmation in the re-interpreted *cogito*. The perils that Sebald's three emigrants experienced are rooted in their isolation and their lack of meaningful involvement.

Self-portraiture, while it is obviously an act of self-representation or self-fashioning, is also an act of self-reflection. It is a form of active relation with the notion we have of ourselves at a specific time and rests on self-affirmation. Self portraits are acts of self-positing by artists, and what makes them possible is a conscious creative self which can project for itself an image of itself which is more than merely visual. Self-portraiture is not just like looking in the mirror. The true relationship of self-portraiture to being begins to emerge thus,

> We "ek-sist" by standing outside of our own being, thus transforming it into an appearance and relating to it as something lost. (Frank, 1995, p.77)

Self-portraits are themselves a manifestation of our existing, our standing-out and relating to our own being as something lost to be regained. And then,

> Lost being is thus represented under the schema of the past, not (yet) Being under that of the future, split between the two, the self loses its strict identity and is transformed into the continuity of a life history. (Frank, 1995, p.77)

First we throw ourselves outside ourselves by creating the self-portrait and then the preservation of the representation of ourselves in self portrait, at one time and in one place, becomes part of the story of our lives and exemplifies its continuity. We can look back on the self-portrait as a representation of what we were, or our being-past, from where we are now in the present. While an ordinary portrait might do this to some extent the privileged nature of self-portraits give these a special place in our own history of being This is because the primary act of self-affirmation, as exemplified in the *cogito*, is singular, so our own self-portrait represents a singular act of self affirmation. This in turn means that the kind of being that can make self-portraits is one that has self-awareness sufficient to attempt to create its own double. Self-portraiture is an attempt to create a sense of Otherness for ourselves and then to gaze upon this Other with recognition that it is our own self. We are thus provided with a means of attempting to affirm and understand ourselves by being able to experience the radical transformation of our own self into an Other. Self portraiture requires a being which is self conscious, capable of projecting its own idea of self, and able to experience itself as an Other. As Gadamer says of portraits,

> The portrait is only an intensification of what constitutes the essence of all pictures. Every picture is an increase of being and is essentially definable as representation, as coming-to-presentation. In the special case of the portrait this representation acquires a personal significance, in that here an individual is presented in a representative way. For this means that the person represented represents himself in his portrait and is represented by his portrait. (Gadamer, 1975, 2004, p.142)

If this is true of portraits then in the *special special* case of pictures that are self-portraits the intensity is both increased and contained within the existing being of the artist. Self-portraits are attempts to affirm identity by re-presenting the self and are produced by a kind of being which is self conscious and capable of projecting and imagining, an active and creative kind of being which both re-presents and questions itself.

Summary

Having roamed widely across the territory of the notion of personal identity I hope that it will now be possible to provide at least a map of the area which connects the various avenues of approach that I have chosen. We should at least be able to enumerate the most important aspects of this most personal idea and this is probably as much as we can expect. I suggest that a number of key concepts have emerged as central to our idea of personal identity; these are, in no particular order; continuity, meaning or purpose, recognition or validation, presence, self-reflection and self-affirmation.

The examples I have used from Sebald's work highlight some of these. The simple loss of his passport in "All'estero" means that the writer is no longer formally recognized and his temporary loss of identity is grounded in this loss of his passport. He has no means of showing the world who is really is and, although this loss is formal and temporary it is none the less disquieting. The three characters from *The Emigrants* have all suffered a loss of meaning or purpose from their lives; they no longer know what they are for anymore. For Paul Bereyter he cannot teach and Ambros Adelwarth has no purpose once Cosmo has died and he has no-one to serve. Henry Selwyn has lost his profession and his origins and lives a life of pointless idleness. All of them have lost the ability to answer the question "Who am I?" or more pertinently "What am I for?" Sebald's Austerlitz stands in much the same position as these three at the beginning of his story but in this case we see the rediscovery of a lost identity, not through the gaining of a purpose, but through the restoration of origins and continuity. Austerlitz's search is a search for his origins and the confirmation of the continuity of his identity. In the same way that Henry Selwyn has been sundered from his origins in Lithuania Austerlitz has suffered the complete loss of his past before the time he arrived in England. He does not know who he was and has no means, through memory, of connecting himself now with the same self as a child. This search for origins, I suggest, reflects our need to understand identity as continuous and ongoing as well as meaningful or purposive. This lack of origin is keenly felt by both Henry Selwyn and Jacques Austerlitz, both have had their names changed and neither is able to connect themselves with who they once were. To this extent their identity is broken and it is only when Austerlitz is finally able to recover his identity and, as Sebald would have it, begin to understand the Czech language, that he is able to avoid the despair that finally overtakes Henry Selwyn. It is essential that Austerlitz goes through this process for himself, no amount of being told about his lost history by his headmaster or even by his nurse Vera can fill the gap in his identity, and he must re-discover his own identity through the experience of searching. These examples from Sebald show both that having a purpose, and the need to connect with the same self at earlier times and thereby recognizing the continuity of identity, are important to us in understanding who we are.

In the case of modern controversies about face transplants and the covering of faces we see that social cohesion or, from an individual's point of view, the recognition given to us by others as one like themselves, or just a simple feeling of belonging, appears to be very important. The problem with the patient in need of a face transplant is that, although they are recognized, they are not recognized as 'one of us' because of their deformity. The yearning for anonymity expressed by these poor individuals is a yearning for acceptance and the validation of their humanity by others. Similarly the wearing of veils deprives those who wear them of the same validation. In this way both the deformed (accidentally) and the veil wearers (deliberately) become apart from the world because they do not participate in the mutual recognition which we all need to realize our own self conscious being. Hegel's abstract reflections are another way of saying the same thing. We need another self-consciousness to recognize us as self-conscious, and we make this possible as a self-conscious being by recognizing this other as one like ourselves. We are thus dependent on each other for the recognition we all need and we can only gain this by accepting our necessary publicness.

In the portrait we come to understand that it is not just visual appearance that leads to identity. Portraits, like Sebald's stories and Bachelard's insistence that we dream, are invitations to our imagination. We see the picture but it is not the visual information which leads us to the person. The identity of the sitter is evoked and it is up to us to open our thinking to this evocation. To focus on the merely visual is to deny ourselves the illusion of presence and to miss the point in the same way that those who only gather the endless facts of history fail to grasp the meaning of historicality.

Self-portraiture is an example of the self-affirmation and self-reflection that we are able to exercise. This means that we have an active relationship with ourselves and are able to put before ourselves the continuity of our own identity and to contemplate our own being. Heidegger is describing this when he says that we are the being which can question itself in our own being.[35] We are, to ourselves, an of object of investigation however paradoxical it may seem, and the making of self portraits is one example of the way that we do this and, as such, shows that we are the kind of being that is capable of reflection on own being.

Although these may seem like relatively meager results for a not inconsiderable effort we have at least avoided the pitfalls and dead ends of some more traditional philosophical approaches to the question of identity. By taking a more oblique and varied approach to the ways that we appear to ourselves, I think that we have revealed some simple and practical truths about this question as well as provoking further thinking.

In the next and final chapter I will summarize the work as a whole as well as providing a practical application of the kind of thinking that I have tried to promote in this book. I will also return to Heidegger for the last word.

Notes

1 Sebald, 2002, *Vertigo*, p.58.
2 Sebald, 2002, *The Emigrants*, p.49.
3 Sebald, 2002, *The Emigrants*, pp.3-23.
4 Sebald, 2002, *The Emigrants*, p.5.
5 Sebald, 2002, *The Emigrants*, pp.65-145.
6 Sebald, 2002, *Austerlitz*, p.98.
7 Sebald, 2002, *Austerlitz*, p.219.
8 Daily Telegraph, 27th October 2006
9 Daily Telegraph, 27th October 2006.
10 Daily Telegraph, 24th September 2001.
11 Daily Telegraph, 25th November 2006.
12 Sunday Telegraph 24th December 2006.
13 Sartre, 1956, Part Three.
14 Sartre, 1956, pp. 252-302.
15 Sartre, 1956, p.259
16 Sartre, 1956, p.255.
17 Sartre, 1956, p.270.
18 Sartre, 1956, p.270.
19 Sartre, 1956, p.263.
20 Hume, 1959, Vol. 1 pp. 239-240.
21 Westerman, 1996, p.131.
22 The original is in the Kunstmuseum, Offentliche Kunstsammlung, Basle.
23 Buck, 1999, p.94. The original is in the Royal Collection, Windsor.
24 Foister, 2006, p.15.
25 The original is in the Alte Pinakhothek Bayerische Staatsgemaldeesammlungen, Munich.
26 Buck, 1999, p.85.
27 Hegel, 1977, p.111.
28 Heidegger, 1962, Part One, Division One, Section IV and elsewhere.
29 This is Heidegger's term and does not mean simply *alongside*. Its more profound meaning is set out in *Being and Time* particularly in Part One, Division One, Section IV.
30 Descartes, 1986, p.17.
31 Hintikka, 1968, pp.108-139.
32 Gadamer, 1975, 2004, p.309, referring to Aristotle, *Politics* and *Nichomachean Ethics*.
33 Kenny, 1993, p.70.
34 Heidegger, 1988, p.66.
35 Heidegger, 1962, H.12, and elsewhere.

CHAPTER NINE

IMAGINATIVE UNDERSTANDING

In this final chapter I will attempt to do three things by way of bringing this book to a conclusion. First I will draw together the four strands of thinking from Bachelard, Sebald, Gadamer and Heidegger that I have developed in the previous thematically structured chapters. I think that by now the similarities between their approaches have become clear, so the task of bringing these strands together should be uncontroversial. I will call the result 'imaginative understanding' and I will then use this term to denote the commonality that I have suggested between these four writers. Second, I will provide a worked example in which imaginative understanding is applied to a specific kind of practical knowledge. I will do this to show that imaginative understanding is no kind of vague mysticism and indeed that it is vital to the accumulation and application of clinical knowledge. I hope that the demonstration of the role of imaginative understanding in clinical practice will dispel any remaining doubts that my readers might have about the value and usefulness of the approach that I am suggesting. I think that any theory which purports to say something about our knowledge of the world must show that it has applications in the real world of everyday practice. The example of clinical knowledge will provide this as well as indicating how imaginative understanding underpins all of our knowledge of the world. Third, and finally, I want to return to some of Heidegger's work. Having shown how effective imaginative understanding can be in helping us to understand how we come to know the world through the way that it appears to us, I want to spend some time addressing the question, What is it about the world and our consciousness which makes imaginative understanding so important? The answer to this question will give at least a clue as to why it is that the approaches set out by, Bachelard, Sebald, Gadamer and Heidegger, have so much in common.

Imaginative Understanding

Heidegger's ideas of emergence and reticence, Sebald's spectral materialism, Bachelard's oneirism, and Gadamer's notion of inescapable Bildung, provide means by which the everyday can be approached and understood in its everydayness. They share a common imaginative approach to the world which allows the world to appear rather than having to be forcibly extracted. They are the observers who watch the butterflies in the meadow rather than the collectors of specimens who insist on pinning the dead insects to a board and making them an object of display. Above all they recognize that that the world is already a display and does not need to be made into one.

All of the writers that I have discussed share an appeal to the imagination and a consequent reversal of the epistemological priority of our thinking, away from the precision of what we might call scientific cognition and towards a more fluid and less precise understanding of the world. In the end it turns out that this apparently less precise approach has more in common with the nature of the world itself and preserves both the unity and the fragility of the onset of the image. We have seen how Severs bold attempt to make the past appear succeeded at 18 Folgate Street, not through a collection of artifacts kept in a museum but through an attempt to create an experience of the past, based on a scene set by Severs and resulting in a strong appeal to the imagination of his visitors. This shows that Severs had an inherent understanding of the nature of history and of time itself, not as an accumulation of moments but as a totality to be experienced and understood as a unity. In Rilke's poetic prose we can feel his anguish, and sometimes his horror, at the world which is exposed in his thinking. The sheer reality of the things he finds in the world overwhelms him and he has to look away. He enables us to begin to see through the surface of what we come across in the world and to experience what is really there. In a different way Sebald's often limpid descriptions nag away at our thinking with quiet insistence, gently calling to us to notice the world and provoking our imagination in ways which we would usually disregard. Bachelard's somnambulistic meanderings provoke in us the same kind of imaginative response as he urges us to drop our frenzied engagement with the world for just a moment longer. He "schools us in slowness" just enough to give free rein to our imagination and to re-establish the priority of imagination in our thinking. By creating this small space Bachelard allows the world to appear to us as we find it, rather than as we have made it, and in just the moment before we destroy it with description. Bachelard perhaps comes closest of all of these thinkers to the "onset of the image" and helps us to gain a fleeting glimpse of the world before it becomes immersed in our activity.

In the works of Gadamer and Heidegger the project of restoring the priority of imagination is much more explicit and their work lacks some of the poetry of the others. Both Gadamer and Heidegger provide essential underpinnings to this kind of thinking and are able to show how it is possible in the first place. In this way they safeguard the imaginative approach from any accusations of mysticism. Gadamer recognizes that we are embedded in the world and that this world makes us what we are and who we are. Our participation in Bildung is not voluntary or even conscious, it is simply inescapable. In common with Severs, Gadamer's discussion of tradition shows us that we can only understand history and time as a continuing unity, and that this is a unity in which we are playing our own continuing part. This understanding of the world can be exhibited through the seemingly frivolous activity of play. Finally, Heidegger directly confronts the philosophical tradition and moves us briskly back to the imagination as the centre for our understanding of the world and our place in it. Heidegger's work is not at all like the poetic prose of Rilke or the quiet dreaming of Sebald and Bachelard. Heidegger wants to achieve a sea change in the way that we think, away from the fragmented post-Cartesian world of the priority of scientific cognition and towards a unified, but equally rigorous, phenomenological epistemology and ontology which does not reject scientific cognition as a mode of knowing, but describes the ground on which it must stand and, in so doing, he points to the origins of scientific cognition.

It is from this perspective of imaginative understanding, a perspective which enables appearance, that all of these thinkers provide us with a means to understand the world. This is not the kind of spectatorial observation offered by the Cartesian and post-Cartesian perspective, it is specifically a kind of understanding which not only recognizes the possibility of engagement but also understands that this engagement will be based on an underlying unity between consciousness and world. The interpretation of our practical engagement in the world leads to a rejection of the conclusion that we are primarily separate from the world, a conclusion which makes the possibility of engagement problematic. However it does not necessarily imply an inevitable pragmatism in which the world can only be revealed to us when we engage. All of these thinkers remind us that that world is there whether we choose to notice it or not.

I will now look at a very important kind of knowledge in which we will see that imaginative understanding is not any kind of esoteric theory but is a way of thinking with significant practical applications. This will finally put to bed any lingering suspicions that the reversal of epistemological polarity in favour of the imagination means a descent into mysticism.

Clinical Knowledge - A Worked Example[1]

Some time ago I spent several years working on a project to implement clinical effectiveness with Family Doctors in the NHS in East Kent.[2] During this time it became clear that the greatest problem with evidence based medicine was finding a method to make sure that it is implemented in practice. The problem was not that the doctors did not know what the science was telling them to do, that much was clear, the difficult bit was putting the science into practice, to implement the evidence in their encounters with individual patients. If the benefits of research are not delivered to real patients in the real world then they are useless, so overcoming the problem with implementation was crucial. It should have been simple, the science was clear, but of course it never is simple in real life. In fact as the project moved forward it very quickly became clear that the doctors, even those who were strongly in favour of an evidence based approach, were using knowledge from a variety of sources, and not exclusively from the evidence that we were giving them. While the evidence was important it was not the whole story. This became especially apparent from our discussion with the doctors of some individual cases where a number of factors had come into play. This kind of thing is now well understood and the reasons for it are quite apparent. First of all there are probably no treatments which have been proved totally effective in all cases. Even the evidence from the best randomized control trials is equivocal to some degree, and therefore insufficient to determine every case. In layman's terms the drugs or procedures don't work for everybody all the time. This is reinforced by the fact that trials are conducted on carefully selected groups of patients who do not represent a representative cross section of real patients. The evidence that trials produce is all about probability and they tend to express likelihood in terms of numbers of patients we need to treat to avoid an adverse event. We may know that as many as five out of every seven or eight patients will benefit from a particular therapy but we don't know which five. The equation is further complicated by the virtual inevitability of side effects, doing good has to be balanced against doing no harm, again with no certainty as to where this may fall. Add into this greater demand for patient involvement in the choice of treatments, and even evidence based clinical decisions become frighteningly complicated and inevitably multi-faceted, to the extent that other sources of knowledge automatically come into play. Our doctors in East Kent were using knowledge drawn from a variety of sources and were then balancing the options in the specific context of each patient. It seems to be the case that the ability of clinicians to implement evidence in practice requires a particular kind of knowing which is not, and cannot be, evidence based or purely scientific. And yet this know-how or practical wisdom is essential if the benefits of scientifically derived evidence based medicine are to be brought into practice.

Knowledge

At bottom, clinical knowledge is not essentially different to any other kind of knowledge that we have about the world, that is, its status as knowledge must be philosophically grounded in the same way that all our knowledge about the world is grounded. Clinical epistemology is a sub-species of everyday epistemology, and in the same way that evidence based medicine forms one part of clinical epistemology so our simple scientific cognition of the world forms only one part of everyday epistemology. In this example I want to show how imaginative understanding grounds the complex networks of knowledge that underpin clinical practice. I want to show how things like the half remembered lessons of medical school, the received experience of senior clinicians, and even the anecdotal experience of colleagues have an essential contribution to make to clinical judgment.

Throughout this book I have been looking abstractly at four different means by which we can gain knowledge and understanding of the world. These are Heidegger's ideas of emergence and reticence, Sebald's spectral materialism, Bachelard's oneirism, and Gadamer's notion of Bildung. All of these represent oblique approaches to the acquisition of knowledge and provide a means by which the world can be approached and understood. Using these approaches I have described ways of talking about the world which avoid the distortion and reduction that simple empirical or evidential engagement necessarily brings. This has not been an argument against empirical or scientific engagement with the world. This engagement is necessary in the sense that it is required to support our everyday existing; the point is that it cannot provide a comprehensive way of understanding the world. Neither, therefore, is this an argument specifically against an evidence based approach to clinical practice. It will however show that any reductive approach, including evidence based medicine, will never be a wholly adequate means to understand and to implement the knowledge we can have about the world, and therefore that effective clinical care can only be delivered on the basis of multi-faceted knowledge based on a multiplicity of equally valid approaches. Finally this is not an argument about hierarchies of knowledge. I am not sure at all what different kinds of knowledge would look like or how we would go about describing or ranking them, nor can I imagine what kind of knowledge we would need to distinguish between them or where the evidence needed to establish such a hierarchy of knowledge could come from. I will now briefly reprise these four approaches and it will become apparent how the work of these thinkers provides the foundation for the knowledge that all clinicians need to ground their practice.

Heidegger

In the section of *Being and Time* headed 'The Existential Constitution of the "There"' Heidegger says, "When irrationalism, as the counterplay of rationalism, talks about the things to which rationalism is blind, it does so only with a squint".[3]

This occurs in a part of *Being and Time* in which Heidegger is trying to show that the ways through which we usually seek to understand the world, our rational scientific, empirical, describing and delineating approach, although apparently rendering the world open to us, in fact close off the world and provide us with only a superficial understanding. So, when irrationalism as the counterplay of rationalism sees and talks about those things which rationalism fails to see, it is as if irrationalism sees by squinting, through the distractions of the everyday, thereby allowing us to encounter the world in a different way. But is it only able to do this by looking at the world with a squint, that is not directly, not in the manner of rationalism, but irrationally in a way that instinctively seems less, not more, appropriate to seeing and understanding. Heidegger is here suggesting a different way of seeing the world by looking past what we might term our rational, or even scientific, kind of engagement and allowing the world to appear as it is, as opposed to how we would make it as something reduced for our own purposes. Heidegger is asking us to take an imaginative approach.

Later he is more explicit about avoiding a kind of confrontational approach to the phenomena of the world when he says, "talking extensively about something, covers it up and brings what is understood to a sham clarity—the unintelligibility of the trivial."[4] It now appears that the way we might think that we will encounter the world in all its richness, by talking about it, is not the way that this can be achieved. This turns out to be an approach that not only misses the target but obscures it at the same time. We will not only fail in our attempt to encounter the world authentically by this route but we will imagine that we have been successful. We will remain in blissful ignorance with no idea of what we do not know. He says,

> Both talking and hearing are based on understanding. And understanding arises neither through talking at length nor through busily hearing something "all around". Only he who already understands can listen." (Heidegger, 1962, H.164)

And later to complete the inversion,

> Keeping silent has been characterized as an essential possibility of discourse. Anyone who keeps silent when he wants to give us to understand something must 'have something to say'. (Heidegger, 1962, H.296)

As well as reminding us that sometimes it is as important to know what we don't know Heidegger is also reversing the position that we would usually assume in which rationalism and discourse bring clarity and definition. Heidegger suggests that, for real understanding and clarity, we must look to apparently deficient kinds of perception, like not-saying and squinting, both of which allow the world to appear as it is and not as we have made it. It seems to be that the way to the world lies in ways of seeing that we may previously have characterized as deficient but which it now begins to transpire, tell us more, not less, about the world. Paradoxically, it is only through reticence that intelligibility is articulated. Our constant striving for the kind of understanding that rationalism promises only confuses, and ultimately defeats, our attempts to understand. We are left to be rescued by the irrational squint.

Sebald

W.G. Sebald tells us more about the places he visits and the people he encounters by not telling us what we expect to hear, his stories are idiosyncratic and often take a quietly unexpected turn. He does not simply give us a description of what he sees, for example *The Rings of Saturn*, the story of a walking tour of Suffolk, is neither a travelogue nor a grown up version of what I did on my holidays, it is a tour de force of history, art, and philosophy because of the stories Sebald chooses to tell and the ways in which he tells them. Sebald is quietly bringing to our attention the usually unaccounted aspects of the world in which we find ourselves. He creates a dream like atmosphere around his characters and his locations, and bids us see them through half closed eyes as a means of gaining not a reduced but a deeper understanding of their history and significance. Above all Sebald has us look again at the apparently inconsequential, and as we do so, the things that we expect to tell us nothing now begin to tell us so much. In Heidegger's terms Sebald invites us to rise above the chatter of idle talk and to encounter the world anew, albeit with a squint. Sebald appeals to our imagination.

Sebald's use of memory and dreams give him powerful devices through which to view the world and which, though they appear to be irrational and often incomplete, provide clarity and a recall which is sometimes astonishing. Sebald shows us that we already know that things are not always what we might think they are and his work brings this knowing to the fore. He makes us aware that what we suppose we know is already conditioned by what we knew before, and in so doing provides a kind of commentary on what we call evidence. The kind of eloquent silence that Sebald conjures up by his crab-like approach to his subject matter allows him to say what he wants to say by almost not-saying at all. Sebald does not so much describe the events that happen to him and his characters as simply bear witness to what is going on, almost as if he were not himself the creator of the characters and scenes. They are not reduced by his descriptions but allowed to appear. So, by not-saying, by suggesting that we stand back and think a little, Sebald appears to say more rather than less and, paradoxically, his descriptions of places and events are the richer and more vivid for his not-saying. We must imagine for ourselves rather than wait for someone to tell us. Our knowledge is thereby increased by this not-quite looking and not-quite saying. This is strongly reminiscent of Heidegger's warning about saying too much and is Sebald's way of letting the world speak for itself. In Sebald's work the world is not described to us but revealed, and the silence that Sebald cultivates becomes eloquent. As Swales puts it in his essay on Sebald,

> Sebald's prose ... never quite manages to say what he wants to say. He can talk round about it; in this way he gives us 'the eloquence of the not quite said'. (Swales, 2003, pp.86-87)

Bachelard

As we have seen in so many respects the work of Gaston Bachelard has much in common with Sebald's spectral materialism, and although his mode of expression often appears more delicately poetic than philosophically rigorous there is without doubt a firm philosophical core to what he has to say. Bachelard takes the enterprise further by specifically emphasizing the oneiric, or dreaming, as a route to the world. The dream and the daydream are the ways in which we penetrate to the core both of the being of the world and our own being. It is clear that Bachelard, like Sebald, is using a method that captures the richness and complexity of experience and avoids any kind of reductionism. Bachelard recognizes that the immediacy of appearance must be preserved.

The same kind of thinking would not be out of place if we were here talking about patients and what we believe to be wrong with them. Bachelard's phrase "the problem of description"[5] shows that he knows well the danger to our understanding posed by reductive empiricism. Bachelard sees that, "the primary virtues",[6] far from being given to us by description are beyond description. In Bachelard's work the image precedes the thought and dreams precede contemplation. It is in reverie that we are sensitive and receptive to the world and he warns us not to wake up too soon because,

> Already when we describe a daydream *objectively* this diminishes and interrupts it. How many dreams told objectively, have become nothing but oneirism reduced to dust! In the presence of an image that dreams, it must be taken as an invitation to continue the daydream that created it. (Bachelard, 1958, 1994, p.152)

Bachelard's point is not only that it is within this dreaming that we can encounter that which is destroyed or lost in the "problem of description" but that without oneiric experience we reduce to dust some of the things that are only clear when we allow ourselves to dream. Differentiating, describing and categorizing lead to a reduction of our encounter with the world, and without these evidential approaches the reduction does not take place. We are then left with all that description would have discarded and which is now left available to our imagination so that,

> The imagination is not … the faculty for forming images of reality; it is the faculty of forming images which go beyond reality, which sing reality. (Bachelard, 1942, 1982, p.16)

Imagination does not curtail experience, it expands it. The singing of reality is that which is all too often drowned out by our systematic process of description and differentiation, and it is by overcoming these problems that we can allow reality to sing out. In simple and less poetic terms, we allow the world to appear as it is, and not as we would make it, in this way we see more, not less, of the world. In the practical terms of clinical judgment Bachelard would have our doctors make sure that they are seeing the patient and not just a set of symptoms or a disease. Bachelard's world is a world of evocation which leads to an immediate, that is an unmediated, awareness of a reality which is felt and lived rather than described and reasoned. Immediacy is vital and forms the cornerstone of this imaginative phenomenology. Rather than have us squint at the world Bachelard would have us see through the half-closed eyes of the daydream. By doing this he has reunited us with a world that we had lost.

Gadamer

In addressing the question, "how is understanding possible?" Gadamer says that,

> This is a question which precedes any action of understanding on the part of subjectivity, including the methodical activity of the interpretive sciences and their norms and rules. (Gadamer, 1975, 2006, p.xxvii)

He also recognizes that "our perception is never a simple reflection of what is given to the senses".[7] Our direction of travel in this argument is already backwards as we are thrown back beyond any action of understanding in the attempt to explain understanding itself. Moreover as we have already learned,

> What we call experience and acquire through experience is a living historical process; its paradigm is not the discovery of facts but the peculiar fusion of memory and expectation into a whole. (Gadamer, 1975, 2006, p. 217)

Experience, understanding and perception are no simple matters and are, as Gadamer indicates, bound up with memory, history and expectation. For Gadamer perception and understanding are inseparable from Bildung. Bildung is usually translated as 'culture' but, as we have seen, this misses out the full richness of Gadamer's idea which includes historical tradition, the structures of language and all of the customs and mores we grow up with, so that,

> Every individual is always engaged in the process of Bildung and in getting beyond his naturalness, inasmuch as the world into which he is growing is one that is primarily constituted through language and custom. (Gadamer, 1975, 2006, p.13)

And, "In Bildung ... that by which and through which one is formed becomes completely ones own." And Bildung goes on,

> The result of Bildung is not achieved in the manner of a technical construction, but grows out of a process of inner formation and cultivation, and therefore remains in a continual state of Bildung. (Gadamer, 1975, 2006, p.10)

All of this provides no more than a background to Gadamer's way of thinking and shows that his view of understanding and of our relationship with the world is not as simple as we might have imagined it to be. In the context of a discussion of clinical knowledge Gadamer can be seen to be telling us that our evidence based knowledge is only part of Bildung, and that we seek to ignore the totality at our peril. We are, as it were, wrapped up in the world to the extent that our own development is our development into Bildung. Bildung is neither something to be avoided nor something to come to terms with, it is just what it is and what we are. Bildung is both unavoidable and essential to our being-in-the-world. This participation is exemplified in the context of our present discussion when we consider some brief remarks, near to the beginning of *Truth and Method*, on the idea of tact.

Gadamer seems to echo some of the things that Heidegger said when he talks about tact in the first part of *Truth and Method*.

> By tact we understand a special sensitiveness to situations and how to behave in them for which knowledge from general principles does not suffice. Hence an essential part of tact is that it is tacit and unformulable. (Gadamer, 1975, 2006, p.14)

And thus,

> To pass over something does not mean to avert one's gaze from it, but to keep an eye on it in such a way that rather than knock into it, one slips by it. Thus tact helps one to preserve distance. It avoids the offensive, the intrusive, the violation of the intimate sphere of the person. (Gadamer, 1975, 2006, p.15)

This "special sensitiveness" and the avoidance of violation and intrusion are again reminiscent of Heidegger's emphasis on reticence and Sebald's not-quite saying. We appear to have, in tact, a way of encountering the world which, while noticing and drawing the everyday to our attention, does not begin the processes of description, designation, categorization and evidential reduction. Indeed the essence of tact is noticing without giving notice. Tact is a deliberate device that we use when we do not wish or need to make explicit our noticing. In the context of Bildung and our inevitable participation in the world we acquire tact as a means of understanding not only the object (of tact) but the whole phenomenological context of our world. Tact and the exercise of tact is not simply a way in which we relate to a particular object, it is a way of being towards the whole complex of objects and Others that make up the world. We notice but we do not share our noticing, nor do we actively make this noticing part of our own existing. Tact is a way in which we notice that which we do not wish to acknowledge but which we take into account all the same, it is certainly not the kind of knowing that we would call evidence based but it underlies all of our explicit knowing. Of all of our ways of noticing, tact lies at the junction of our active participation in the world; it is both a way of noticing and a way of remaining silent. Tact is the sidelong glance (or squint) at the world, a knowing glance but one that remains unspoken, a way of looking at the world in which we conspire with others not to notice the world. Under the glance of tact we can know the world without calling it forth, without tactful regard and the store of knowledge it brings we cannot function.

Squinting

Gadamer's tact, Heidegger's reticence, Bachelard's oneirism and Sebald's oblique approach to his subjects, all these tell of ways of encountering the world which may appear to be unnecessarily laboured, superficial or even pretentious. However we have now begun to see that if we want to see what is important about the world, and in particular to see the structures which enmesh us in the world, these avenues of approach will prove much more fruitful than the directly confrontational evidential, scientific and pseudo-scientific methods which we might have hoped would tell us what we want to know. From all of these thinkers it is clear that a purely evidence based approach to the world is inadequate because it is necessarily reductionist, and consequently deficient in not allowing us to see the things we really need to see. To achieve this we must, regard tactfully or as Heidegger puts it, see with a squint. In the same way clinicians must use an unspoken and tacit knowledge in making their judgements. It is this knowledge that provides the bridge between evidence and real live patients; it is this unspoken know-how that brings the benefits of evidence to real live patients.

Putting it into Practice

It should be clear by now where and how this kind of thinking relates to the debate about evidence based medicine, and in particular to the different kinds of evidence that are used in the process of clinical judgement. Evidence based medicine has produced a multitude of benefits for patients but the application of evidence requires a distinctly different kind of knowing, without this knowing the opportunities of evidence based medicine cannot be turned into patient benefit. To do this we need imaginative understanding, an approach which, by refusing reduction, goes beyond simple scientific cognition, and which recognizes the ground on which this cognition rests. From my own experience of working with doctors in East Kent it is clear that many lives were extended through the use of an evidence based approach. However it was also clear that, in practice, the approach was tempered and mediated through the imaginative understanding and practical wisdom of individual doctors, and that this imaginative understanding was the key to the successful implementation of the project. It is perhaps significant that some clinicians find it difficult to respond to the demands of evidence based medicine not because they are unaware of the evidence, but either because they lack the imaginative understanding needed to put it into practice, or perhaps because they fear the uncertainty that this approach necessarily brings with it .

The ways in which the evidence based medicine has been thrust into a predominant position in clinical practice has led to a reduction in the richness of clinical judgments and the progressive devaluation, and even discrediting, of other approaches which are not based on the kind of reduction that evidence based medicine demands. However these other sources of knowledge provide an essential component of effective care. Anecdotes, narratives of patients and clinical practitioners, accumulated experience, past and ongoing episodes of education and training, even informal discussions with colleagues, all of these are not examples of evidence based practice but neither are they detrimental or incidental to the accumulation of the knowledge which has to inform practice. These often unspoken understandings are central to clinical practice because they make it possible for the evidence derived from carefully constructed and controlled trials to be implemented in large and diverse populations which do not match the composition of the trial groups. They are also the ways of knowing that Heidegger, Sebald, Bachelard and Gadamer are describing. Clinicians, even those who are devotees of evidence based medicine, cannot afford to forget the value of all the other sources of their knowledge, neither can they allow anyone to devalue or deprecate the importance of these sources. They are the essential components of

Bildung, the eloquent silence, the unexpected recollections and memories, and the dream which precedes reduction. Seeing with a squint involves seeing not only what is clear and distinctly presented but seeing that which disappears from sight when we look too hard, and this makes it a vital component of effective clinical practice.

Heidegger Again

In this concluding section I will take the analysis a little bit further by looking a bit closer at some of the things that Heidegger has to say about knowledge and world. One of the aims of his work is to reverse the epistemological polarity between theory and practice, in simple terms this means that, in Heidegger's world everyday experience takes priority over what we might call scientific cognition. It is through our engagement with the world that we can come to know the world rather than gaining engagement through the acquisition of knowledge. However, as we shall see, this does not mean that Heidegger is some kind of naïve pragmatist. Engagement is one route by which we may approach the world, and it is the route by which we most commonly come to know the world, but this engagement itself is made possible by the primordial relationship we first have with the world, which must come before any engagement can take place. It is this relationship which grounds not only our everyday engagement, but also scientific cognition itself. Fell sets out Heidegger's primary thesis about how we come to know the world like this,

> Heidegger indicates specific pragmatic entities by the term "equipment" and by the ontological category "readiness-to-hand". The praxis by which this kind of being is disclosed he calls a kind of "concern" whose pre-theoretical way of seeing is "circumspection". What Heidegger especially wishes to show us is that the disclosures of this circumspective practice are *intrawordly* – that they are orientated and made possible by a totality of references or significative meanings that Heidegger calls a "world." (Fell, 1995 p.65)

This not only stresses the inevitability of engagement and describes the reversal of ontological polarity from theoretical contemplation towards practical activity, but also affirms the existence of the whole world as the referential context for our activity. The reason for this affirmation will become clear as the argument progresses. Heidegger himself describes "The Being of the Entities Encountered in the Environment" and how we can come to know them when he says,

The achieving of phenomenological access to the entities which we encounter, consists rather in thrusting aside our interpretative tendencies, which keep thrusting themselves upon us and running along with us, and which conceal not only the phenomenon of such 'concern', but even more those entities themselves as encountered of their own accord in our concern with them. (Heidegger, 1962, H.67)

These are the same tendencies which Bachelard urges us to put aside and the tendencies which Sebald manages to suppress in his writing about places and history. All of them show us that we need to find a new way to understand the world if we are to gain phenomenological access. It seems as if the way that we had previously supposed would lead us to the world (scientific cognition) obscures rather than reveals, and that other avenues of approach, (dreams, daydreams and play) which we might have considered deficient, could be more productive. The centrality of engagement to our understanding is given vividly and famously when Heidegger says,

the less we just stare at the hammer-thing, and the more we seize hold of it and use it, the more primordial relationship to it becomes, and the more universally it is encountered at that which it is—as equipment. (Heidegger, 1962, H.69)

If this is true of hammers then it should also be true of all the possible equipment that we could encounter. We are to look to our engagement with the world of things and to the equipmental nature of these things to understand how this engagement is possible, but there is more to it than practice. Heidegger is not a naïve pragmatist, and the way he wants us to understand the world is precisely not in terms of things.

Heidegger wants us to appreciate two distinct ways of understanding the world, one of which echoes through the works of both Sebald and Bachelard, and he gives us a simple example,

The botanist plants are not the flowers of the hedgerow; the 'source' which the geographer establishes for a river is not the 'springhead in the dale'. (Heidegger, 1962, H.70)

We have here a juxtaposition of the poetic and the scientific views of the world, and we have already seen that the poetic has much more to offer than we may have first thought, in the ways in which it liberates and broadens our conceptions of the worldly circumstances in which we find ourselves. This means that the interest here is not in the truth or otherwise of Heidegger's assertion's about flowers and springs but more in the reason why it appears to be true, and perhaps in the way that it makes us think of the landscapes painted by the Dutch painters. Our own imaginative understanding leads us to feel that there is something missing in the descriptions of the botanist and the geographer. Neither makes an appeal to our experience of the phenomena, and therefore neither gives us phenomenological access to either the flowers or the springhead, or for that matter to anything like the world we know from our experiences. Specifically the access that scientific cognition gives us is access to individual entities, or things, but not to a world, and significantly not to the world in its totality. It does not matter how many things we come to know they will never add up to a totality, in the same way that however many facts about the past we accumulate it will never give us a sense of history, and however much Austerlitz is told about his childhood it will not give him back his identity. Phenomenological access is given to us in our primordial and pre-theoretical experience and this can only be found when we "thrust aside" our tendency to interpret, or as Bachelard would have it, when we dream. This propels us towards pragmatism because interpretation is most often thrust aside in our unreflective and practical everyday activity; that is when we act apparently without thinking about what we are doing. Therefore while this does represent a reversal of epistemological polarity between scientific cognition and experience, it is not a demand that we discard scientific cognition. As we have seen in the example of clinical knowledge, both kinds of understanding are required and, as Fell puts it,

> Heidegger is not asking us to choose between the validity of science and the validity of ordinary experience. He is broadening and deepening the phenomenon of truth, not transferring it from one set of disciplines to another. (Fell, 1995 p.73)

Reduction blocks our access to the world and is the enemy of truth. It is not a matter of choosing one way or another to approach the world, without both we are lost. The problem is not that one way forward is right at the expense of another, nor even that we must try somehow to combine approaches which will at times contradict. Scientific cognition points us towards the botanist's flowers and the geographer's source, but this implies a model of world which is a collection of entities, with our knowledge growing ever larger as our stock of known entities increases. The world which Heidegger wants us to understand is not like this at all. In simple Heideggerian terms the world is not revealed as any kind of thing but in its 'worldness' or being as world, the decisive shift is between the noun and the verb, from things to doing. This is the kind of world that

Rilke is giving us in his account of the remaining wall of the demolished house. If we pursue the endless accumulation of scientific knowledge we will never encounter the world as a whole and as what it is, we will only have a more or less partial understanding, based on a percentage of the total things in the world that we might encounter. To achieve a complete understanding we must approach the world from a different direction, a direction which will give us the world complete. This will be a very different kind of thing from the world of things which we had supposed under the direction of scientific cognition, and it is in fact the way of understanding that underpins scientific cognition itself so that,

No matter where and however deeply science investigates the what-is it will never find Being. All it encounters, always, is what-is because its explanatory purpose makes it insist at the outset on what-is. But Being is not an existing quality of what-is, nor unlike what-is, can Being be conceived and established objectively. (Heidegger, 1968, p.384)

To encounter the world as a hermeneutic totality we must first find an alternative to scientific cognition which will itself ground scientific cognition, a poetic means of approaching the world like those given to us by Sebald and Bachelard. In doing this we will reverse the epistemological polarity and place everyday experience at the centre of understanding. We will also come to understand a world that we can recognize from our experience, a world that is rich and complex, and a world from which we can only then begin to extract the entitles which we encounter. We have already seen in Chapter Seven how this must also be true of history which cannot be complete as a collection of facts about the past. However large this collection might get it can never give us the whole of history which must be understood as a totality if it is to have any meaning at all. We have also seen in Chapter Eight how Austerlitz is only able to recover his lost childhood time existentially through his own experiences. This means that time itself must also be understood in the same way, not as a collection of moments but as fundamental and unified temporality. Time, like world, must be grasped as a whole if we are to understand our lived reality. We are in time like we are in a world, or more accurately; just as we are worldly so we are temporal. This is the spirit of the works of writers like, Sebald, Rilke and Nemirovsky and the spirit that grounded Severs' enterprise at 18 Folgate Street.

Angst and Nothing

All that remains now is to understand how Being can be conceived and established, if not objectively. To do this it will be necessary to return to the discussion of the importance of mood which links Heidegger with Sebald, Bachelard and Gadamer, and to look more specifically at what Heidegger has to say about angst[8] and Nothing. Heidegger's most epic account of this coming to the world is given in his rather messianic essay "What is Metaphysics?" I hope that we can navigate his elaborate prose and somewhat gothic imagery to arrive at some simple understanding of what he is trying to say. To begin with Fell remarks that,

> Even though ones' "first and for the most part" experience is a praxis disclosive of practical things that praxis is already a response to what it tries to conceal and forget: an original anxious disclosure of contingent and unmeaning nature. (Fell, 1995, p.77)

Thus pointing towards a ground on which practical engagement itself must rest and suggesting a mood through which it might be disclosed. I have already shown how Sebald, Bachelard and Gadamer all use something like mood. Sebald is bored and melancholic, Bachelard stresses the importance of the dream and Gadamer uses the notion of play and tactful regard. While dreams, play and tact may not in the technical sense qualify as moods they produce the same disinterested and disconnected feelings which are common to Sebald's boredom and melancholia and to the angst of Heidegger's work, they all rely on provoking an imaginative response. In Heidegger we will find a much more decisive and significant role for mood and for the mood of angst in particular. He begins by acknowledging a particular kind of boredom with a passage that also illustrates his use of poetic language,

> Real boredom comes when "one is bored". This profound boredom, drifting hither and thither in he abyss of existence like a mute fog, draws all things, all men and oneself along with them, together in a queer kind of indifference. This boredom reveals what-is in totality. (Heidegger, 1968, p.364)

The key word here is "indifference" as he tries to emphasize the sheer disconnection we experience in profound boredom. Sebald has shown how powerful this can be in his writing about place and history in which boredom provides him with the metaphysical space in which the world he encounters can appear, and Severs uses his term 'the space between' to denote the same phenomenon.

For Heidegger this disconnection is brought to the fore in the case of angst (or dread, or anxiety, depending on the translation). It is in angst that the world is disclosed to us, but disclosed in a very different way to the way that entities are disclosed in any of the other moods that Heidegger considers. Heidegger makes a critical distinction between the mood of angst and other moods like fear and curiosity, and this is a distinction which opens up the discussion and leads ultimately to the disclosure of world. Unlike angst, these other moods arise out of our preoccupation with the things in the world; we are afraid of something and we are curious about some things, we are therefore led from them to a world of things, a world which, as we have seen, can never be complete. In the mood of angst our discomfort has no object; it is nameless dread or fear of nothing, it is uncanniness and a sense of being not-at-home. It is therefore in the experience of angst that Dasein surpasses itself towards a world that is not-itself; that is, it recognizes the world as other. It is in angst that the sheer strangeness of this otherness is disclosed. In Heidegger's rather more gothic terms he says,

> An experience of Being as something "other" than everything that "is" comes to us in dread, provided that we do not, from dread of dread, i.e. in sheer timidity, shut our ears to the soundless voice which attunes us to the horrors of the abyss. (Heidegger, 1968, p.385)

This is the experience that Rilke so vividly describes in his account of the wall and it is also the kind of experience that Sebald is trying to provoke in his quiet prose. The reward for listening to this soundless voice is clear,

> Man alone of all beings when addressed by the voice of Being experiences the marvel of all marvels: that what-is is. Therefore the being that is called in its very essence to the truth of Being is always attuned in an essential sense. The clear courage for essential dread guarantees that most mysterious of all possibilities: the experience of Being (Heidegger, 1968, p.386)

In angst the world is not disclosed to us as a collection of entities or things, the world is to be no accumulation of objects accrued and examined as our 'knowledge' supposedly increases. In angst the world is disclosed as 'world'; that is, as everything that which we are not, and as such it is disclosed as a totality. It is in the mood of angst that we encounter our worldliness by experiencing ourselves as not-world. We are not removed from the world we are simply given to see it and our place in it, for what it is. Sebald with his bored melancholia, and Bachelard with his dreaming both encourage us to see and to understand the world and ourselves in this way, and in so doing they show us the foundation of the everyday.

The strangeness of the world is not the strangeness of the things that we find in it, it is the strangeness of the 'otherness' of the whole world, and this is revealed to us in angst. In angst the fact of the world is given to us as just that. This understanding is not dependent on the nature of any contents of the world that we might encounter; it is not an understanding of things but an understanding of world. It is only in this way that we can understand what it is to be in-a-world, and consequently, through this understanding, the only way in which we can come to understand ourselves as beings-in-the-world. This primordial relationship to world provides the ground for all of our further interactions. It is only when faced with world as that which we are not that we can come to understand both ourselves and world. Angst is a special case of mood because it is the mood that we experience in the face of nothing; it is in angst that we are brought face to face with the world as it is, and it is in angst that we understand the world as not-us, or as Heidegger puts it,

> Nihilation is not a fortuitous event; but understood as the relegation to the vanishing what-is-in-totality, it reveals the latter in all it's till now undisclosed strangeness as the pure "other"—contrasted with nothing. (Heidegger, 1968, p.369)

This means that, "The essence of Nothingness as original Nihilation lies in this: that it alone brings Dasein face to face with what-is as such." [9]

We can see this from the other side if we consider what is going on when we avoid angst, that is when we maintain a pre-occupation with our everyday activity and, as it were, look away from the sheer unknown meaninglessness of the world and the sheer contingency of our being in it at all, Heidegger calls this state of mind 'falling' and says,

> When in falling we flee into the "at home" of publicness, we flee in the face of the "not at home"; that is we flee in the face of the uncanniness which lies in Dasein as thrown being-in-the-world, which has been delivered over to itself in it Being. This uncanniness pursues Dasein constantly, and is a threat to the everyday lostness in "the they" though not explicitly. (Heidegger, 1962, H.189)

The language here is the language of flight, of the uncanny, and of threat. We do not wish to face nothingness and we run back to the everyday and in so doing avoid the world altogether. We preoccupy ourselves with or everyday activity and avoid understanding our primordial relationship with the world, even though it is this relationship which makes this activity possible in the first place. Heidegger puts it in even more exotic terms with,

> The dread felt by the courageous cannot be contrasted with the joy or even the comfortable enjoyment of a peaceable life. It stands—on the hither side of all such contrasts—in secret union with the serenity and gentleness of creative longing. (Heidegger, 1968, p.374)

And again perhaps less emotively, "Nothingness is the not of being and thus is Being explained from the point of view of being".[10]

It is angst that brings us to turn and face the 'not at home', the nothingness at the heart of being. This means that,

> An experience of Being as something "other" than everything that "is" comes to us in dread."(Heidegger, 1968, p.386)

This mood of angst, anxiety or dread, is unique in leading to this disclosure of the world as world, and world not as a collection of things but as that which is not-me and thus as a totality. In angst we come to know the being of the world as world, or as Heidegger might say in its worldness. It is because of this, and through this disclosure, that the world is revealed to us as a totality. The unity of the world is that which belongs to world as world, and it is only in the radical distinction between Dasein and world that this unity and totality can be revealed. This is a very long way from the conception of the world as a collection of things, but it is a conception that grounds our later scientific cognition of the world of things, or as Heidegger puts it, "Being may be without what-is but never what-is without Being."[11] Until we understand Being as such we can have no conception of things.

Heidegger's articulation of the role of angst validates the approaches of all of the other thinkers that I have discussed; they all seek to bring us to an understanding of the world though the evocation of one kind of mood or another. The common strand between them is that they promote disconnection from the world of things and encourage us to see in a different way. From Sebald's wistful musings, to the dreams of Bachelard, and Gadamer at play, there is a clear path to Heidegger's angst and the world as it is disclosed and as it appears. At this point it is time to let

Heidegger have the last word, words which reverberate through all of the writers that I have discussed,

> Only because Nothing is revealed in the very basis of our Dasein is it possible for the utter strangeness of what-is to dawn on us. Only when the strangeness of what-is forces itself upon us does it wonder and invite our wonder. Only because of wonder, that is to say, the revelation of Nothing, does the "Why?" spring to our lips. Only because this "Why?" is possible as such can we seek for reasons and proofs and a definite way. Only because we can ask and prove are we fated to become enquirers in this life. (Heidegger, 1968, p.378)

Notes

[1] This section is based on my own paper, "Four Alternatives to a Reductive View of Knowledge".
[2] Spooner, Chapple, Roland, 2000.
[3] Heidegger, 1962, H.136.
[4] Heidegger, 1962, H.164.
[5] Bachelard, 1958, 1994, p.6.
[6] Bachelard, 1958, 1994, p.4.
[7] Gadamer, 1975, 2006, p. 78.
[8] Angst may be the better term to use here since it has less misleading connotations than the translation 'anxiety'.
[9] Heidegger, 1968, p.369.
[10] Heidegger, 1969, p.3.
[11] Heidegger, 1968, p.385.

BIBLIOGRAPHY

Ackroyd, P. *London - The Biography*, Vintage, London, 2001.
Alpers, S. *The Art of Describing*, University of Chicago Press, 1983.
Ayer, A.J. *Descartes: A Collection of Critical Essays*, Edited by. Doney, W., Macmillan, London, 1968.
Bachelard, G. *The Psychoanalysis of Fire*, Routledge and Kegan Paul Ltd., London, 1938, 1964.
—. *Water and Dreams*, The Pegasus Foundation, Dallas, USA, 1942, 1982.
—. *Air and Dreams*, Dallas Institute Publications, Dallas, USA, 1943, 2011.
—. *The Poetics of Space*, Beacon Press, Boston, Mass, 1958, 1994.
Bailey, Martin, *Vermeer*, Phaidon Press, London, 2001.
Barthes, R. *Camera Lucida*, Vintage Books, London, 2000.
Borges, Jorge Luis *Fictions*, John Calder, London, 1965.
de Botton, A. *The Architecture of Happiness*, Penguin, London, 2007.
Boureanu, R. *Holbein*, Abbey Library, London, 1977.
Brilliant, R. *Portraiture*, Reaktion Books Ltd., London, 1991.
Brown, Christopher. *Dutch Painting*, Phaidon Press, London, 1998.
—. *Scenes of Everyday Life – Dutch Genre Painting from the Mauritshuis*, Ashmolean Museum, Oxford, 1999.
Buck, S. *Hans Holbein*, Konemann, Cologne, 1999.
Caton, H. *The Origins of Subjectivity – An Essay on Descartes*, YUP, London and New York, 1973.
Descartes, R. *Meditations on First Philosophy*, Cambridge University Press, 1986.
—. *Philosophical Writings,* Nelson University Paperbacks, London, 1954.
Descartes, R. *Selected Philosophical Writing*, Cambridge University Press, 1988.
Eichler, A-F. *Durer*, Konemann, Cologne, 1999.
Einberg, E. *Hogarth the Painter*, Tate Gallery, London, 1997.
Fell, J.P. "The Familiar and the Strange: On the Limits of Praxis in the Early Heidegger." *Heidegger: A Critical Reader*, Edited by Dreyfus, H.L. and Hall, H., Blackwell, Oxford, 1995.
Five Hundred Self Portraits, Phaidon Press. London, 2000.
Foister, S. *Holbein In England*, Tate Gallery, London, 2006.

Frank, M. "Philosophical Foundations of Early Romanticism", *The Modern Subject – Conceptions of the Self in Classical German Philosophy*, Edited by Amerikas, K and Sturma, D., University of New York, Albany, 1995.

Gadamer, H-G. *Truth and Method*, Continuum, London, New York, 1975, 2004.

—. *The Relevance of the Beautiful and Other Essays*, Edited by Bernasconi, R., Cambridge University Press, 1986.

Goffman, E. *The Presentation of Self in Everyday Life*, Edinburgh University Press, 1956.

Gombrich, A. *Art and Illusion*, Phaidon Press, London, 1960.

Glendinning, S. *On Being with Others*, Routledge, London and New York, 1998.

Guignon, C.B. *Heidegger and the Problem of Knowledge*, Hackett Publishing, Indianapolis, 1983.

Hegel, G.W.F. *Phenomenology of Spirit*, Oxford University Press, 1977.

Heidegger, Martin, *The Basic Problems of Phenomenology*, Indiana University Press, Bloomington and Indianapolis, 1988.

Heidegger, M. *Being and Time*, Blackwell, Oxford, 1962.

—. *The Essence of Reasons*, Northwest University Press, 1969.

—. "Origins of the Work of Art", *Basic Writings*, Edited by Krell, D.F., Routledge, London, 1994.

—. "The Question Concerning Technology", *Basic Writings*, Edited by Krell, D.F., Routledge, London, 1994.

—. "What is Metaphysics?" *Existence and Being*, Vision Press, London, 1968.

Hintikka, J. "Cogito, ergo, Sum: Inference or Performance", *Descartes: A Collection of Critical Essays*, Edited by Doney, W., Macmillan, London, 1968.

Hockney, David, *Hockney on Art – Conversations with Paul Joyce*, Little, Brown, London, 2008.

—. *Secret Knowledge*, Thames and Hudson, London, 2001.

—. *That's The Way I See It*, Thames and Hudson, London, 1993.

Hume, D. *A Treatise of Human Nature*, Vol. I, Everyman, London, 1959.

—. *A Treatise of Human Nature*, Vol. II, Everyman, London, 1959.

—. *Enquiries Concerning Human Understanding*, Clarendon, Oxford, 1970.

Kenny, A. *Descartes: A Study of his Philosophy*, Thoemmes Press, Bristol, 1993.

McCulloch, M. *Understanding W.G. Sebald*, University of South Carolina Press, Colombia SC, 2003.

Mitchell, D.R. "Four Alternatives to A Reductive View of Knowledge", *Journal of Evaluation in Clinical Practice*. 17,: 899-904. doi: 10.1111/j.1365-2753.2011.01724.x.

—. *Heidegger's Philosophy and Theories of the Self*, Ashgate, Aldershot, 2001.

Nemirovsky, Irene, *Suite Francaise*, Chatto and Windus, London, 2004.

Pepys, S. *Pepy's Diary,* Selected and Edited by Latham, R., Folio Society, London, 1996.

Pevsner, Nikolaus, *The Buildings of England – Suffolk*, Penguin, Harmondsworth, Middlesex, 1961.

Richardson, John, *Existential Epistemology - A Heideggerian Critique of the Cartesian Project*, Clarendon, Oxford, 1986.

Rilke, Rainer Maria *The Notebooks of Malte Laurids Brigge*, W.W. Norton, London and New York, 1992.

Santner, Eric *On Creaturely Life, Rilke/Benjamin/Sebald*, University of Chicago Press, 2006.

Sartre, J-P. *Being and Nothingness*, Philosophical Library, New York, 1956.

Schama, S. *Landscape and Memory*, Fontana Press, Bath, 1996.

Schiller, F. *On the Aesthetic Education of Man*, Dover Publications, Mineola, New York, 1795, 2004.

Schneider, Norbert,), *Vermeer – The Complete Paintings*, Taschen, Koln, 2000.

Searching for Sebald – Photography After W.G. Sebald. The Institute of Cultural Inquiry, ICI Press, Los Angeles, USA, 2007.

Sebald, W.G. *After Nature*, Penguin, London, 2002.

—. *Austerlitz*, Penguin, London, 2002.

—. *Campo Santo*, Penguin, London, 2006.

—. *The Emigrants*, Vintage, London, 2002.

—. *The Rings of Saturn*, Vintage, London, 2002.

—. *Vertigo*, Vintage, London, 2002.

Severs, D. *18 Folgate Street – The Tale of a House in Spitalfields*, Chatto and Windus, London, 2001.

Sontag, S. *On Photography*, Penguin. London, 1979.

Spooner, A., Chapple, A., Roland, M. *East Kent Primary Care Clinical Effectiveness Project Evaluation Report,* National Primary Care Research and Development Centre, Manchester, 2000.

Steadman, P. *Vermeer's Camera*, Oxford University Press, 2001.

Swales, M. "Intertextuaility, Authenticity, Metonymy - On Reading W.G. Sebald", *The Anatomist of Melancholy*, Ed. Gomer, R., London

Institute of Germanic Studies, University of London School of Advanced Study, 2003.

Uglow, J. *Hogarth – A Life and a World*, Faber and Faber, London, 1997.

Upshur, R. Four alternatives to a reductive view of knowledge: a commentary. *Journal of Evaluation in Clinical Practice*, 17: 905–906. doi: 10.1111/j.1365-2753.2011.01749.x.

W.G. Sebald – A Critical Companion. Edited by Long, J.J. and Whitehead, A., Edinburgh University Press, 2004.

West, S. *Portraiture*, Oxford University Press, 2004.

Westerman, M. *The Art of the Dutch Republic 1585-1718*, Wiedenfeld and Nicholson, London, 1996.

Williams, B. "The Certainty of the Cogito", *Descartes: A Collection of Critical Essays*, Edited by Doney, W., Macmillan, London, 1968.

INDEX